James M. Buchanan and
Liberal Political Economy

James M. Buchanan and Liberal Political Economy

A Rational Reconstruction

Richard E. Wagner

LEXINGTON BOOKS
Lanham • Boulder • New York • London

Published by Lexington Books
An imprint of The Rowman & Littlefield Publishing Group, Inc.
4501 Forbes Boulevard, Suite 200, Lanham, Maryland 20706
www.rowman.com

Unit A, Whitacre Mews, 26-34 Stannary Street, London SE11 4AB

British Library Cataloguing in Publication Information Available

Library of Congress Cataloging-in-Publication Data

Library of Congress Control Number: 2017934167
ISBN 9781498539067 (cloth: alk. paper)
ISBN 9781498539081 (pbk. : alk. paper)
ISBN 9781498539074 (electronic)

Printed in the United States of America

Contents

Preface

James M. Buchanan (1919–2013) was one of the premier economists of the twentieth century, as attested by his being awarded the Nobel Memorial Prize in Economic Science in 1986. His approach to economics, however, was in no way ordinary. His brand of economics made such strong contact with law, ethics, and political science that he could easily have served as a poster-child for the programs in politics, philosophy, and economics which have been gaining momentum in recent years. He spoke for a style of economics that made wide and firm contact with the full range of the humane studies, in contrast to the inward-looking narrowness of orthodox economics.

The life of a thinker can be told largely through his or her ideas. Buchanan is typical of thinkers in this respect. After leaving the Navy in 1945, he devoted his life to thinking and writing about political economy. The topics he thought about are the objects this book addresses. This book, however, is not an intellectual biography. It features neither archival work nor excerpts from correspondence, though I should note that Buchanan's archives are currently being assembled for public use at George Mason University under the supervision of Dr. Solomon Stein. This book is my interpretation of the contemporary meaning and significance of Buchanan's oeuvre, as filtered through my 50-year association with him as a student, colleague, and coauthor. The book offers my rational reconstruction of Buchanan's oeuvre. It is less concerned with Buchanan's past contributions per se than it is with the present and potential relevance of his scholarly contributions and insights. I do not seek to describe the steps Buchanan took in arriving at the formulations with which he is associated. Rather, I seek to explain what insight for their work contemporary scholars might acquire by becoming familiar with some of those formulations.

While my presentation of Buchanan's thought is cognizant of the chronology of his work, the book proceeds thematically and not chronologically. To proceed chronologically unavoidably reflects an antiquarian quality by locating a scholar in the past. Yet Buchanan had limited antiquarian interests, as illustrated by his repeated reminders that "we have no option but to start from where we are." In this respect, Buchanan embraced George Shackle's (1961) recognition that the present is but a knife-edge that separates a dead past from a possible future. All scholars unavoidably must incorporate work from the past into their current work, but Buchanan's orientation was always on moving forward from the present. In presenting his Adam Smith Lecture before the National Association of Business Economists, Buchanan (1989) noted that "I am not an exegetist," and explained that his "concern is not what Adam Smith may have said or failed to say. My concern is, instead, with articulating what I think would be a consistent position, for Adam Smith, in the context of the United States political economy in the late 1980s." In line with this orientation, I emphasize those features of Buchanan's thinking about philosophy, politics, and economics that seem relevant for contemporary scholarship within the broadly liberal tradition of political economy.

In this effort, I treat Buchanan as participating in what Kenneth Boulding (1971) describes as the "extended present" in explaining why Adam Smith is still relevant more than two centuries after his death. This book is especially concerned with exploring how Buchanan, as a participant in this extended present, might have carried forward his interests and lines of thought into the near future. While I present the prime contours of Buchanan's thought, my purpose in doing so is to probe the contemporary relevance of his thought. Buchanan was a classical political economist who entered the scholarly world during the heyday of the neoclassical period of economics. Consequently, he was often misconstrued as a neoclassical economist with right-wing ideas. That view is wrong; it reflects the common tendency of people to interpret other people and events in terms of the main currents in play at the time. While Buchanan worked during the heyday of the neoclassical period in economics, he was a classical political economist in the style of Frank Knight and not a neoclassical economist of post-war Chicago vintage.

Buchanan stood for the construction of a different type of economics, one that would serve as a contemporary version of the liberal political economy that grew out of the Scottish Enlightenment associated with such scholars as David Hume and Adam Smith. Buchanan, like Friedrich Hayek, was an incipient theorist of social complexity whose theoretical activity preceded development of the computational tools with which ideas about social complexity are now explored. Buchanan was concerned with the borderland between individual liberty and the collective actions that are often necessary for people to live well together. He also recognized that actual life is far richer and more nuanced than any whiteboard can capture, no matter how many equations adorn it. Buchanan recognized the positive value of liberty along with the responsibility that liberty entails, while also acknowledging the need for appropriate collective action to promote the common flourishing that societal living together enables but doesn't guarantee. This setting provided the mental environment inside of which Buchanan constructed his body of scholarship.

Chapter 1 introduces the reader to Buchanan and his thought, and explains what I mean in asserting that Buchanan worked within and extended the tradition of classical political economy, and was not a standard neoclassical economist. Chapters 2–7 represent a book within the book, so to speak. These chapters offer my rational reconstruction of Buchanan's body of work. That oeuvre resembles a large oak tree when viewed some 64 years after it was planted as a sapling in 1949. The several significant lines of thought he created over his life are all traceable to the first article he published in 1949, though he didn't think of his work as reflecting this degree of organization. This book within the book presents this organization as a six-themed rational reconstruction. The book closes with an Appendix that reprints a memorial I published in the *Journal of Public Finance and Public Choice* soon after Buchanan's death.

For several helpful thoughts and suggestions, I am grateful to several people in Italy where I presented some of this material in seminars in Lecce and Rome. These include Manuela Mosca and Michele Giuranno in Lecce and Emma Galli, Giampaolo Garzarelli, Giuseppe Eusepi, and the late Domenico da Empoli in Rome. The F. A. Hayek Program for Advanced Study in Philosophy, Politics, and Economics held a seminar on the book in its early stages, from which I received valuable advice and suggestions from Paul Dragos Aligica, Neera Badhwar, Peter Boettke, Donald Boudreaux, Christopher Coyne, Stefanie Haeffele-Balch, Bobbi Herzberg, Jayme Lemke, Solomon Stein, Virgil Storr, and Lawrence White. Although he died three years before I decided to write this book, I am grateful all the same to the helpful advice and suggestions Jim Buchanan provided through me throughout the fifty-years association we had, even including or perhaps especially including the modest points of disagreement we had along the way.

Chapter One

Introducing James Buchanan

James M. Buchanan was a prolific author. His collected works (Buchanan 1999–2002) required 20 volumes to hold, and this collection only contained most and not all his work. Moreover, Buchanan continued to publish after 2002, with one book even published two years after his death (Buchanan and Yoon 2015). Yet there are scholars who publish similar volumes of work without attaining Buchanan's standing. What caused Buchanan to stand out was less the volume of work than it was the ability of his work to capture the attention of readers and to direct their scholarly efforts toward lines of inquiry that Buchanan set forth. It is the distinctive quality of his work more than its quantity that catapulted Buchanan into his place of prominence among contemporary economists. Buchanan inserted new themes into economics, thus expanding the domain of economics and political economy. For this insertion, Buchanan was awarded the Nobel Memorial Prize in Economic Science in 1986 "for his contributions to the theory of political decision-making and public economics." While the distinctive quality of Buchanan's scholarship was present in his first published article on public finance (Buchanan 1949), that distinctiveness came into prominence with Buchanan's move to the University of Virginia in 1956, where the analytical path he blazed through his scholarship came to be known around 1960 as Virginia Political Economy.

While Nobelity came Buchanan's way at age 67, he started modestly. Buchanan spent his boyhood in rural Tennessee, near Murfreesboro where he learned to milk cows, drive a tractor, and undertook the many other activities that farm boys practiced at that time, with Buchanan (1992) containing 12 autobiographical essays and Kyle (2012) being a biography of the Buchanan family from its arrival in Tennessee late in the eighteenth century until Buchanan's receipt of the Nobel Prize. After finishing high school in Murfreesboro, Buchanan had hoped to attend the University of Tennessee, some 200 miles away in Knoxville. The austerity of the Great Depression didn't allow that, however, so he stayed home and attended Middle Tennessee State College in Murfreesboro, receiving his Bachelor's degree in 1940.

At that time, he received scholarship support to attend the University of Tennessee, where he received a Master's degree in economics in 1941. Subsequently, he entered the U.S. Navy, underwent officer's training, and spent the war in the Pacific, mostly stationed at Pearl Harbor. Upon his discharge from the Navy in 1945, Buchanan enrolled in the economics Ph.D. program at the University of Chicago for the winter quarter 1946, receiving his degree in 1948. After spending three years at the University of Tennessee, Buchanan moved to Florida State University where he stayed until he moved to the University of Virginia in 1956. Save for spending 1968–1969 on the faculty of UCLA, Buchanan spent the rest of his academic career in Virginia, 1956–1968 at the University of Virginia; 1969–1983 at Virginia Tech, and 1983 until his retirement in 2007 at George Mason University, though he continued his professional activity, including still working at his office, until his death in 2013.

Unlike many prominent economists who spend large parts of their lives engaged in political activity through working with legislatures or executive agencies, Buchanan spent his career almost exclusively as a thinker, thinking mostly about matters pertaining to the relationships among politics, economics, and social philosophy. Occasionally Buchanan gave testimony or wrote opinion editorials, but he dedicated his life to his scholarship. Besides his writing, Buchanan also engaged significantly in academic entrepreneurship. Upon moving to the University of Virginia, Buchanan, in conjunction with Warren Nutter, a classmate from the University of Chicago, established in 1957 the Thomas Jefferson Center for the Study of Political Economy and Social Philosophy. The Thomas Jefferson Center helped in the recruitment of such additional faculty as Ronald Coase, Gordon Tullock, and Leland Yeager, as well as in supporting graduate students and sponsoring lectures and conferences. The Thomas Jefferson Center also sponsored semester-long visits from such noted scholars as Maurice Allais, Duncan Black, F. A. Hayek, Terence Hutchinson, William Hutt, Frank Knight, Bruno Leoni, Bertil Ohlin, Michael Polanyi, and Overton Taylor, which Buchanan (1986a) recollects.

Buchanan in conjunction with Gordon Tullock established the Committee on Non-Market Decision Making in 1963. This Committee was the forerunner of what became the Public Choice Society in 1968. In 1963 and again in 1964, the Committee assembled some 20 scholars who were interested in questions pertaining to economic organization outside of normal market processes and institutions. Those scholars included representatives from philosophy and political science as well as economics. Among these were Edward Banfield, Otto Davis, Anthony Downs, Gerald Garvey, John Harsanyi, Stanley Kelley, Gerald Kramer, James March, Roland McKean, Mansur Olson, Vincent Ostrom, John Rawls, William Riker, and Jerome Rothenberg.

Buchanan's organizational and entrepreneurial efforts continued after he moved to Virginia Tech in 1969, with that effort now carried out within the framework of the Center for Study of Public Choice. The program in Charlottesville was centered on classical political economy, as conveyed by the ability of human interaction within a system of free markets to generate beneficial social properties, and with politics being treated mostly normatively as operating to maintain the system of market interaction. Inspired by the change in analytical focus set in motion through the meetings of the Committee on Non-Market Decision Making, the program in Blacksburg centered on the construction of explanatory theories of political processes and institutions. In Charlottesville, the theory of markets and social organization through markets occupied the analytical foreground of the program. In Blacksburg, explanatory theories of politics moved into the foreground. The interest in market theory was still present, only that interest was displaced by public choice as occupying the analytical foreground.

BUCHANAN: A HEDGEHOG OF A THINKER

In *The Hedgehog and the Fox*, Isaiah Berlin's (1953) celebrated essay on Leo Tolstoy, Berlin distinguished between thinkers who had one large idea and thinkers who had many smaller ideas. Buchanan was a hedgehog, as this book explains through its rational reconstruction of Buchanan's body of work. To be sure, Buchanan did not appear to himself as a hedgehog. He did not operate with any consciousness of pursuing some grand scheme of work that he created early in his career. Indeed, he often noted that he responded to various topics that caught his attention at different times during his career, and certainly did not operate with any sense of developing a unified body of ideas. All the same, a rational reconstruction of his scholarly oeuvre shows Buchanan to have been a hedgehog. Buchanan's first article was published in 1949 in the *Journal of Political Economy*. It was titled "The Pure Theory of Government Finance: A Suggested Approach." Nearly all of Buchanan's subsequent work contributed to building the scholarly edifice that was inchoate in this 1949 paper. Buchanan's subsequent contributions to the theory of political decision-making and public economics were inchoate in his initial paper, as were his subsequent works on ethics, social philosophy, and constitutional political economy.

That initial paper resembles an oak sapling that Buchanan planted in 1949. Over the following 64 years that sapling grew into a massive oak tree whose branches and leaves covered wide territory of great interest to many people. While various of those branches of thought might have seemed to

Buchanan to have had little if any connection with his 1949 paper, it becomes apparent that they were connected when they are viewed from the end of his career. Rational reconstruction of Buchanan's oeuvre shows that his mind was that of a hedgehog even though his self-description might have asserted that he was a fox, though quite an energetic fox. His 1949 sketch of what he perceived to be an alternative approach to the theory of public finance required that he theorize about how the constitution of groups influences collective action, including the study of alternative structures by which groups are constituted. That sketch also required that Buchanan think about how principles of the rule of law play out in democratic settings, about the relationship among liberty, entitlement, and responsibility, and about the place of the moral imagination within a scheme of liberal political economy.

James Buchanan started his scholarly career as a theorist who wanted to develop a different approach to public finance than what he encountered during his student days at the University of Chicago, as Marianne Johnson (2014a) explains. Buchanan wanted to avoid all theories that placed governments and their activities into some form of black box whose workings could be neither observed nor explained. To do this required Buchanan to bring to life the people within a democratic polity who in some fashion ultimately shape fiscal outcomes. This bringing individuals to life within a democratic system of self-governance required Buchanan to develop an alternative approach to public finance. The prevalent approaches were of no use because they treated public finance as the playground of a few experts who designed taxing and spending schemes to pursue what they thought were good societal objectives, and then complained when their plans were rejected through the political process. In Buchanan's dissertation research, as Johnson (2014a) explains, Buchanan came across work by Knut Wicksell (1896; 1958) and Antonio de Viti de Marco (1936; 1888), both of which pointed away from the orthodox approach to public finance. Nearly the full body of Buchanan's scholarship can be reconstructed as a development and refinement of themes that he sketched in "The Pure Theory of Government Finance," and which serves as an organizational blueprint for presenting the primary lines of thought that Buchanan injected into the scholarly world.

RATIONALLY RECONSTRUCTING BUCHANAN'S OEUVRE

Chapters 2–7 offer a rational reconstruction of Buchanan's oeuvre. Chapter 2 locates the theory of public finance as the analytical point of departure from which Buchanan developed his body of work. Buchanan (1949) is a form of call to arms in which he sets forth a bottom-up approach to public finance wherein people are construed as governing themselves, in contrast to the orthodox approach to public finance where the state is treated as some in-

governments. Central to Buchanan's refinement of this interest was his recognition that cost and choice are obverse faces of human action (Buchanan
1969a and the essays collected in Buchanan and Thirlby 1973). Any choice
implies the existence of an alternative action that could have been chosen but
wasn't. Cost is thus the perceived value of the option that was not chosen.
This recognition Buchanan set forth in *Cost and Choice*, with this slim book
packing perhaps as much theoretical punch per page as any book in the
history of economics. Buchanan's orientation toward cost and choice, moreover, ramifies throughout his political economy and social philosophy, as this
orientation toward the relation between cost and choice is vital for any effort
to explain the emergence of concrete fiscal phenomena. Among other things,
the typical aggregate magnitudes so popular with economists are typically
irrelevant for human action because relevance resides with how those magnitudes are perceived by those individuals on the ground who are in positions
to take action.

Chapter 5 explores various paths along which Buchanan sought to take
account of the passing of time, which is integral to the classical but not the
neoclassical orientation toward economic theory. As a continuation of classical political economy, Buchanan theorized mostly in terms of processes and
not equilibrium states. To be sure, equilibrium models appear throughout his
work, though mostly as providing background for developing his point of
interest. Buchanan (1964a; 1969b) conveyed this point sharply when he advanced catallactics or exchange over resource allocation as the focal point
around which to organize economic theory. As Buchanan developed his ideas, moreover, it was clear that he focused on processes of development more
than on states of equilibrium throughout his explorations in constitutional
public finance and political economy. Democratic processes entail significant differences from market processes, which Buchanan explored along
several avenues, as illustrated by Buchanan (1954a) and Buchanan (1954b).
This chapter pays attention to the operation of political processes within time
in democratic settings where people can make commitments today for which
they might not be responsible until tomorrow or even the day after tomorrow.
Issues pertaining to credit in several ways occupied the foreground of Buchanan's attention, with public debt occupying a place of prominence. All these
topics are unified through Buchanan's concern with developing an explanatory theory of public finance.

Chapter 6 explores Buchanan's treatments of individual responsibility as
the obverse of his treatment of individual liberty. Buchanan recognized that a
political regime grounded on individual liberty could not sustain itself without individuals acting responsibly to maintain that system of liberal governance. Liberty without responsibility is license, recognition of which led Buchanan to explore the place of entitlement within a constitution of liberty.
While most of Buchanan's work emphasized liberty, responsibility and liber-

scrutable entity that magically injects taxes and spending into socie
with individuals responding to those injections but in no way causin;
Buchanan recognized that public finance necessarily had to rest o1
form of political philosophy because public finance deals with the ecc
activities of states. Without political entities, there would be no theo
public finance. Any work in public finance must reflect some foundati(
political philosophy, even though theorists rarely articulate their philo
cal principles and presuppositions. Traditional public finance reflected
litical philosophy of absolutism, in that taxing and spending programs
construed as the province of rulers who are pursuing their objectives as
choose them. Buchanan wanted to reconstruct public finance to ren(
suitable for democratic regimes where people governed themselves a
posed to being governed by a class of rulers. For people to govern t
selves, some scheme for constituting relationships among those peop
necessary. One cannot speak of people governing themselves withou1
dressing how such governance is constituted. Buchanan's interest in cons
tional political economy bears intimate connection with his interest in
individualist approach to public finance.

Chapter 3 examines how Buchanan's alternative orientation toward p
lic finance led to his placing strong emphasis on the constitutional frar
work through which groups are constituted (Munger and Munger 2015). 1
phenomena of public finance arise through group action and not individ(
action, which means that a theory of public finance must concern itself w\
how groups form, acquire, and deploy their powers. Groups can't act, f
only individuals can act. Groups are constituted through some organization
framework that establishes relationships and positions among the membe1
of the group. It is individuals within a group who act, and with the group'
constitutional structure channeling individual desire into group action. I\
short, Buchanan recognized that a theory of public finance that pertains t(
democratically organized polities must reflect the presence and operation o1
transactional and contractual principles within democratically constituted
groups. Buchanan found no help within the Anglo-Saxon tradition to which
he was exposed at Chicago, but did find help in Sweden and Italy.

Chapter 4 continues from chapter 3 by exploring several ramifications
that reside within Buchanan's recognition that collective action is group
action that is rendered possible through some constitutional framework. Alternative constitutional frameworks should generally be associated with different group choices due to the influence of different power relationships
among the membership. Pragmatically speaking, large governments will necessarily entail much administrative decentralization. That decentralization,
however, can be accommodated within either unitary or federal forms of
state. Buchanan's interest in liberal political economy, as well as his being an
American, led to his enduring interest in federal forms for constituting

ty are inseparable, just as are cost and choice. The 1776 Declaration of Independence asserted that Americans are entitled to life, liberty, and the pursuit of happiness. But 1776 is far back in our rear-view mirrors, and the world of entitlement has expanded massively, necessarily restricting freedom of action as a complementary necessity. In any case, Buchanan recognized that the political economy of entitlement is inseparable from the political economy of liberty, and with the two being antagonistic in some instances.

Chapter 7 explores Buchanan's normative interests as these are reflected in his work on ethics and social philosophy. While Buchanan approached economic theory from a scientific orientation, he also recognized that the subject matter that economics treated resonated with the interest people have in the quality of the lives they lead. Economic theory can cast useful light on the problems people face in living well together, but a political economy that is cognizant of morality is also necessary (Buchanan 1982a; 1982b). Any constitutional structure can be described as a network of nodes put together in a particular way, with different forms of assembly denoting different constitutional structures. One prominent claim is that changes in structure can promote different outcomes. Another claim is that the same structure can also yield different outcomes, depending on the moral imaginations of the people who occupy positions in that constitutional structure. Hence, ethics and moral philosophy are also significant for the theory of democratic action that represented the analytical core of Buchanan's scholarly oeuvre.

BUCHANAN AND THE ORIGIN OF VIRGINIA POLITICAL ECONOMY

There is something unavoidably arbitrary about locating the origin of any scheme of thought. A thinker's thought always takes place against a background of preceding thought, even if it also entails a projection of a thinker's imagination into new analytical territory. While today's thought might have some original aspects, it also will bear the imprint of preceding thought that can reasonably be described as precursory to the present thought (Lovejoy 1936). Despite this unavoidable arbitrariness, it is often informative for readers to know something about the most significant precursors of a scheme of thought to locate it within the broader *Commons of the Mind* (Baier 1997) in which all thought occurs. With this caveat in view, I locate Buchanan as the proximate originator of what has become known as the Virginia tradition of political economy, though he had significant help, particularly from Warren Nutter (1962; 1983), in doing that. The origins of this tradition most certainly does not reside in the neoclassical theory of rationality applied to voting and politics. To the contrary, it resides in the confluence of classical political economy (Robbins 1952; Samuels 1966) and Italian public finance (Bucha-

nan 1960; Fausto 2003), though with modest reservations I could also extend
that origin to the nineteenth-century tradition of *Staatswissenschaften*, along
the lines of Backhaus and Wagner's (2005a; 2005b) examinations of the
Continental tradition of public finance in contrast to the Anglo-Saxon tradition. One significant reason for selecting this point of origin, in addition to its
truth value, is that it opens naturally into a multi-faceted exploration of the
problems involved in people living together in close geographical proximity,
and with such explanation being by-passed by the standard neoclassical orientation toward comparative statics in contrast to emergent dynamics (Wagner 2010).

Constructing scholarly genealogy entails significant subjective elements
that are absent from biological genealogy. At any moment, a scholar stands
inside a chain of being (Lovejoy 1936), where one end points backward to
some sense of origin while the other end points forward to work that remains
to be done. The construction of such chains belongs not to the realm of
necessity but to the realm of volition, out of recognition of the ability of
language to encapsulate sentiment and emotion and not to serve simply as an
instrument for conveying fact, as Viktor Klemperer (2006) illustrates beautifully in his examination of the use of language in Nazi Germany. Alternative
narratives regarding origins point toward different directions for future scholarship as part of the highly contested quality of scholarly activity, as Melvin
Reder (1999) explores for economics and Randall Collins (1998) examines
for scholarly competition in general. In presenting my thesis, I start with
Kenneth Boulding's (1971) treatment of past thought as belonging to what he
called the "extended present."

Economists are notorious for having disdain for old books. Few doctoral
programs offer fields in the history of economic analysis and many of them
don't even offer courses on the topic. Many reading lists feature few items
more than five years old, and with many of the featured items having yet to
be published. The image created by such reading lists is that past scholarship
has little to offer present scholars. This image reflects what appears to be the
widely held presumption that whatever was once valuable in the past has
already been incorporated into present economic theory, so avoiding old
books avoids wasting time in exploring blind alleys, which in turn makes
economic theory more progressive than it would otherwise be. We can honor
the past by recognizing that we are standing on the shoulders of giants, but
there is no need to read the contributions of those giants because those of
their formulations that are still useful are already incorporated into current
theory.

This widely held belief is just that, a belief or an article of faith. It has
neither theory nor evidence in its support. Indeed, as theory it entails a
thoroughgoing embrace of the theory of perfect competition applied to the
present state of economic scholarship, along with the claim that perfect com-

petition pertains to that generation in each instant of time. Yet very few economists believe, and for good reason, that the theory of perfect competition gives a good description of actual economic processes or arrangements. Furthermore, that belief runs afoul of the micro-theoretic basis of the constitution of economic theories, as Arthur Lovejoy (1936, 3–23) explains in his treatment of "The Study of the History of Ideas." An economic theory is packaged as a macro-theoretic entity. That entity, however, is constituted as a string of micro-theoretic entities. Consider the use by some theorists to explain involuntary unemployment due to firms paying workers efficiency wages that are above the competitive wage. While this idea is packaged as a macro entity, or what Lovejoy described as a "unit-idea," it is constituted through stringing together several micro bits of theory. Among those bits are assumptions about business firms, agency theory, compensation schemes, marginal productivity theory, and the meaning of competition, among other bits, all of which can be combined in numerous ways.

The construction of an economic theory is thus an exercise in combinatorial arithmetic. A deck of cards can provide a simple illustration of the complexity that arises quickly from this type of arithmetic. There are some 635 billion ways that a sequence of 13 cards can be drawn from a deck of 52 cards. Keeping with this illustration, suppose a theory of involuntary unemployment of the efficiency wage variety requires a sequence of 13 micro bits to be strung together from among 52 bits that are available. If so, there are some 635 billion ways a theory of efficiency wages can be articulated. Furthermore, suppose it takes a speedy theorist one day to organize and articulate one such theory. If a thousand scholars are involved in constructing efficiency wage theories, it will take 635 million days to articulate all such theories, or around two million years. It is surely implausible and even unreasonable to claim logical support for thinking that present theory inexorably incorporates the best from the past. To be sure, one could recur to argument about statistical sampling to assert that full enumeration would be wasteful. Even a sample size of one percent, however, would require 20,000 years to allow an inference reasonably to be made by standard statistical procedures. Claims on behalf of the proposition that competition among theorists generates some objective notion of Truth are undecidable, as Chaitin, da Costa, and Doria (2012) explain in their exploration of the world of undecidability that arises in pursuing Kurt Gödel's insights about the unavoidably arbitrary character of any closed scheme of thought.

When Kenneth Boulding (1971) asked who needs Adam Smith after Paul Samuelson, Boulding's effective answer was "everyone," and he justified his response by locating Smith within the "extended present." Boulding's poetic prose and my combinatorial arithmetic lead to the same recognition that past scholarly contributions and formulations can often provide valuable insight for current theoretical effort. There is no guarantee that what is carried forward from past to present will prove to be the most useful of all the possibilities. Someone in 1876 looking back to 1776 might select some things for usefulness and discard others. Yet someone in 1976 looking back to 1776 might make a different selection due to any number of things: the questions to be addressed by current theories might have changed; alternatively, new methods of analysis might have been created that brought tractability to formerly intractable ideas. Adam Smith's use of the diamond-water paradox was kept alive for the better part of a century before being abandoned. Adam Smith's interest in increasing returns was set aside in favor of the tractability of constant returns, with increasing returns revived two centuries later when new schemes of thought made it possible to work with those ideas, as Paul Romer (1986) set forth and with Buchanan and Yoon (1994) collecting a set of essays on increasing returns.

Nicholas Vriend (2002) illustrated nicely Boulding's theme about the extended present when he asked: "Is Hayek an ace?" By "ace," Vriend meant an economist who works with agent-based computational models. As a literal matter, there is no way Hayek could have been an ace because those techniques weren't around when Hayek (1937; 1945) argued that the central problem of economic theory is to explain how coherent macro patterns can emerge in societies when no micro entity knows but a pittance of the knowledge that would be needed to construct that pattern. In doing this, Hayek was, among other things, denying the meaningfulness and usefulness of standard theories of perfect competition as based on postulated conditions of full awareness of relevant knowledge. The analytical challenge for Hayek was to explain how orderly patterns tended to emerge in the face of limited and divided knowledge. This challenge could never be met by postulating equilibrium and supporting that postulation with econometrics because doing that gave no insight into the actual workings of the social world. Hence, Vriend argued that Hayek most surely would have been an ace had those schemes of thought been available when he was wrestling with his ideas about divided and distributed knowledge. Someone who can now work with agent-based computational models can find illuminating formulations in Hayek, and formulations that are much more open to agent-based techniques than the subsequent equilibrium-centered presumptions that such economists as Grossman and Stiglitz (1976; 1980) have worked with, though it should also be recognized that agent-based modeling also unavoidably butts against the same problems of unavoidable incompleteness, as Stephen DeCanio (2014) examines in exploring the limits of genuine knowledge about economy and society.

VIRGINIA POLITICAL ECONOMY:
THE PERSONS AND THEIR IDEAS

Individual theorists rarely assign themselves explicitly to a school of thought, for they mostly think of themselves as forming their own traditions. A school of thought is a construction someone applies to a group of scholars to facilitate the making of points about a set of people and a body of scholarship, even if those points pertain to no particular scholar in precise detail. Sometimes the points made are negative, with the designation of a school serving to concentrate that negative energy. Virginia political economy became a recognizable term in this manner. As David Levy and Sandra Peart (2013) document, around 1962 the central administration of the University of Virginia hired a consultant to prepare a report to give the administration leverage to undermine the program that had been under construction in Charlottesville since 1956. That report opened by stating that: "It is generally recognized that at the top professorial levels this Department is staffed by unquestionably capable men and that it enjoys a considerable repute in the profession. On the other hand, the Committee has received considerable adverse criticism of this Department by reason of its close association with a particular viewpoint; and we have been given to understand that the repute enjoyed is regarded by the vast majority of economists as of a distinctly unfavorable character. It does not need to be emphasized here that the Economics Department has associated itself firmly with an outlook now known as that of the 'Virginia school.'" In identifying a distinctive Virginia approach to political economy, that report helped to marshal the administrative force required to destroy the program in Charlottesville, though part of that program resurfaced in Blacksburg at Virginia Polytechnic Institute under the rubric "public choice."

Such negative association aside, schools of thought are an emergent feature of scholarly competition for scarce attention space, as Randall Collins (1998) explains in his analysis of the birth and death of schools of thought. The contours of that attention space can be constructed in various ways, as those contours are products of human craftsmanship. For instance, several distinct forms of attention space can be constructed through the marriage of principles of economizing action and an interest in bringing together political and economic phenomena. One such space can be organized around the twin presumptions of utility maximization and societal equilibrium, as illustrated by the well-known Stigler-Becker proposition about utility being invariant across people and time. Another such space can be organized by inverting that Stigler-Becker proposition, as Ross Emmett (2006) illustrates by contrasting Frank Knight's classical orientation toward political economy with George Stigler and Gary Becker's neoclassical orientation. Furthermore, Emmett (2009) amplifies Knight's approach to political economy, which Buchanan (1968a; 1976; 1991) embraced in the large, while also examining the chasm that separates Knight's (and Buchanan's) political economy from what became known as Chicago-style neoclassical economics in the 1950s.

The tradition of Virginia political economy, which is only one attention space within the territory of political economy, clearly falls within the Knight-Buchanan-Tullock-Nutter ambit of political economy, as Emmett recognizes. Any scholarly tradition can be identified in terms of a hard core of ideas from which various lines of thought are fashioned, as Lakatos (1978) explores in general and as Weintraub (1993) explores for general equilibrium theory. As both Boettke and Marciano (2015) and Wagner (2015a) examine from different but complementary angles, the hard core of Virginia political economy incorporates recognition of the limited and divided quality of knowledge in conjunction with human creativity, both of which lead to inquiry within a mode of plausible reasoning (Polya 1954). That hard core further treats collective action within the same comprehensive vision of collective action that emerged within the Italian tradition of public finance and fiscal sociology. To be sure, public choice and Virginia political economy arose during the height of the neoclassical period in economic theory, and has been often misidentified with ordinary neoclassical economics. But misidentification it is, for the central theoretical claim of neoclassical economics is the formal identity of liberalism and collectivism as systems of economic order. This formal identity reflects recognition that the first-order conditions for an optimal allocation of resources are identical under capitalism and socialism. This identity of liberalism and collectivism was not a claim that would have been advanced within the classical tradition, nor was it a claim that appeared sensible within the tradition of Virginia political economy, for reasons Milton Friedman (1953, 277–319) identified in his reviews of separate books by the socialist theorists Oskar Lange and Abba Lerner, where Friedman contrasts a focus on the technical identity of necessary conditions with a focus on the different operating properties of alternative institutional arrangements for the governance of human interactions. In this regard, Nathan Rosenberg's (1960) recognition that Adam Smith's analytical foreground focused on institutional arrangements, and with resource allocations being relegated to the analytical background surely comports with the analytical core of Virginia political economy.

The Virginia theorists to a man focused on process and coordination, and not on resource allocation. Warren Nutter's (1962) massive treatise on economic growth in the Soviet Union challenged forcibly what had been western hysteria over Soviet growth. It had long been claimed by western economists that Soviet growth was outpacing western growth by significant margins. The challenge for the western world was how to reorganize the economy to approach Soviet growth rates while maintaining a modicum of traditional western liberties. Nutter exploded this hysteria, though it took several years of sometimes savage disparagement before the correctness of Nutter's analysis become generally recognized. In developing their estimates of Soviet growth, western economists accepted Soviet data as truthful and discarded observations from years of war, famine, and persecution. In contrast, Nutter reasoned that Soviet-type systems were held together by lies and persecutions, and with war and famine being products of that type of economic organization. One could not sensibly treat the Soviet economy as a western economy that encountered negative shocks of severe magnitude. When Nutter examined Soviet growth within a reasonable theory of systems of political economy, he explained that the Soviet Union was no threat to catch the western world—unless, perhaps, the western nations moved toward a Soviet-style system. Even more, Nutter showed that growth was significantly higher in czarist Russia than it was after the Russian Revolution.

Ronald Coase joined the Virginia faculty in 1958, staying until he moved to Chicago in 1964 in the aftermath of the efforts of the University administration to suffocate what by then was known as Virginia political economy (Buchanan 2006). Coase, who received the Nobel Prize in 1991, operated within the liberal tradition of classical political economy with its focus on the generation of institutional arrangements inside of which people interact. Coase (1960) is especially known for its explanation of the strong ability of market transactions to overcome what had been thought to be situations of market failure. Coase's key point of departure was that any situation described as one of market failure simultaneously implied that profit opportunities were present. This didn't mean that market failures would automatically evaporate, but it did mean that market processes contained generally strong forces operating in the direction of capturing the gains from trade that are latent within a society.

Leland B. Yeager, who joined the Virginia faculty in 1957, reflected the same coordinationist approach to economics as did Buchanan, Coase, Nutter, and Tullock. In a collection of essays, Yeager (1962) showed that a system of sound money was a pivotal feature of any system based on a belief in a rule of law. While the book's dozen essays varied in nuance and emphasis, they were united in recognizing the centrality of sound money to a society whose self-identification was that it was based on a rule of law. Differences in emphasis and nuance aside, the essays in Yeager (1962) reject the Keynesian support for government manipulation of money in favor of removing money from direct political control because sound money facilitated peaceful human interaction within society, in contrast to the instability that results from political domination over monetary arrangements. In this respect, Buchanan (1987a) amplified the essays Yeager (1962) collected by describing the "Keynesian Follies" that captured the attention of so many economists. In a related line of analysis, Buchanan (1986b) explained that the Employment

Act of 1946 which created the Council of Economic Advisors reflected the fundamentally erroneous Keynesian presumption that free markets could not be generally relied upon to promote flourishing within a society. Buchanan's recognition of the Keynesian follies led him to advocate abolition of the Council of Economic Advisors because economic-theoretic expertise was not capable of improving upon the socially coordinative processes that free markets generate.

BUCHANAN AND THE ASSEMBLY OF VIRGINIA POLITICAL ECONOMY

James Buchanan and Warren Nutter both joined the economics faculty at the University of Virginia for the 1956–57 academic year. During their days as students at the University of Chicago in the late 1940s, they had agreed that they would create some center for academic research should they ever come together at the same university. The invitation to join the faculty in Charlottesville was spearheaded by Rutledge Vining (1956; 1984), who was a few years ahead of them as a student at Chicago and who shared the same intense admiration for Frank Knight as Buchanan and Nutter held. In 1957, Buchanan and Nutter established the Thomas Jefferson Center for Studies in Political Economy and Social Philosophy, with the reference to Social Philosophy soon removed because the longer title was thought to be unwieldy. Leland Yeager joined the faculty in 1957, with Ronald Coase joining the faculty in 1958. Also in 1958, Gordon Tullock visited for one year before taking up a faculty position at the University of South Carolina, then returning to Virginia in 1962.

The nucleus of Buchanan-Coase-Nutter-Tullock-Yeager provided a coherent orientation toward political economy that differed markedly from the orientation that was generally characteristic of economics at the time. That time was the heyday of the neoclassical period in economics wherein theoretical work had become mathematical exercises on models of utility maximization and market clearing, and with models subject to econometric testing. The founding participants in the program of Virginia political economy stood far outside this mainstream presumption, both methodologically and normatively.

Normatively, they all stood squarely within the classical liberal tradition that reached back to Adam Smith and David Hume, was associated strongly with John Stuart Mill, and was central to Chicago-style economics during the time of Frank Knight and Henry Simons. The classical liberal outlook operated from a default position that people should be free to pursue their desired activities so long as they did not violate the similar rights of other people in the process. This default in favor of laissez faire, it should be noted, was only a point of departure and not a destination. The initial presumption was in favor of individual liberty and not collective control, giving to proponents of collective control the burden of showing how individual liberty violated the rights of other individuals, thereby creating a case for collective action. Lionel Robbins (1952) and Warren Samuels (1966) illustrated how this classically liberal perspective could play out in a variety of cases.

To be sure, the ability to make an intellectual case for collective participation does not imply that actual collective action will work out in the manner the argument in favor of collective participation claimed. For instance, one could argue for the collective provision of elementary education by claiming that many parents would lack sufficient motivation to provide education for their children. To argue that such an outcome is possible or even plausible does not imply that actual collective supply of education will work to overcome the problem associated with laissez faire in education. Collective schools might not be capable of accomplishing what the arguments on their behalf envision them as accomplishing. Among other things, the provision of collective schooling will require the establishment of bureaucratic agencies to operate schools and will involve legislative bodies in overseeing schools. The result might even be worse than doing nothing at all collectively, and, in any case, is a topic that deserves further examination. Examinations of this type, and the competence with which such examinations might be performed, are topics that would fall within the rubric of the individualistic approach to public finance that Buchanan (1949) adumbrated.

Besides the classically liberal orientation of the faculty Buchanan and Nutter assembled, that faculty also operated with a significantly different orientation toward the scope and method of economics than what had become of economics in the post-war period. Perhaps most significantly, the Virginia faculty were incipient theorists of complex social systems long before tools of thought that would enable one to work with those ideas had been developed. They all disdained any presumption that systemic equilibrium was a reasonable way of perceiving reality, as distinct from providing some useful insights into reality. For instance, one could recognize that any statement one makes about the demand side of a market requires a complementary statement to be made about the supply side, without at the same time accepting the proposition that existing prices are equilibrium prices that in turn can be used in reaching scientifically useful conclusions. For the Virginia faculty, as for Hayek before them, the knowledge contained within an economic system was distributed throughout the economic system and never collected at one point in that system. This distributed character of relevant knowledge was, moreover, a methodological rather than a normative reason for adopting the classical liberal default position in support of laissez faire.

The establishment of Virginia political economy was a joint enterprise of Buchanan and Nutter, though the term is now identified with Buchanan alone. The intervening history has much to do with this. Starting early in the 1960s, the central administration of the University of Virginia had its way in destroying the program that Buchanan and Nutter began in 1956. That administration made no effort to retain Ronald Coase, who left for the University of Chicago in 1964. It made no effort to retain Gordon Tullock, who left for Rice University in 1967. And Buchanan left for UCLA in 1968, before moving to Virginia Tech in 1969, joining Gordon Tullock, who had moved from Rice to Virginia Tech in 1968. While Nutter and Yeager remained in Charlottesville, the core was gone. Furthermore, Nutter died in 1979; moreover, he was away from academic life during 1969–1973 when he served as Assistant Secretary of Defense for National Security Affairs. With Buchanan and Tullock together again in 1969 at Virginia Tech, and joined by Charles Goetz, a 1964 graduate of the Virginia program, Virginia political economy shifted onto a different trajectory.

VIRGINIA POLITICAL ECONOMY AS CLASSICAL POLITICAL ECONOMY ITALIANIZED

Public choice as a scientific term originated in 1968 in Chicago at a meeting of what until then had been known as the Committee on Non-Market Decision Making. This Committee was established by James Buchanan and Gordon Tullock in 1963 and 1964 to bring together scholars who were interested in bringing economic-theoretic insights to bear on non-market phenomena. From this initial meeting, the annual volume *Papers on Non-Market Decision Making* was established, with the first issue published in 1966. When the Committee was formalized as the Public Choice Society in 1968, the journal Tullock edited was renamed *Public Choice*. While the term was embraced in Chicago in 1968, several years would have to pass before public choice styles of thinking became an object of general scholarly awareness.

In those early meetings of the Committee on Non-Market Decision Making, the participants were aware that they were dealing with distinctive material that did not fit within established disciplinary boundaries. Indeed, the Preface to the *Calculus of Consent* noted this quality by referring to plowing a field next to a fence. The soil was likely to be more fertile than in the middle of the field; however, such obstacles as rocks could be encountered because the territory was unfamiliar. The Committee participants recognized that they were out of step with ordinary disciplinary conventions with respect to American academic practice circa 1960. The material that was discussed in those early days stood clearly outside the territory of conventional thinking about economics, politics, and political economy, as Tullock (1997) set forth in his discussion of "Origins of Public Choice." But this reality speaks only to American academia circa 1960. As an act of conjectural imagination, suppose a set of such Italian scholars as Antonio de Viti de Marco, Maffeo Pantaleoni, Vilfredo Pareto, Amilcare Puviani, and Luigi Einaudi fell asleep in Rip Van Winkle fashion, only to awaken in Charlottesville in 1963 during the first meeting of the Committee on Non-Market Decision Making or in Chicago in 1968 at the meetings during which the Committee on Non-Market Decision Making transformed itself into the Public Choice Society. I do not think it takes any daring leap of faith or imagination to conclude that those Italian scholars would have felt quite at home with respect both to the topics that were discussed and to the orientations taken toward those topics. Nor do I think the assembled participants would have thought that the Italian participants were visitors from some different scholarly planet. To be sure, the breadth of the public choice enterprise would have widened and acquired new topics in the presence of those visitors, but all the participants would surely have recognized the similarity of scholarly interest they held in common.

For now, let me use Amilcare Puviani to support my conjecture about Italian origins. In 1960, Gunter Schmölders, known at the time for work on what he called fiscal psychology (Schmölders 1959), and with fiscal psychology being a precursor of behavioral economics, sponsored a German translation of Amilcare Puviani's (1903) *Teoria della illusion finanziaria* [Theory of Fiscal Illusion]. In his Forward to Puviani's book, Schmölders explained that "over the last century *Italian public finance has had an essentially political science character*. The political character of fiscal activity stands always in the foreground. . . . This work [Puviani's book] is a *typical product of Italian public finance*, especially a typical product at the end of the nineteenth century. Above all, it is the science of *public finance combined with fiscal politics*, in many cases giving a good fit with reality" (my translation and italics). It should be noted that Schmölders recognized that Puviani's book was not some unusual outlier, but rather was a *typical* illustration of how the Italian theorists of the time had been working to bring political and fiscal phenomena within the same conceptual ambit, making due allowance for differences in institutional arrangements, both between political and market interaction and between governments today and governments in feudal times.

Had he been so inclined, Schmölders would surely have written to similar effect in writing a Foreword to Giovanni Montemartini's (1902) book on the municipal provision of rail services, not to mention Antonio de Viti de Marco's (1888) initial effort to articulate his vision of the theoretical character of public finance, a treatment that he revised and expanded four times until 1934, and with the 1934 version translated into English in 1936. Similar statements could be made about such Italian notables as Maffeo Pantaleoni, Luigi Einaudi, and Vilfredo Pareto, among others. These scholars and their contributions are surely part of the extended present of public choice theorizing, and one that points in some different analytical directions from what would arise from other notions of the core of public choice, and with Wagner (2007; 2016a) illustrating some of those differences in direction.

Particularly relevant for the origin of the Virginia political economy is the Italian tradition in public finance that arose with De Viti de Marco (1888), and with Buchanan (1960) and Fausto (2003) surveying this body of scholarship, with Manuela Mosca (2011; 2016) presenting an informative treatment of De Viti's character and work, and with Giuseppe Eusepi and Richard Wagner (2013) locating De Viti as a significant precursor to public choice theory. De Viti sought to locate public finance as an explanatory and not a hortatory theory. He did so by conceptualizing alternative forms of political-fiscal process, and with reality being some admixture of those forms. One form treated political-fiscal processes as reflecting something like consensus within society, while the other form construed political-fiscal processes as operating for the advantage of ruling sets of people within a society, as illustrated by the essays collected in de Viti (1930). De Viti's framework of consensual governance, it is worth noting, is similar to Wicksell's notion of approximate unanimity. To be sure, Wicksell didn't recognize this affinity with De Viti, perhaps because Wicksell took Ugo Mazzola and not De Viti to be the prime representative of Italian fiscal scholarship. It is also worth noting that a principle of consensual governance is not the same as a rule of unanimity because the former pertains to plausible reasoning while the latter pertains to demonstrative reasoning (Polya 1954).

In 1888, De Viti published *Il carattere teorico dell'economia finanziaria* [The theoretical character of public finance]. This small book was expanded three further times during De Viti's lifetime, culminating finally in the 1934 publication of *Principii di economia finanziaria*. This book was translated into English (De Viti 1936), and is the only book-length statement of the classical Italian orientation toward public finance available in English. In the Preface, De Viti explains that "I treat public finance as a theoretical science, assigning to it the task of *explaining* the phenomena of public finance in their historical setting" (De Viti's italics). James Buchanan (1960) was the primary source of bringing attention of English readers to the Italian tradition. To be sure, the Italian theorists did not speak with a single voice with respect to political economy, other than to treat the political within society as an object to be examined and understood. Michael McLure (2007), for instance, contrasts the comparatively hedonistic constructions of De Viti and Pantaleoni, which emphasize the similarities between economic and political phenomena, with the contributions of Pareto and Fasiani (1949) which emphasize the differences between the logical action found in markets and the non-logical action that characterizes politics. These kinds of differences aside, the Italian tradition in public finance arose as an effort to incorporate political activity into the explanatory framework of economic theory. Within this tradition, political processes reflected the same principle of economizing action as did market processes, and with differences between market phenomena and fiscal phenomena arising because of differences in the institutional environments that governed interactions among participants. The schemes of thought associated with any scholarly tradition resemble a river into which numerous scholars contribute. With multiple schemes of thought and research programs being in play at any moment, it is not unusual to find admixtures among schemes sometimes occurring due to strategic and competitive elements entailed in the generation of scholarship (Collins 1998) as scholars compete for attention space, sometimes making tactical borrowings from other analytical cores despite inconsistencies between those borrowings and the cores of the parental research programs.

BETWEEN STASIS AND CHAOS:
BUCHANAN'S ECONOMIC THEORY

Buchanan (1964a; 1990) distinguished between an economic theory centered on choice and allocation and one centered on interaction and coordination. This distinction entails a relationship between foreground and background, and is not a matter of one being right and the other wrong. Ross Emmett's (2006) examination of the different orientations toward economics taken by Frank Knight on the one hand and that associated with the contemporary Chicago economics of George Stigler and Gary Becker on the other hand conveys the difference crisply, and with Buchanan residing on the Knight side of the divide. Buchanan did not deny that economic theory had predictive content. To the contrary, he asserted it did have such content, and asserted it strongly and repeatedly. At the same time, however, he asserted equally strongly and continually, that people could not be reasonably modeled as rats responding to incentives in a maze and brought wholly within the rubric of ethology. Humans are among the higher mammals, and much human action is habitual and predictable. There is a great deal of predictive content within the corpus of the economic theory of pricing and allocation.

That theory, however, provides but incomplete guidance for any effort to understand the course of human interaction within society. People are reflexive creatures. They have scope for choosing to change what economists denote as utility functions. People are also creative and imaginative creatures who often try new things just to avoid the boredom that comes with too much repetition. A theory of choice based on maximizing given utility functions in the presence of given prices and incomes (Stigler and Becker 1977) will carry much predictive content, and yet it will leave out of consideration the internal generation of change as people act creatively and innovatively. Buchanan wanted economic theory to maintain its predictive content while also recognizing that the same principles of economizing action are in the foreground of injecting change into society. In holding this orientation toward economic theory, Buchanan faced the same conundrum as his mentor Frank Knight (1921) faced. Knight avoided the conundrum by separating the theory of perfect competition from the theory of entrepreneurial action in *Risk, Uncertainty, and Profit*. Buchanan faced the conundrum by placing the theory of market equilibrium in the background and bringing into the foreground the various forces and processes that continually are in motion to disrupt what might otherwise be states of equilibrium, as Buchanan's (1982c) one-page essay conveys crisply. Where equilibrium theory is presented within a framework of demonstrative reasoning, Buchanan's orientation toward economic theory called for plausible reasoning (Polya 1954). Where an equilibrium theorist would seek to demonstrate conditions under which a competitive equilibrium would be Pareto efficient, Buchanan's approach to economic theory would recognize that demonstrability was not a reasonable objective of a social theory. To be sure, one could always validate an equilibrium theory by claiming that its predictions were close enough. This validation would not be wrong, though it would probably misdirect analytical attention all the same.

In the spirit of Thomas Schelling's (1978) experiment with pieces on a checkerboard, suppose a torus is divided into squares. There are 100 people on that torus, and they constitute a society. With respect to the spirit of Schelling, constituting a society can be described in terms of two rules that govern the movement of pieces on the torus. First, by the principle of private property no piece tries to move onto a square occupied by another piece. Second, asserting that the 100 people constitute a society means that no piece will allow more than two squares to separate it from its nearest neighbor. We can describe the initial distribution of squares on the torus as a social equilibrium. To continue in the spirit of Schelling, suppose five of the 100 pieces seek a new location, perhaps illustrating entrepreneurs seeking to situate new products in some abstract commercial space. That entrepreneurial action will require locational adjustments among some of the other members of the society to maintain adherence to the second rule.

Suppose this entrepreneurial process is continued for several periods. At each period, five entrepreneurs will seek new commercial locations, and the other 95 will respond to maintain their adherence to the second rule. By the principle of constructive mathematical analysis (Bishop 1967), I have described a society that is in continual motion, and with that motion led by five outliers among the social mass (Gladwell 2008). By standard tests of statistical significance (McCloskey and Ziliak 2008), the hypothesis that society is properly described as being in equilibrium could not be rejected. It could be categorized as an equilibrium disturbed by exogenous shocks. Yet by construction, the society is in continual motion and with the direction of movement determined by entrepreneurial action to inject novelty into society. Buchanan (1989) recognized that societies were generally orderly, but he also recognized that change was being injected continually into society. Equilibrium theory had explanatory merit, but it didn't carry a full explanation of social processes. Contrary to Frank Knight, however, Buchanan wanted to keep predictability and change on the same analytical plane, which required that he work with open rather than closed analytical concepts and theorize through plausible rather than demonstrative reasoning.

Buchanan often worked with equilibrium models to take advantage of their simple elegance, but he never allowed such models to displace his recognition that creativity, imagination, and the internal generation of change were also central features of a social economy that an economic theory must embrace. An equilibrium theory by itself countenances reduction of a society to the maximizing choices of a representative individual because the presumption of equilibrium reconciles all individual desires into a consistent whole. Hence, nothing is lost by theorizing about society through a model of a representative individual or, equivalently, a societal average. From this analytical point of departure, the only way change can occur is as an exogenous shock. For Buchanan and his scheme of thought, however, change is not exogenous at the level of society because societies are filled with people who at any moment are seeking to inject changes into society. For most people most of the time, change appears as exogenous. Buchanan recognized, however, that you cannot get to society simply by adding over individuals. One hundred Crusoes living on the same island will generate phenomena that would be unrecognizable to any of the 100 Crusoes scattered across their individual islands. For instance, the individual Crusoes will not establish property rights and will not experience quarrels, nor will they be inspired by someone's example to change some established habit or pattern. Buchanan recognized that theories that pertain to societies are not reducible to theories of individual action, even though he also recognized that the same principles of individual action carry forward to societies. Buchanan's economic theory sought to embrace enough predictability to avoid chaos while avoiding embracing so much predictability as to generate stasis.

Jason Potts (2000) distinguishes between fields and networks as providing alternative frameworks for the construction of economic theories. While Buchanan came to maturity during the heyday of field-based theorizing, Buchanan's intuitions always ran in terms of networks of interacting agents, and in two respects, one vertical and the other horizontal. Vertically, all thinking that entails the emergence of complex phenomena out of interaction among simpler elements requires a conceptualization in terms of different levels of phenomena. For instance, Bruto Latour (2005) notes that a genuine explanation of social phenomena must explain how that phenomena is assembled through interaction among simpler elements that themselves are pre-social. Latour described his orientation as actor-network theory, and illustrates a vertical scheme of thought where higher-level orderliness emerges through lower-level interaction, much as Mitchel Resnick (1994) sets forth in explaining how failure to organize thought in a suitably vertical manner leads to misunderstanding of myriad forms of social phenomena where social-level observations are emergent products of micro-level interaction.

Horizontally, a social theory can have both foreground and background. For classical theory, the institutional arrangements that governed human interaction occupied the theoretical foreground, with the resource allocations that emerged through those interactions occupying the theoretical background. For the classical mind, and for Buchanan's, this made sense. For one thing, resources have no ability to allocate themselves. Only people can allocate resources. Furthermore, no person has the mental capacity to allocate resources for an entire society outside, perhaps, of a small tribe. Hence, resource allocations will be emergent features of some institutional arrangement or conventional practice that governs interactions among the members of a society. The foreground of classical economic theories was occupied by different institutional arrangements for governing human interactions.

The neoclassical movement in economic theory that got underway in the 1870s and was dominant by the 1920s and the years of high theory (Shackle 1967), elevated resource allocation into the foreground of economic theory. Institutional arrangements receded into the theoretical background, and were regarded as pretty much inessential, as conveyed by common claims that the first-order conditions for economic efficiency were identical under liberalism and socialism. To regard institutional arrangements as inessential background was central to the neoclassical movement in economic theory. While Buchanan came to scholarly maturity during the heyday of the neoclassical period in economics, he most certainly was not a neoclassical economist. Buchanan's theoretical orientation was that of a classical political economist who understood the significance of actions at the margins and so, unlike Adam Smith, did not get tripped up by the diamond-water paradox.

All the same, Buchanan worked in an environment where editors inclined more strongly toward neoclassical styles of thought than he did. In this situation, Buchanan often responded by developing analyses that contained both neoclassical models and literary discussions that extended beyond the models. In this practice, Buchanan resembled Alfred Marshall. For both Marshall and Buchanan, the properties of different arrangements by which people might govern themselves occupied the foregrounds of their attention space, and with various neoclassical formulations of equilibrium conditions occupying the background. In developing this style of theorizing, Buchanan improved on Frank Knight (1921) who theorized in terms of two disjunctive models: competitive equilibrium and entrepreneurial action. Where Knight sought separation between the disjunctive models, Buchanan sought to bring them together by placing them into a relationship of foreground and background.

Chapter Two

The Theory of Public Finance

Buchanan's Scholarly Sapling

Buchanan titled his first professional paper (Buchanan 1949) "The Pure Theory of Public Finance: A Suggested Approach." This short piece was the sapling from which grew nearly the entire corpus of his subsequent work, which 64 years later had grown into a mighty oak tree that cast a large shadow over the territory of political economy. Buchanan's idea was strikingly simple on hindsight, as are most good ideas. That idea enabled the emergence of a new school of thought known variously as public choice, constitutional political economy, and Virginia political economy (chapter 3). This new orientation toward the traditional material of public finance led to the creation of new literatures on federalist forms of government (chapter 4), on money, credit, and debt (chapter 5), and on the relationship among liberty, entitlement, and responsibility (chapter 6). It also led to new insights into ethics, social philosophy, and the myriad problems associated with ever larger populations living together in an ever-shrinking world (chapter 7).

My reference to the ability of Buchanan (1949) to set in motion the emergence of a new school of thought is advanced in the context of the scholarly world Buchanan entered at mid-century in the United States. That world was one where what passed for theory in public finance were a set of ideologies parading as scientific-sounding maxims. One maxim might proclaim that taxes should be based on ability to pay, and use a utilitarian logic to convey the idea. Another maxim was that equals should be taxed equally. As Louis Eisenstein (1961) recognized, such maxims lacked scientific content but they offered a platform from which public finance economists could inveigh on topics of public discussion. Buchanan found no scholarly inspiration in the public finance he encountered during his student days, and yet he wanted to pursue work in public finance. Thanks to Marianne Johnson's (2014a) investigation into Buchanan's days as a doctoral student at the University of Chicago during 1946–1948, we know that his doctoral dissertation on federalism contained references to Knut Wicksell (1896) and Antonio de Viti de Marco (1936). Wicksell and de Viti pointed toward an orientation toward public finance that differed sharply from the orientations that Buchanan encountered at Chicago. Buchanan's "Pure Theory of Government Finance" was Buchanan's effort to incorporate those insights into the creation of a new orientation toward public finance, one that would be explanatory and not hortatory. The rest of the story is history, as they say. Before examining Buchanan's sapling and the branches that emerged from it, some useful context can be acquired by examining the scholarly landscape that Buchanan encountered at mid-century.

PUBLIC FINANCE AT MID-CENTURY

Buchanan completed his dissertation under Roy Blough's supervision in 1948 on problems of equity in federal systems (Buchanan 1950). The other members of Buchanan's committee were Harvey Perloff and Frank Knight. While Buchanan often identified Knight as one of the two inspirations for his scholarly work, the other being Knut Wicksell, Buchanan was not attracted to the work done by the other members of his dissertation committee. Yet he wanted to write his dissertation on public finance, and Blough was the prime figure at Chicago at the time. Henry Simons had died in June 1946, though Buchanan took a course from Simons during the spring 1946 quarter. One could speculate that had Simons not died, Buchanan would have chosen Simons to supervise his dissertation, for Buchanan was attracted to the classically liberal orientation he found in Knight and Simons. But this is just speculation about something that might have been but wasn't. Besides, it's unlikely that Buchanan would have found Simons' orientation toward public finance any significant improvement on the other orientations toward public finance that dominated the American scholarly landscape, for Simons too thought of public finance in terms of offering maxims for practical statecraft. While Buchanan was attracted to Simons' liberalism, he would not have been attracted toward Simons' orientation toward public finance.

Marianne Johnson (2014b) examines the emergence of public finance as a field of study in the United States between 1880 and 1930 at four major universities: Chicago, Columbia, Harvard, and Wisconsin. She explains the role that progressivist ideas played in shaping the construction of academic public finance over what was its formative period. The period between the end of Johnson's narrative in 1930 and Buchanan's arrival in Chicago in 1946 saw continued consolidation of the trends Johnson identified, but no kind of fundamental change in orientation. This meant that public finance was dominated by historical and institutional descriptions in the service of social reform. In that formative period, public finance had been to a significant extent imported from Germany, more from Americans taking their advanced degrees in Germany than from Germans moving to America. Johnson reports that one of the major public finance professors of that early period, Henry C. Adams, who pursued graduate study in Germany, organized his teaching around two questions: (1) what are the legitimate and necessary wants of a State and (2) how might those wants be most advantageously supplied? While this phrasing is Adams', the sentiment was common to the study of public finance understood to be the search for lessons useful for practical statecraft. Simons would have accepted those questions as reasonable, though he would surely have addressed them in a classically liberal manner. In contrast, Buchanan would have objected to those questions, and with that objection heralding Buchanan's (1949) expressed desire to set public finance on a different footing from what he found during his student days.

Buchanan's dissertation supervisor, Roy Blough, had a joint appointment in economics and political science. He also was highly active in politics, serving both in the Roosevelt and Truman administrations, including as two-year stint on Truman's Council of Economic Advisors. Harvey Perloff's interests were in urban design and planning, and he later became dean of the Graduate School of Architecture and Urban Planning at UCLA. Also in attendance at Buchanan's dissertation defense, Johnson (2014a) reports, was Richard Goode, another public finance economist, who spent the bulk of his career at the International Monetary Fund. The other attendees at Buchanan's dissertation defense were T. W. Schultz, H. G. Lewis, and L. W. Mints, all serious academic theorists outside of public finance. Johnson offers some plausible speculation that Buchanan might have been attracted to public finance from a course he took with Simon Leland in his first (winter 1946) quarter at Chicago, and with Buchanan also taking classes that quarter from Frank Knight and Theodore Schultz. Leland was a Chicago graduate from 1926 who was well known for his work on state and local public finance, and with Johnson further speculating that Leland probably wrote his dissertation on property taxation with Jacob Viner, who was teaching public finance at that time. Leland, however, left Chicago for Northwestern at the end of the spring 1946 quarter, replaced by Blough.

While Buchanan took a class from Henry Simons during the spring 1946 quarter, Simons died in June 1946. Although Buchanan was closer to Simons regarding orientations toward government than to Leland. Buchanan had great respect for Leland's talents all the same; moreover, Buchanan's dissertation topic on fiscal equity in a federal system would have been broadly compatible with Leland's work on property taxes and state and local public finance. Yet, neither Simons nor Leland were options when it came time for

Buchanan to write his dissertation. So Roy Blough became the supervisor of record, though it's also clear, both from reading the dissertation and from conversations with Buchanan, that Knight was the prime source of advice that Buchanan sought while writing the dissertation. Regardless of whether Leland or Simons might have supervised his dissertation had the period 1946–1948 worked out differently for Leland and Simons, Buchanan's distance from what he experienced as public finance at Chicago almost surely would not have narrowed.

Buchanan did not care for the heavy historicism and institutionalism that dominated American public finance at mid-century. His attitude in this respect was similar to Frank Knight's intense dislike of what was then known as institutional economics combined with a strong sense of the desirability of making social institutions more central to economic theory. American public finance offered no help in this regard. Nor did the British alternative, replete with what Buchanan regarded as a sterile utilitarian mysticism as exemplified by the dominating figures of F. Y. Edgeworth (1897) and A. C. Pigou (1928). In looking at the options then in play for pursuing a career in public finance theorist, Buchanan must have found himself between the proverbial rock and a hard place. On one side, there was the historicist-institutionalist motif illustrated by Edwin Seligman, Harold Groves, and Roy Blough. On the other side was the utilitarian neoclassicism associated with Edgeworth and Pigou, and which also characterized Henry Simons, though Simons worked within more of a libertarian framework than did most utilitarian theorists.

For Buchanan's theoretical proclivities, the prime exemplars of theoretical public finance were surely Francis Edgeworth (1897) and A. C. Pigou (1928). Edgeworth and Pigou both addressed public finance within the spirit of the two questions Henry Adams advanced for students of public finance to explore noted above: what are the economic wants of the state and how might these be best satisfied? Edgeworth and Pigou addressed such questions more systematically and formally than did the American institutionalists, losing much contact with actual experience in the process. While Buchanan was always attracted to formal styles of inquiry over discursive expositions of the same material, Buchanan also disliked formality that was unanchored to some institutional mooring through which all human interaction occurred.

Francis Edgeworth's (1897) "Pure Theory of Taxation" posed a simple question: how can a government that wants to collect some stipulated amount of revenue from its subjects do so in a manner that imposes the least sacrifice of welfare on those subjects? This formulation represents an organismic political philosophy where the state stands apart from the citizenry and imposes its will on them. Edgeworth assumes that the state will impose its will in beneficent fashion, indicating that Edgeworth assumes the state is a benevolent form of despot. To be sure, benevolence is determined from the perspective of the state, as individual subjects have nothing to say about state action. The state asserts its benevolence in Edgeworth's organismic framework, and that ends the matter. The state does not inquire into individual desires in Edgeworth's formulation because Edgeworth takes that knowledge as data. Armed with those data, the state is instructed to impose taxes to minimize the sacrifices that its chosen quantity of taxation will impose on the population. This knowledge does not come through any inquiry into the desires, dreams, or aspirations of subjects. Rather it comes about by analytical supposition or ethical intuition by the presumed ruler of the state.

That ruler is presumed to know that subjects care only about their consumption of goods and services that are available within the economy. This presumption is formalized by positing a functional relationship between a subject's income and the utility a subject derives from that income along the lines that figure 2.1 illustrates. Individuals are assumed to receive utility from their income, and with that utility increasing at a diminishing rate as income increases. Figure 2.1 illustrates this diminishing marginal utility of income for two individuals denoted as A and B, with the two individuals having the same functional relationship between income and utility. The imposition of a tax lowers an individual's income and the utility associated with that unit of income. Should both subjects be taxed at the same rate, the loss of utility is greater the lower the income. A unit of tax reduces utility by MU_A for A and by MU_B for B. By shifting that tax from A to B, an increase in aggregate utility of $MU_A - MU_B$ results. In Edgeworth's basic framework, state spending, which is presumed to return nothing of value to subjects, is a pure reduction in utility to subjects. This simple framework yields one simple implication for public finance: tax extractions should pare down incomes from the top until the desired amount of revenue is collected. So long as the amount of revenue to be raised is less than $I_B - I_A$, the entire amount should be collected from B to minimize the aggregate amount of sacrificed utility the tax imposes on subjects.

Edgeworth, as well as subsequent theorists, recognized that this simple framework was one extreme case in a field of theoretical options. Edgeworth also recognized that the 100 percent marginal rates of tax his scheme imposed on those who would be subject to tax would reduce the incentive such taxpayers have to earn income. Why would someone work 60 hours a week if everything earned beyond working 40 hours was taxed away? Recognition of this simple point led Edgeworth to amend his initial formulation to account for the ability of taxes to reduce the effort people would put into earning income. That amended formulation still supported a progressive structure of tax rates, though the highest rate stopped short of 100 percent.

Edgeworth's formulation ran in terms of minimizing the loss of utility from raising some stipulated amount of revenue. Frank Ramsey (1927) amended Edgeworth's formulation by converting the amount of revenue to be raised into a variable to be determined within the model rather than being

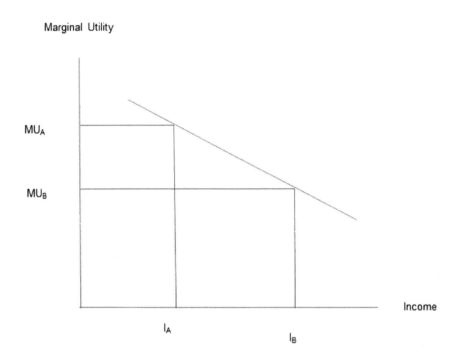

Marginal Utility

MU_A

MU_B

Income

I_A

I_B

Figure 2.1.   Edgeworth and Utilitarian Redistribution through Taxation.

exogenous to the model. This amendment inspired what became known as the theory of optimal taxation, of which Atkinson and Stiglitz (1980), Mirrlees (1994), and Salanié (2003) are clear illustrations. This contemporary literature still rests wholly within the notion of an organismic state that stands apart from its subjects. Only now the state taxes some people and subsidizes other people, with the budget reflecting a desire to maximize some concept of societal welfare. Within this style of formulation, taxes reduce the utility of subjects while subsidies increase it. If taxes are imposed on people with high incomes and subsidies given to people with low incomes, income is transferred from units of income with low utility to units with higher utility, increasing aggregate societal utility in the process.

While the contemporary literature on optimal taxation posits the problem of public finance as being one of redistributing income to maximize some measure of aggregate utility, it does not follow that this approach generates strong support for redistributive taxation. The strength of such support these models generate depends on the strength of response to taxes and transfers. Taxes and subsidies both discourage the supply of effort to earn income. For taxpayers, why work if earnings are taxed away? For recipients of subsidies, why work if you will receive subsidies anyway? The answer to such questions depends on the rate at which taxpayers reduce their effort to earn income as the marginal rate of tax increases, and on the rate at which subsidy recipients will reduce their effort as the marginal rate of subsidy increases.

What is surely most notable about this organismic formulation is its fictional or magical character. The taxes and spending that comprise the objects of any theory of public finance simply appear like the proverbial rabbit springing from a hat. No one does anything to cause the phenomena of public finance to appear. Not even a ruler truly enters the scene, nor do subjects. All that exists are functional relations between income and utility that are manipulated analytically by some theorist who exists in a different world. The organismic model of the state certainly does not offer a useful model of public finance within democratic regimes. Nor does it offer a useful model for monarchical and despotic regimes. The Edgeworthian framework asks us to imagine a despot or monarch who has a single-minded devotion to maximizing the aggregate utility of the regime's subjects. Yet that monarch has no staff of courtiers who roam about the countryside trying to ascertain incomes or the desires and aspirations of subjects. The organismic model offers a fairy tale that perhaps allows readers to feel good upon hearing justifications for fiscal measures that they would have supported without reading the fairy tale.

It would be possible to develop despotic, monarchical, or ruling-class models of public finance in a realistic vein, but such models would be realistic stories and not fairy tales. Several efforts to this effect were undertaken by Italian contemporaries of Edgeworth. For instance, Amilcare Puviani (1903) inquired into how a ruler might conduct his fiscal activities when those activities can influence his hold on his position, and with Buchanan (1967, 126–43) summarizing Puviani's ideas about fiscal illusion. After all, a ruler won't hold power tomorrow simply because he holds it today. Power invariably has more claimants than there are positions to claim, and a current holder must work to maintain that hold. What this implies for a theory of public finance depends on numerous institutional details that vary across time and space. For instance, Puviani thought that a ruler would maintain a firmer hold on power by imposing numerous small taxes than by imposing a few large taxes because smaller taxes would generate less resistance from taxpayers.

Alternatively, a monarch might employ some agents to collect taxes from his subjects, as illustrated by the practice of tax farming. A monarch in that position faces two types of problem. One is that he wants the agents to turn over their collections to him. The other is that he wants those collections to avoid inciting rebellion among the subjects. A monarch in this position might handle his first problem by stipulating a volume of tax revenue he wants to receive from his tax farmers, and letting them keep the rest of what they collect. He might handle his second problem by instructing his farmers to avoid collecting taxes from subjects whose support the monarch values especially heavily. Along such lines of inquiry, an explanatory theory of public finance could be constructed for monarchical and despotic types of regime. That theory would have a realistic as distinct from a mystical or magical character, to recall a distinction James Burnham (1943) set forth in contrasting Dante and Machiavelli as exemplifying alternative tacks toward political phenomena, and with Dante reasoning mythically and Machiavelli reasoning realistically.

Arthur Pigou's (1928) *Study in Public Finance* is the other prime English-language option to institutionalist public finance that was relevant when Buchanan was a student. Pigou operated without Edgeworth's mathematical formalism, but theorized to much the same effect. Pigou's focus was always on how a government can intervene into existing patterns of market activity to increase some notion of aggregate social utility. In this book, Pigou examines two versions of sacrifice theory for guiding the imposition of taxes, siding in the end with Edgeworth's notion of minimizing aggregate sacrifice over imposing equal sacrifices of utility on everyone. As befits the author of the *Economics of Welfare* (Pigou 1920), opposition to which inspired Coase (1960) and Buchanan and Stubblebine (1962), Pigou (1928) explores the use of taxes and bounties to correct what Pigou perceives to be maladjustments in market relationships. Much of the book is concerned with the effects of taxes under various circumstances and conditions, with the analysis having a generally sharper focus than what characterized most institutionalist writing on public finance, so there are grounds for thinking that Buchanan might have found this style of thinking marginally more attractive than the institutionalist style that dominated American public finance. Neither style of public finance, however, was remotely competitive in Buchanan's judgment to what he encountered in his dissertation-writing exposure to Wicksell and de Viti.

Fortunately for Buchanan, he encountered sources of inspiration for a third way in his dissertation research from two directions. One direction was from Sweden, where Buchanan's dissertation contained references to Knut Wicksell and Erik Lindahl, along with Richard Musgrave's (1939) paper on the voluntary exchange theory of public finance. The other direction was from Italy, where Buchanan cited Antonio de Viti de Marco's (1936) English translation of de Viti (1934), which itself was the fourth version of de Viti (1888), though with changes in titling between 1888 and 1934. Buchanan (1949) is Buchanan's response to the scholarly conundrum he faced, and with that response being the sapling that became the massive tree that could not even be contained within the 20 volumes collected in Buchanan (1999–2002).

WHAT DID WICKSELL BRING TO BUCHANAN?

These days, Wicksell's approach to public finance is typically summarized by asserting that he favored some scheme of qualified majority voting over ordinary majority voting, as illustrated by requiring something like three-quarters or four-fifths support. It is true that Wicksell spoke of approximate unanimity in this manner, but Wicksell's formulation entailed much more than replacement of majority voting within parliaments with a rule that required higher than majority support for a measure to be enacted. Wicksell's support for approximate unanimity was accompanied by a set of institutional arrangements that departed significantly from any incorporation of approximate unanimity into the American fiscal system, whether at the federal or the state level of government.

Wicksell envisioned a political system in which public output reflected the desires of citizens as these were reflected in their demands for public output. Figure 2.2 illustrates schematically what Wicksell sought to accomplish, as further formalized by Erik Lindahl (1919). Shown there are three individuals with different demands for some collective activity. Under unanimity, Q^* would be the desired amount of public output, given the configuration of cost and demand shown there, and with the three individuals paying different marginal prices that reflect their different demands for the collective activity. Figure 2.2 illustrates what became known as the benefit principle of public finance. The idea that public output should reflect the desires of citizens has a long history that can be traced to contractual formulations of idealized state activity. But it has been generally thought that this is one of those ideal schemes that rarely can be put into practice. A city might be able to impose charges for installing sewer lines along the lines that figure 2.2 depicts, but the benefit principle has modest scope for being put into practice, most theorists have thought. Indeed, Paul Samuelson's (1954; 1955) articulation of the theory of public goods expressly denied that the benefit principle could be put into practice, leaving the only option someone's reaching into a black box to impose some social welfare function.

Charles Tiebout's (1956) well-cited "Pure Theory of Local Expenditure" was written as an answer to Samuelson, by explaining that a system of local government could resemble a market in the provision of public goods. While Tiebout's formulation attracted strong attention, it has been generally thought that his formulation was a special case and not a theory of general applicability. In two books published one year apart, James Buchanan (1967; 1968b) sought to articulate elements of a catallactic and explanatory theory of public finance, placing him in opposition to Samuelson's denial of that possibility. Buchanan's articulation occurred against a background of American institutional arrangements, and did not consider the gamut of com-

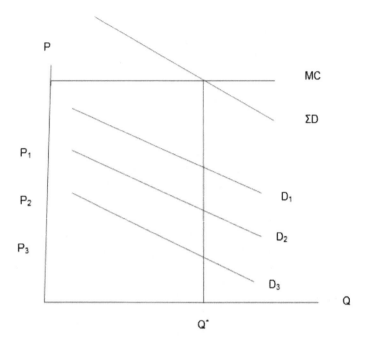

Figure 2.2.   Wicksell's Theory of Fiscal Catallactics.

plementary arrangements that would be necessary to implement the benefit principle.

Wicksell, like Buchanan, started from a normative point of departure that fiscal actions should reflect the preferences of individuals, as against being impositions by some ruler or ruling class. Wicksell's central question concerned how to embed such a normative point of departure within the Swedish fiscal system of his time (Wagner 1988). It is fine to assert that fiscal choices should reflect the consent of those affected by those choices, as figure 2.2 illustrates. But how actually to accomplish this outcome is the puzzle that Wicksell explored. Simply to require unanimity or near-unanimity might be sufficient for a small town of a few hundred people, but it wouldn't be sufficient for a nation of many millions of people. A relative handful of people can reasonably have a multi-sided conversation and come to some reasonable consensus. There is no way that millions of people could do this without developing auxiliary institutions that made the challenge of achieving consensus manageable.

Wicksell's approach to public finance within an individualist motif had two facets. One was recognition, contrary to Edgeworth, that people should participate in making the fiscal choices with which they will live. For Wicksell, there was no sense of a ruler imposing his or her will on ruled subjects, for there were no ruled subjects in Wicksell's analytical framework, nor were there in Buchanan's. There were citizens rather than subjects, and those citizens governed themselves rather than being governed by some ruler. This alternative formulation doesn't deny the presence of political offices staffed by people who execute fiscal actions. Rather, that formulation examines the way the pattern of political offices might influence the extent to which the actions of political officials reflect the interests of citizens. This pattern of scholarly inquiry is similar to that which economists bring to corporations. For a corporation, there are a set of offices through which officers choose patterns of corporate activity. Within an institutional framework grounded in private property and freedom of contract, those officers will be strongly motivated to channel corporate activities in directions that corporate customers would choose if they were in position to direct those activities. Within a generic democratic template, there are numerous institutional patterns of democratic governance that could be created. Wicksell suggested one pattern for the Sweden of his time which he thought would operate reasonably well in reflecting the consent of the governed within a Swedish organization of public finance.

Several things were notable about Wicksell's formulation. One was that Wicksell perceived Sweden to be comparatively homogeneous, which meant that opinion would be more narrowly distributed within Sweden than within larger nations. This suggested to Wicksell that a system of proportional representation with a relatively small number of political parties could result in the selection of a parliamentary assembly that would come close to being a scaled-down version of Swedish society. To the extent this presumption is accurate, a fiscal measure that secured 90 percent support within parliament would have secured something like 90 percent support within the nation. So long as this presumption is reasonably accurate, securing approximate unanimity within parliament would correspond to something like securing approximate unanimity within the nation.

This theory of the demand side of fiscal activity must be joined by a theory of the supply side to create a full theory of public finance. For Wicksell, the supply side of public finance would operate through a monarch who was construed as an executive or entrepreneur who would propose programs for parliamentary decision. In proposing programs, Wicksell's executive would be constrained in two ways. One constraint was that the monarch's proposals had to secure a high degree of support within parliament. The other constraint was that the monarch operated not as a salaried civil servant but as a residual claimant on the net revenues he derived from supplying services to parliament. One may reasonably doubt the efficacy with which the Wicksellian scheme could be put into effect, at least without being subject to substantial refinement. Whatever degree of refinement might be thought necessary, ranging from modest revision to starting over, Wicksell succeeded in sketching the contours of an individualistic approach to public finance, recognizing that the identifier "individualistic" denoted some scheme in which people participate in generating the fiscal outcomes they experience.

Buchanan's initial interest in constructing a different approach to public finance from what he encountered during this student days in Chicago found inspiration both from Wicksell and de Viti, and with Buchanan's interest in de Viti's orientation being amplified by spending the 1955–1956 academic year in Italy. Buchanan's 1949 paper on "The Pure Theory of Government Finance" was truly the sapling to which most of subsequent work can be traced, provided one reads back from the present rather than reading forward from the past. One who reads "The Pure Theory" and tries to locate pieces of that paper in Buchanan's later works will have but modest success. But one who reads instances of his later work will typically be able to draw a connection from that work to "The Pure Theory." For instance, a reader will not find tax earmarking mentioned in "The Pure Theory"; however, it is easy to understand how Buchanan's (1963) treatment of earmarking emerges out of the mental orientation of the author of "The Pure Theory." Indeed, the type of parliamentary procedure required to implement Wicksell's approach required universal tax earmarking, where any proposed program of expenditure would be accompanied by a proposal for financing it.

More generally, to describe fiscal phenomena as arising through interaction among citizens within a democratic fiscal process must entail the construction of a theoretical framework through which political action is constituted. Buchanan's well-known interest in constitutional political economy stems directly from his interest in avoiding organismic theories of the state. To do this requires effort to explain how collections of individuals are able actually to undertake fiscal activity. By itself, a collection of people is just a mob. The energy contained within that mob can be released and channeled in several ways. One way or set of ways is despotic, of which Edgeworth advanced a benevolent form of despotism, though we should surely recognize that this is more wish or myth than reality, along the lines of James Burnham's (1943) contrast between Dante and Machiavelli. An alternative way, the democratic way and Buchanan's way, is to bring some organizational form to that mass of people, and with different particular forms channeling social energy in different ways. In this instance, each form would denote a constitutional arrangement, and the theory of democratically organized public finance would reflect a constitutional focus on how different frameworks of rules through which people are organized into groups channel fiscal outcomes in different directions.

WHAT DID DE VITI BRING TO BUCHANAN?

Richard Musgrave (1939) brought to English readers the central ideas of what he described as the voluntary exchange theory of public economy articulated by Knut Wicksell and Erik Lindahl. While Musgrave's exposition was clear, it was also skeptical that the principle of taxing according to benefits that people receive in their capacities as taxpayers could be put into practice. Accordingly, Musgrave became an advocate of what he called a planning approach to public finance and what Buchanan (1949) described as an organicist approach. In de Viti (1936), Buchanan found a noted public finance economist who thought public finance should be a theoretical field of study and not just some maxims to guide applied statecraft, whereby the economist would speak truth to power (Wildavsky 1979). Furthermore, de Viti had served some 20 years as a member of the Italian parliament, which would surely give an outside observer some basis for thinking that the activities in which a politician would undertake as a member of parliament would find some degree of correspondence with the academic theories that this part-time politician wrote about in his capacity as a professor of public finance at the University of Rome. Sure, the role of a politician is different from that of a professor of economics, just as the role of the owner of a small business is different from that same person's role as a professor of economics. Yet the central activity of an academic economist in de Viti's and in Buchanan's judgments is to illuminate the world of practice in which a business person or politician engages. The scholarly and practical activities are different, so the practical person should not expect to find practical recipes in theoretical formulations. All the same, the practical person should be able to recognize the general contours of his or her activities in the abstract renditions of the theorist.

De Viti (1888; 1936) sought to incorporate politically organized activity into the explanatory rubric of economic theory. De Viti recognized and worked with the category of collective wants, which he attributed to wants that arose in conjunction with people living together in close geographical proximity. There was no normative thrust coming from de Viti to create some technological dichotomy between private and public goods along the lines of Samuelson's (1954; 1955) dichotomy. For de Viti, public finance was not to be a form of social engineering where the public finance theorist assigns activities to market or governments according to some conceptual construction. For de Viti, the task of the theorist was not to tutor politicians about how they should conduct their political activities. Rather, their task was to explain the underlying and heretofore unseen logic by which societies operated. If the world operated with both privately provided and politically provided parks, the task of the theorist was not to say how parks should be supplied. It was rather to uncover the principles and forces at work that generated the observations about the actual organization of parks.

De Viti (1936) incorporated two antipodal frameworks into his analysis. One was a formulation in terms of a cooperative state. This model of the state, which stems from de Viti (1888), has the same general features of the voluntary exchange theory that Musgrave (1939) attributed to Wicksell and Lindahl. To be sure, de Viti did not think in terms of individuals coming together to organize trades within some group, thereby raising concerns about direct democracy on large scales. De Viti took political organization as data. People would be organized into political units, and they would select governing officials through elections. De Viti did not engage in discussion about the problems created by free riding that Musgrave (1939) raised against what he called the voluntary exchange theory because de Viti was not trying to explain how a mass of people without structured relationships among themselves could secure such structure. Instead, de Viti began by observing such structure and inquired into its operating qualities and principles. Here, de Viti recognized a limiting case where collective action captured gains from trade among the participants, reflecting much the same result as Wicksell's principle of unanimity. De Viti also recognized that this was a limiting case, and that democratic action could often secure advantages for some set of people at the expense of others in the society.

Between Wicksell and de Viti, Buchanan found a path along which to pursue his interest in bringing public finance within an explanatory rather than the planning rubric that Musgrave (1939) advanced. In Buchanan's Pantheon of scholarly gods, only two figures appeared by his own reckoning: Frank Knight and Knut Wicksell. From Knight, Buchanan acquired an attitude and orientation toward the world of scholarship and his place in that world. He also acquired a friendship that remained until Knight's death. Buchanan's substantive work occupied different territory than did Knight's, though it is possible to find reflections of Knight throughout Buchanan's oeuvre, typically more in terms of attitude toward material than in substantive text. In contrast, Wicksell's presence was rarely far removed from Buchanan, both in attitude and in text. In attitude, Buchanan was an individualist who was interested in marching to his own internal drummer and not in trying actively to sell his ideas to others. In text, Buchanan incorporated Wicksellian themes throughout his oeuvre. Steven Medema (2005) argues that Wicksell spoke to Buchanan's reformist urgings where the Italians, about whom Buchanan did much to bring to the attention of English readers, did not. This appears to be the case, though it is also the case that the Italian theorists operated in a more explanatory motif than did Wicksell. Buchanan pursued both motifs throughout his career, with a mix that changed somewhat toward exhortation as he aged.

ITALIAN PUBLIC FINANCE TRANSFORMED INTO PUBLIC CHOICE

It is easy to see how Buchanan's initial interest in constructing a different approach to public finance led to the emergence of public choice in the aftermath of his immersion in the Italian literature during 1955–1956. To illustrate the congruence between Italianate public finance during its classical period and the Virginia style political economy associated with Buchanan, I shall consider briefly Attilio da Empoli (1926; 1941). Instead of da Empoli, I could have done the same with such more familiar and somewhat older theorists as Maffeo Pantaleoni, Vilfredo Pareto, or Luigi Einaudi, but I use da Empoli to widen the net of relevant theorists. Attilio da Empoli was in the process of making significant contributions to the classical Italian tradition of public finance when he died in 1948 at the age of 44. He was also the father of the founding editor of the *Journal of Public Finance and Public Choice*, Domenico da Empoli, who held that position until Domenico's death in December 2016. Attilio da Empoli's conceptual orientation sought continually to develop means of theorizing about public finance in bottom-up fashion. For instance, in his *Teoria dell' incidenza delle imposte*, da Empoli (1926) set forth the concept of oblique incidence. This concept stands in sharp contrast to the standard dichotomy of forward and backward shifting, and illustrates how da Empoli stood apart from the standard neoclassical orientation by thinking in terms of structured patterns of interaction rather than working with the standard dichotomy where those interactions are reduced to a single relationship between consumers and producers. Within the standard dichotomy, taxes are shifted either forward to consumers or backward to producers. In developing his concept of oblique incidence, da Empoli not only sought to develop analyses of types of horizontal shifting but also in so doing thought in terms of a disaggregated network of economic interaction that was ahead of his time because the tools and techniques of network-based theorizing were not in play at that time. Da Empoli's concept of oblique incidence could surely have been put to good use in seeking to explain concrete fiscal phenomena, even though that concept might have little to offer for a hortatory approach to public finance. A theory of oblique shifting opens directly into recognition that many regulations redistribute wealth among firms and consumers in often complex patterns.

In chapter 8 (pp. 91–136) of his *Lineamenti teorici dell'economia corporativa finanziaria*, da Empoli (1941) sought to establish a framework for integrating collective action into the economic process. Da Empoli explained that any such effort must confront two snares that beckon the theorist and which must be avoided if a genuinely explanatory theory of public finance is to be developed. To fall into either of these snares would pull the author into pursuing public finance within the organicist orientation. One branch of the organicist snare is to avoid the analytical challenge by ignoring the lack of a theoretical bridge between the taxing and spending sides of the budget. This branch of the snare treats taxes as uncaused causes (*imposta grandine*), and is illustrated by analyzing taxes in terms of their excess burdens. As da Empoli recognized, a tax can't be wholly a source of loss because the revenues are spent on objects and activities that at least some people desire, and perhaps many do. The tax is part of a fiscal transaction, and it's possible that that transaction will be value enhancing and not value degrading within some overall societal scheme of things. Whether enhancing or degrading, taxes are always caused by desires held by someone somewhere in a society that becomes manifested through political action. To build a theoretical bridge between the taxing and spending sides of the fiscal account might be a difficult challenge, as Buchanan (1967) recognizes and as Marlow and Orze-chowski (1997) amplify, but taxes are components of fiscal transactions all the same. An explanatory theory of public finance must wrestle with the transactional process through which fiscal phenomena arise. A cousin to this branch of the snare is to postulate that collective action is not susceptible to economic explanation. This is the approach Paul Samuelson (1954; 1955) took, and which James Buchanan sought to oppose in setting forth an approach to fiscal catallactics (1967; 1968b).

The other branch of the snare da Empoli identified is to assume that fiscal processes are just market process by another name or means. It's easy enough to understand the power of this snare to capture a theorist's attention. This branch of the snare is illustrated cogently by Donald Wittman's (1989; 1995) arguments that democratic public finance has the same efficiency properties as do competitive markets. Indeed, democracy is just a different form of competition, and with competition being a universal source of allocative efficiency in Wittman's framework. This form of theorizing commits what Mitchel Resnick (1994) calls the centralized mindset, which is to ascribe outcomes to some choosing agent even though those outcomes emerge through some process that currently is not well understood. To compare democratic forms of competition with market forms, it is necessary to develop explanations of the properties of these different processes. Buchanan (1954b) undertook to do that in comparing voting and markets with respect to individual rationality. Wagner and Yazigi (2014) extended Buchanan's analysis from individual rationality to systems of competitive selection. All competition selects for excellence among competitors, but different forms of competition select for different qualities. One wouldn't assemble a swimming team after doing nothing but watching the candidates dive.

The image of a parliamentary assembly as a *peculiar* form of investment bank is one way to avoid both these snares because parliaments are organizational bridges between taxing and spending, as Buchanan (1967, 88–97) explains. This assembly could not be a simple investment bank, for this would be to fuse the taxing and spending sides. Yet it is an arena within which the conflicting desires of people for programs are intermediated. In many respects, a parliament is like a partnership of investment bankers, in that it intermediates between the political enterprises that supply services and seek revenues on one side and the citizens who have the means to support those enterprises, whether or not they want to, on the other side, as McCormick and Tollison (1981) and Leibowitz and Tollison (1980) explain. As an investment bank, the legislative partners seek to develop connections between people who have enterprises for which they are seeking support and people who have the means available to support political enterprises. To say they have the means of support does not imply that they turn it over voluntarily, for if they did that the polity would be a regular investment bank and not a *peculiar* investment bank. It is almost surely the case that there is complementarity between decisions about the support of enterprises and the ability of legislatures to generate revenue, which provides a budgetary bridge between the two sides of the fiscal account, provided only that people who are attracted into the legislative form of investment banking prefer to do more business rather than to do less.

A bridge always exists that connects sources of revenue provided by citizens to sources of service provided by political enterprises. To be sure, political enterprises do not operate by the same rules that govern market-based enterprises, but the connection between revenue and service must be there all the same. It would always be possible to make that connection as direct as it is with ordinary commercial transactions. Knut Wicksell's (1896; [1958]) well-cited formulation articulated one approach to doing just this. In Wicksell's formulation, the legislature would serve explicitly as an intermediary to connect those who supply services with those who demand them. The organization of legislatures along non-Wicksellian lines does not deny the connection between service and revenue, but it does render that connection complex and ambiguous, and something to be explored and illuminated. A good deal of that complexity comes about because of the large number of political enterprises that run some of their financing through the legislature, along with the large number of revenue sources that legislatures tap.

As Eusepi and Wagner (2011) explain, a society contains numerous enterprises distributed across public and market squares. Some of those enterprises are supported through a legislative process and so operate with inalienable ownership. These enterprises bear a parasitical relationship to the system of market pricing (Pantaleoni 1911): they don't generate prices and yet must use prices to guide economic calculation (Boettke 1998; 2001). All of the enterprises are seeking to expand their custom, only with the different forms of enterprise governed by different rules of organization that in turn generate differing patterns of conduct. Zones of conflict and cooperation would arise among different enterprises, and the political arena would expand or contract depending on the organizational efficiency this peculiar investment bank is able to attain, and with efficiency perceived in terms of a political and not a directly commercial calculus. Government would be a factor of production in society, and its operation within society would radiate throughout society in thoroughly oblique and knotted fashion, to recur to da Empoli's analysis of oblique incidence. Governments would be participants within the complex adaptive system that society represents, not necessarily all to the good by any means but there all the same as societal phenomena for a theorist to explain.

BUCHANAN'S PURE THEORY OF GOVERNMENT FINANCE

Buchanan (1949) explains that any theory of public finance must rest on some political foundation. After all, public finance is about the economic activities of governments, especially their taxing and spending. Therefore, the economics of public finance must connect with some theory of politics. One cannot truly theorize about public finance without having some theory of the state close at hand to form a platform for theorizing about public finance. Typically, theories of the state are thought to be the domain of political theory or philosophy, and with a menu of theories and theorists that reach back to ancient Greece. Yet when an economist speaks of matters pertaining to the taxing and spending activities of governments, the economist is necessarily making contract with the territory of political theory, even if economists mostly do not recognize that they are doing this. For the most part, economists develop their theories of public finance unaware that they have buried presuppositions about political theory within their work. Buchanan (1949) brought those presuppositions to light.

The historical record contains numerous forms of government. We know them by such names as despotism, monarchy, oligarchy, and democracy to mention some long-standing forms. For each form of government, there would be economic manifestations that would be amenable to analysis through a theory of public finance. For a monarchy, the material of public finance would stem from a monarch's choices and actions, and observing those choices and actions would tell us something about the monarch. For a monarchical form of government, an economist could reasonably use a theory of choice to explain a monarch's taxing and spending. It would be the same for despotic forms of government. Both a monarch and a despot rule over subjects, and how they exercise that rule is their business. For governments of this form, a theory of public finance would proceed much like an ordinary theory of choice, with allowance made for recognition that a monarch or despot is more than an ordinary person, and operates instead with some form of Big Player status (Koppl 2002). The monarchs of old were well known for often seeking to borrow from wealthy subjects. Monarchs were not subject, however, to the ordinary rules of property and contract. A monarch who failed to redeem a debt could not be sued by the subject he did not pay, though the monarch might try to make good on many such debts to maintain a good reputation. Still, the monarch was a Big Player, meaning that the rules of commerce that applied to subjects did not apply to the monarch.

For an oligarchical form of government, the task of explanation would be more difficult than for a monarchical or despotic form. A simple theory of choice would not be suitable for an oligarchic form because the phenomena of public finance arise through a committee-based process of decision making. For an oligarchy, much of significance would reside in the procedures through which the oligarchs reach their decisions, and with different procedures for reaching those decisions leading to different fiscal outcomes, as Duncan Black (1958) explains in setting forth a theory of action within committees. A committee-based theory of public finance could not be reduced to some ruler's choices because fiscal outcomes would emerge through interaction among the oligarchs. That interaction would proceed through some set of conventions that governed those interactions. Those conventions could even be codified explicitly, in which case they would represent a constitutional framework that governed oligarchical interaction, with Michels (1962) and de Jouvenel (1961) theorizing about democracies as effectively oligarchic.

For a democratic form, the task of explanation would be more challenging still because everyone has some say in the budgetary outcome, at least according to standard democratic ideology. To be sure, this ideology becomes more fantasy than reality as the population of the democratically governed entity increases. For a club or a village with a few hundred residents, it would be relatively easy to have open discussions and reach some consensus in which everyone can be said to have participated. For a city with two or three million residents, however, such direct participation is impossible. No longer can fiscal outcomes be said *ipso facto* to reflect consensus among those affected by fiscal actions. Whether they do or don't, or under what circumstances they might or might not, is something to be explored and not something to be assumed. For democratic public finance far more than for oligarchic public finance, fiscal phenomena arise through interactions among participants. The patterns of those interactions comprise the constitutional framework that shapes the relevant public through which fiscal phenomena emerge.

Buchanan (1949) set forth two polar models of public finance, which he described as "organismic" and "individualistic." In the preceding description, both despotism and monarchy would be forms of government where fiscal phenomena arise through some ruler's choice, and so can be theorized by using the organismic framework. In contrast, neither oligarchy nor democracy are suitable for theorizing through the organismic framework without embracing a clear fiction in place of trying to explain reality. To be sure, theorists of public finance readily embraced fictions, mostly ones that sounded pleasant. A common fiction was to treat the state as a benevolent despot that used its budget to maximize social welfare. A wish or a hope was substituted for an explanation of the operation of actual political processes (Eisenstein 1961). To explain outcomes under democracy, and under oligarchy, requires use of some theory of interaction among the participants who are able to generate collective outcomes. It further requires explanation of how people acquired such positions and how relationships of power or precedence is established among governing officials. With oligarchy, the numbers of people involved are small. With democracy, however, the numbers can be large, and with the difficulties of analysis increasing with the number of participants. With either form, however, an explanatory approach to public finance and collective action requires an individualistic point of analytical departure.

Buchanan's reference to the organismic notion of the state is consistent with both despotic and monarchical regimes. Public finance within regimes where governments are despotic or monarchical would reflect the various interests and desires of rulers. A fiscal theorist could use observed fiscal outcomes to make inferences about the ruler's values and constraints. One monarch might be interested in conquest, another in luxury and amusement. The different patterns of expenditure between those monarchs would speak to differences in the monarch's preferences and values. A theory of public finance for a monarchical or despotic regime would have the same formal structure of a relationship between preferences and constraints as the theory of consumer choice, for observations of a consumer's budget also yield information about the consumer's preferences and values.

Public finance would differ for oligarchic and democratic regimes because there is no person who makes choices for a regime. Under these forms of institutional arrangement, what are described as outcomes are not some person's choices but are products of interaction among the people whose participation leads eventually to the observed outcomes. Yet, theorists of public finance nearly universally have treated fiscal outcomes as if they were simple products of choice. Knut Wicksell (1896 [1958]), who along with Frank Knight were Buchanan's two most admired theorists, lamented that

> with some very few exceptions, the whole theory [of state activity] still rests on the now outdated political philosophy of absolutism. The theory seems to have retained the assumptions of its infancy, in the seventeenth and eighteenth centuries, when absolute power ruled almost all of Europe. . . . Even the most recent manuals on the science of public finance frequently leave the impression . . . of some sort of philosophy of enlightened and benevolent despotism. (Wicksell 1958: 82)

Buchanan's distinction between organismic and individualistic theories of the state as providing different political foundations for a theory of public finance reaches back to Wicksell's lament with respect to the theory of public finance. Buchanan recognized that contemporary scholarship in public finance, just as it had when Wicksell wrote, treated public finance within democratic regimes as if those regimes were despotic or monarchical. By contrasting organismic and individualistic approaches to public finance, Buchanan was seeking to erase Wicksell's lament. The organismic approach to public finance would be suitable for despotic and monarchical regimes. For democratic regimes, however, an individualistic approach would be required. In 1949 Buchanan did not address how that individualistic approach might be constructed, but the challenge of construction became the generative source of much of Buchanan's subsequent analysis of collective phenomena of all sorts.

Buchanan similarly found inspiration for pursuing an alternative approach to public finance in Antonio de Viti de Marco (1936). In his Preface, de Viti explains: "I treat Public Finance as a theoretical science . . . [that has] the task of explaining the phenomena of Public Finance as they appear in their historical setting." With respect to historical settings, de Viti went on to explain that the fiscal phenomena of the middle ages differ from those of modern times, along with further explaining that the phenomena of public finance will differ for states based on slavery than for states based on parliamentary government. With respect to parliamentary government, de Viti further explained that fiscal phenomena could differ among types of parliamentary regime. In this respect, de Viti distinguished between cooperative and monopolistic models of the state. While the cooperative state for de Viti bore a close resemblance to Wicksell (1896), de Viti also recognized that democratic public finance could be highly monopolistic, as de Viti (1930) shows.

The central objective in Buchanan's 1949 paper was to set forth the possibility of an alternative to treating fiscal phenomena as products of some despot, whether that despot is real or imagined. With this formulation, Buchanan took the first step in shifting public finance from a despotic to a democratic institutional framework. Buchanan's reference to an individualistic theory of the state does not imply some embrace of a social philosophy of rugged individualism. It means only that governments are comprised of individuals who rule themselves in some fashion, in contrast to people being ruled by monarchs or despots. Therefore, any explanation of what governments do must be traced to those individuals who in ruling themselves act in the name of government. Just how those individuals might rule themselves depends on their preferences, values, and ideologies. They might operate in the name of liberalist or collectivist ideologies, or any other ideological formulations one might imagine. Whatever the ideology, however, governmental action is action that is initiated by some set of individuals. Just what set of individuals depends on numerous institutional features through which a democratic government is constituted.

An individualist approach to public finance, in contrast to an organismic approach, holds that the explanation of governmental activity must be resolvable into actions favored by individuals within a society who invoke the mantle of government. Those individuals might comprise but a small set within the society or they might comprise most of the society. Either way, fiscal phenomena are not some ruler's choices but rather are products of participation and interaction among a set of people within the society. In this respect, Buchanan's embrace of an individualistic approach to public finance was methodological and not substantive. With respect to substance, one could well think that a flourishing society required a rich variety of politically sponsored activity. Still, the organization and operation of those activities would be pursued by individuals, and in this respect political activity is no different from commercial activity, as conveyed by Wagner's (2016a; 2016b) examination of entangled political economy. Polities are no more genuinely acting entities than are firms. As convenient modes of expression, we refer to governments as doing things, but we recognize that behind these expressions stand the ordered interactions of individuals who operate those entities. Those operations, moreover, respond to the clienteles those organizations serve.

Buchanan's scholarly career started with his creation of the disjunction between organismic and individualistic theories of the state, along with embracing the belief that the individualistic construction offered scientific advantage because it offered a path through which a genuine understanding of the etiology of governmental activity could be constructed. By contrast, the organismic approach to the state created a form of black box, the internal operations of which were not open to explanation. For democratically grounded political systems governed by the ideology of self-governance, black boxes are surely normatively unacceptable in addition to being scientifically unsatisfying. Normatively, Buchanan was a liberal democrat; his normative inclination thus merged with his scientific interest in the conduct of government, leading to his methodologically individualistic orientation toward government that guided construction of his scholarly oeuvre.

RECIPROCAL RELATION BETWEEN COST AND CHOICE

For Buchanan, economics at its foundation was a theory of society organized principally through exchange, and not a theory of choice (Buchanan 1964a). It is this distinction that renders it more accurate to describe Buchanan as continuing within the classical tradition of political economy after incorporating considerations of marginal utility, as against being a neoclassical economics as this tradition was understood during the middle of the twentieth century. During this period, neoclassical economists pretty much believed that the theory of general equilibrium was a reasonably good model of the economic organization of societies. This theory had two central presumptions within its hard core (Reder 1982). One was that people should be treated as utility maximizers as conveyed by models of constrained maximization. The other is that societal observations pertain to states of equilibrium as described by generalized market clearing. Should a theorist observe a situation where one or both presumptions are thought not to hold, the theorist is most likely wrong and should rethink what he or she thought had been observed. Alternatively, the observation pertains to an instant of transition from one equilibrium to another, set in motion by some exogenous shock.

Buchanan accepted neither of these presumptions. He accepted the notion that people operated with objectives in mind and sought to pursue them efficiently. But he also incorporated a self-referential quality into his conception of the individual. He did not regard people as being directed rigidly by utility functions, whether those functions were programmed into them genetically or were habits that were impressed on them through social or cultural interaction with other people. To the contrary, he thought people had scope for constructing their biographies, though the ability to do that required that they live as free persons and not as slaves. This belief implied that reflective individuals could continually insert new data into society, which rendered Buchanan incapable of believing in the ubiquity of market clearing. He recognized that market clearing could be a useful way of looking at social processes, but not the only way because he also recognized that changes were continually inserted into society.

Most economists going back at least to Alfred Marshal treat utility and cost as distinct conceptual concepts. The classical economists tried to explain prices of different products through variations in their costs of production. Utility or demand would influence the amount of a product people would buy, but the prices of products would be governed by their costs of production. To the contrary, Marshall explained that prices were set by intersections between supply and demand, recognizing that cost and utility were independent forces whose joint interaction yielded price.

Within this neoclassical scheme of thought, the cost of a product stems from the efforts of producers to produce those products. The neoclassical framework envisions a two-step sequence where production precedes cost, with a cost function being derived from a production function. A production function is a form of recipe, for it relates output to some combination of inputs. Inputs are the ingredients that when combined yield the output that producers offer to consumers. The producer must hire inputs to produce output, so the cost of output derives from the price and quantity of inputs that are employed in producing output. The valuation consumers place on that output determines demand for outputs. Demand and supply are separate forces operating on market prices, though there are limiting cases where only one of the two forces act on price. If average cost is constant as output increases, cost alone governs price, with demand only governing the amount of the output that consumers demand. If total cost is fixed independently of output, cost has no influence on price, and price is governed wholly by demand. Those limiting conditions aside, supply and demand or cost and utility operate independently in governing the pattern of market prices, according to post-Marshallian thinking.

Not all economists accepted the post-Marshallian scheme of thought, and Buchanan, and Philip Wicksteed (1910) before him, was one of those who did not, as he set forth in 1969 in *Cost and Choice*. Within the Marshallian scheme of thought that characterized neoclassical economics, there is a conceptual disjunction between producers and consumers. Different theories are thought to pertain to the different categories of persons. Even though it would be recognized that a producer was also necessarily a consumer, separate theories could be applied to each category because there was little overlap between the categories. As producers, people specialized in producing one or a few items. As consumers, they consumed a wide variety of products, only a meager share of which they produced. As a conceptual simplification, it would surely do no harm to assume that people did not consume what they produced, especially in industrial settings even though it might be allowed that a farmer might consume some of the products he produced.

This neoclassical scheme of thought starts from some preconfigured world where there is one set of positions to be filled designated as producers and another set to be filled designated as consumers. Each person occupies a position of each type. In contrast, Buchanan was a theorist who theorized in a manner that can be described variously as generative, constructivist, or emergent, all of which speak to a program of generating the social world from some pre-social point of analytical departure. In proceeding in this manner, Buchanan showed that he was an incipient theorist of societal complexity before any such concepts were in play within the scholarly world. To be sure, ideas relating to societal complexity were set forth during the Scottish Enlightenment and the efforts made then to explain how useful social practices and conventions can arise that were not part of any person's direct intention. The Scottish theorists were the precursors of contemporary theorists of social complexity, for all were concerned with explaining how interaction among individuals generated social configurations and conventions that were not intended by anyone and yet could be socially beneficial.

Buchanan's treatment of the reciprocal relation between cost and choice reflected this Scottish tradition which he amended by incorporating neoclassical ideas about the significance of actions that can be subject to marginal variation. Hence, a person faces a parade of choices. At each instant of choice there are options. In choosing one of those options, the person is rejecting the other options that could have been chosen. The chosen option will be the option the person valued most highly at that moment, even though regrets might ensue later. The options that were not chosen were also valued, only not as highly as the option that was chosen. The most highly valued of those rejected options is the cost of the option that was chosen. Value and cost are both present at the moment of choice.

Buchanan's treatment of cost and choice can explain everything that the Marshallian framework can explain, only it does so differently, and in a manner that is consistent with generating the social world rather than stipulating its existence. An individual realizes that he needs to secure a source of income to support his desire to buy products on the market. How might he do this? He faces options. He might choose to work as a clerk in a department store. He might decide to open a shop to sell bicycles. He might decide to open a shop to repair bicycles. In any case, the person faces options regarding how he will earn income. For each option, the person forms some image of probable ensuing consequences. Working in the department store might pay more than working in the bicycle shop, but working in the bicycle shop might have more inherent interest than working in the department store. Establishing a repair shop might have the most inherent interest of all, but it would also mean longer hours of work and the need to bear the possibility that the business will not be able to cover the expenses of its operation. Whichever option the person chooses, the cost of making that choice is the value the person placed on the option not chosen. Robert Frost, in "The Road Not Taken," had the theory of cost exactly right when he described following the road not taken. Buchanan's treatment of the reciprocal relation between cost and choice ramifies throughout economic theory.

COST AND CHOICE WITH PUBLIC AGENCIES

For Buchanan, cost is a projection of the utility that could have been attained by a rejected possibility, as George Shackle (1968; 1972) also pursues. Cost cannot be separated from choice because it is inseparably connected with choice. For someone concerned with collective action, a significant question concerns whether it is meaningful or plausible to think of public officials as facing the same cost conditions as private citizens. Buchanan's theory of cost suggests this is not possible.

Consider first an entrepreneur who has decided to establish a park on 100 acres of land. That land had other uses, and the entrepreneur decided to devote that land to a park and not to some alternative use. The cost of the park is what the owner regarded as the sacrificed gain that he thought might stem for an alternative use. The entrepreneur's projection of the value he could derive by establishing the park would be based on plans he developed regarding the architecture of the park and the various ways that he thought he could derive revenue from the park. Those plans for deriving revenue would include projections about what kind of activities would attract users and the pattern of pricing, such as comparing a general price admission with charging individual prices for different attractions, along the lines Walter Oi (1971) examined. Throughout construction of the enterprise and development of its policies and programs, the entrepreneur bears the value consequences of the choices he makes. If he installs playground equipment that attracts little usage, he loses the revenue that could have been generated by equipment that attracted greater usage. That revenue might have been collected directly from prices for individual rides or activities. But it could also have been collected indirectly through a larger number of general admissions. The central point in any case is that the entrepreneur's operation in profit maximizing fashion is identical to operating his enterprise in cost minimizing fashion. After all, an entrepreneur who fails to choose the least-cost option is failing to maximize his net worth because he is rejecting the option he values more highly than the option he chooses.

Suppose alternatively that the park is established by a Department of Recreation within a city. What does it mean to compare cost for a city park with cost for a privately created park? The first thing to be noted within Buchanan's framework of individualistic public finance is that the relevant choosers must be identified. Set aside various complexities regarding the form of city governance and the relation between the recreation department and the rest of the city by assuming that the head of the recreation department has the same 100 acres to convert into a park as the private entrepreneur had. We can even assume that the recreation department has the same access to capital that the private entrepreneur had.

Constructing a plan for the park will entail managerial effort. How much effort, it might be asked? As a matter of pure formality, it could be asserted that the manager would devote effort to designing the park so long as he thought the additional revenue generated by increased attractiveness exceeded the value he placed on his time. This formulation isn't helpful as a calculational template, but it does advise one to ask how the political manager values his time as compared with a private entrepreneur. The private entrepreneur will devote additional time to refining his plan for the park so long as he senses that the resulting gain will exceed the value he placed on alternative uses of his time. The political manager faces the same situation speaking in a formal manner; however, the political manager is not a residual claimant to gains that take the form of an increase in the market value of the park.

Any choice entails a rejection of some alternative option under the belief that the value the chosen option will bring will exceed the value the option not taken would have brought. It should be noted in this formulation that a choice is made prior to the experience of the result of that choice. The combination of choice and the consequences associated with that choice requires some interval of time. This recognition creates a conceptual problem for equilibrium theories because those theories do not pertain to the passing of time. It's not that those theories deny time, whatever that might mean or entail, but that there is no work that is accomplished by or during the passing of time. Equilibrium theory is constructed outside of time. To do this requires the theorist to work with a prefabricated world, because the fabrication of anything requires the passing of time, along with whatever else might be associated with the passing of time. For instance, as time passes people as inquisitive and experimental creatures can acquire knowledge that will disrupt preceding equilibrium patterns.

Buchanan distinguished between choice-influencing and choice-influenced concepts of cost. This distinction pertains to the place of time in economic theory as this place is seen both by an individual chooser and that same individual later appraising past actions. From the actor's orientation, cost influences choice because it denotes the anticipated values of different projected courses of possible action. Choice-influencing costs exist in the minds of choosers at the moments of choice, and with the cost of the chosen option being the projected value of the option that was not chosen. There is nothing that a chooser can do about choice-influencing costs, other than perhaps to learn some useful lessons in the event the choice subsequently is regretted.

Choice-influenced costs are historical manifestations that in some cases can be measured by accountants. A lighthouse entrepreneur might decide to acquire dockage rights at harbors rather than to enlist political support to establish a public agency to collect tolls at harbors. With the entrepreneur's dockage enterprise in business, its accounts can be developed. The resulting transactions might show the enterprise to be more profitable than what the entrepreneur originally thought was possible. Those accounts could alternatively have shown the enterprise to be much less successful, perhaps even leading the entrepreneur to wonder whether he might be wise to see if he could obtain political support for transferring the collection of tolls to a public agency. The cost figures that would appear in the accounting statements of this enterprise would be choice-influenced costs, in that they would emanate from earlier choices.

As a formal matter, choice and the consequence of choice are separated by some interval of time. Action precedes the ability to experience the consequence of action. Equilibrium theory ignores this passing of time because time has no work to do within the prefabricated world of equilibrium theory. Recognition of the inescapable operation of time brings into focus questions regarding leadership and animal spirits. Invariably, people must choose an action or course of action prior to experiencing the results of that choice. All action thus has the formal character of leaps of faith. In many cases, the distance leaped is short and the faith entailed is small. But there will also be cases where the distance is long and the faith required to attempt the leap is strong.

SUMMARIZING BUCHANAN'S ASPIRATION FOR PUBLIC ECONOMICS

Between Wicksell and de Viti, Buchanan found exemplary encouragement for his desire to do public finance differently than what he had experienced during his student days. Public finance needed to be pursued in an explanatory direction, considering historical and geographical variation in institutional arrangements. Figure 2.3 offers an equilibrium-based summary of the intuition that must have informed Buchanan (1949), recalling that states of equilibrium were placed in the background of Buchanan's approach to economic theory because the foreground was occupied by institutionally governed processes of human interaction. The axes describe a conventional production frontier PP that portrays a tradeoff between public and private output. Production is portrayed as occurring at R on PP, which yields the equilibrium distribution of output of G public output and M private output. These amounts of public and private output are aggregations that correspond to the data incorporated into the national income and product accounts. The amount of private output, M, is the object that the theory of markets seeks to explain. In standard public finance, G denotes governmental contribution to national output, which is a topic that Buchanan and Forte (1961) examined.

Aggregate market output, M, is the object that the theory of markets seeks to explain. To be sure, no economist thinks that market equilibrium pertains over the year to which annual GDP data pertain or believes that so-called false trading doesn't exist. The equilibrium portrayal is a fable that simplifies a complex reality, often though not always in a useful way. The truly significant work of economic theory is not directed at developing calculations for M, but is in explaining how the complex network of economic activities manages to form a generally coordinated pattern that renders efforts to develop measures of aggregate market activity a generally reasonable thing to do. M denotes a scalar that is derived by multiplying a vector of outputs by a vector of prices. No economist or politician, however, has the ability to make M appear or happen. Economists direct their inquiries to explaining how a generally coordinated pattern of economic activity emerges when human interactions are governed by the private law principles of private property and freedom of contract. Market outcomes are not created by some societal

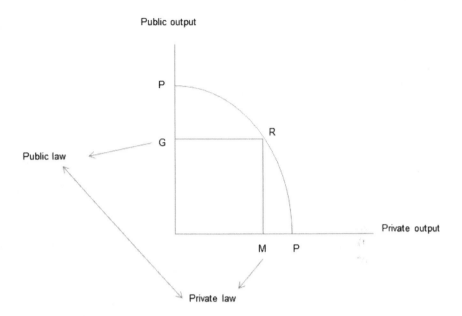

Figure 2.3. Summarizing Buchanan's Explanatory Approach to Public Finance.

planner, but rather emerge through interaction within the institutional framework characterized as private law or private ordering.

Buchanan's vision for a theory of public finance was to accomplish the same thing with respect to public output. The scholarly challenge Buchanan sensed was to describe a set of institutional arrangements that would yield the state of public output denoted by G as an outcome of political competition within a democratic system of public finance. Musgrave (1939) denied that such a theory could be constructed, and called instead for recognition that decisions regarding public finance must be directed by some cadre of experts. In contrast, Buchanan rejected that position, which required him to proceed in the direction of constructing explanatory approaches to public finance. Several scholars have remarked on the significantly different readings of Wicksell that Buchanan and Musgrave have presented, as illustrated by Bernd Hansjürgens (2000) and Marianne Johnson (2006). Musgrave, who embraced the concept of merit wants, was comfortable working with concepts of governing elites acting for the good of society. Buchanan was not, and was determined to reduce collective action to the same explanatory categories and principles that economists brought to bear on market activity. It can be fairly said that Buchanan did not complete the challenge that he set for himself, but it must also be recognized that he made considerable progress in this direction, both through his own massive body of work and through the inspiration he transmitted to others. .

Within the standard neoclassical presumption that economics is primarily a theory about resource allocation, the explanatory task is ended with the determination of R or the (G, M) division. For Buchanan's institutionally oriented public finance, there is much more required for satisfactory explanation. Subtended to M is the designation "private law." This is to recognize that the theory of markets pertains to a setting where people relate to one another through the principles and conventions of private property and freedom of contract. People have rights of ownership, and can transfer those rights either in whole or in part through their freedom of contract. This institutional framework designated "private law" is an idealization that appears only incompletely in historical settings. Until late in the eighteenth century, someone who owned real estate in the west typically could not subdivide that estate. Among other things, this practice of primogeniture led often to second- and third-born sons migrating from Europe to America because they wanted to practice agriculture but could not obtain land in Europe. As another illustration, until late in the nineteenth century, married women typically could not own property, for it had to be held in the names of their husbands. Economic interactions were still governed by principles of property and contract, only those principles played out differently under primogeniture and coverture than they did after those practices disappeared. In any case, the subtended designation "private law" conveys recognition that the allocative outcome denoted as M in figure 2.3 does not reflect some person's choice but rather reflects the product of human interaction when those interactions are governed by the principles of property and contract.

In his seminal conceptualization of public goods, Paul Samuelson (1954; 1955) claimed that there was no market-like process that would generate the outcome denoted as G. In other words, there was no meaningful scheme of public law subtended to G that would generate G as an emergent outcome of individuals pursuing their interests within a political setting. In contrast, Buchanan (1949) asserted the desirability of constructing such an explanatory approach to public finance, with Buchanan (1967; 1968) making starts in this direction, and with Wagner (2007) making some effort to carry forward this research program. In this respect, Roland McKean (1965; 1968) called for construction of invisible hand theories pertaining to governments, which is a challenge that remains to be met but which Buchanan articulated in 1949.

In figure 2.3, the double arrow connecting "private law" and "public law" denotes the unavoidable connection between the two sources of law, what Wagner (2016a) describes as entangled political economy. Among other things, this means that there will continually arise interpenetration between the domains of public law and private law. No rigid separation between public law and private law is possible. Taxation is the domain of public law;

prices are the domain of private law. Yet taxes are impositions on market transactions, which modify prices in the process. There is no such thing as neutral government activity, any more than there is such a thing as neutral money (Bilo and Wagner 2015). Where Musgrave looked to public policy as the administrative locus for generating G within society, Buchanan looked to political competition within a property designed scheme of public law to do this. In any case, Buchanan (1949) raised the challenge of placing the theory of public finance on an explanatory footing. It's unlikely that Buchanan recognized the hydra-headed quality of the challenge he set forth in 1949. But a hydra-headed challenge it truly was, and remains so today as many analytical challenges remain to be explored in developing an integrated treatment of social organization and social processes without embracing the mythology of the "centralized mindset" (Resnick 1994).

Chapter Three

Collective Action and Constitutional Political Economy

Going forward from his initial paper in 1949, Buchanan sought to bring analytical life to his belief that a theory of public finance that was suitable for a democratic regime should reflect an individualistic and not an organismic motif. This belief had both normative and explanatory branches. Normatively, Buchanan rejected progressivist and elitist presumptions that governance was the province of a special class of rulers to whom ordinary people owed thanks and deference. For Buchanan, governance was not properly conceptualized as something that governors did to or for a set of governed masses. Superficially, the situation might look this way because a society can be divided between those who hold political office and those who do not. The holders of political office, however, are not accurately perceived as bossing or imposing on the rest of the society. To the contrary, they are regarded as ordinary citizens who use their offices to reflect desires and urgings that reside within the society at large.

This, anyway, is the predominant thrust of democratic ideology, and is embraced by Buchanan in his liberal political economy and social philosophy. But do democratic regimes work automatically and inexorably in this manner simply because they hold periodic elections to fill a few political offices? This seems to be the thrust of contemporary democratic ideology which holds that anything political that is democratic is *ipso facto* superior to anything that is not. Within this type of contemporary ideology, regimes are graded on a 0–1 scale. Democratic regimes are graded a 1; other regimes are graded a 0. In contrast, Buchanan thought regimes could and should be graded along a continuum. One end would be anchored by regimes where most people were slaves of a ruling few. The other end would be anchored by an idealization of Wicksell's vision of consensual collective action. The presence of a continuum meant that there could exist democratic regimes that were inferior to instances of authoritarian regime, recognition of which led Buchanan to develop his theory of constitutional political economy.

The explanatory problematic for a theory of public finance starts with recognition that groups themselves can't act. Action is a property of individuals, not of groups. When we speak of groups acting, we are referring to individuals within that group promoting the action in question. For a group to take what we recognize as action, it must be constituted as a group (Munger and Munger 2015). Otherwise, a group is just a formless mass. A mass is constituted as a group through leadership and rules. Buchanan often invoked images of several people gathering to play poker. Before they started to play, they had to agree on the rules by which they would play. From this simple image, Buchanan developed the distinction between constitutional and post-constitutional politics. This distinction is relatively accurate for parlor games, though probably not completely so because the people who gather to play poker generally already know one another and so to some extent have already been constituted. Or if they don't know one another, they will have gathered at a casino where the rules by which they will play are data they must accept. With respect to the human drama, as distinct from a parlor game occurring inside that drama, Buchanan's distinction between constitutional and post-constitutional politics is an abstraction that is sometimes useful and sometimes not, and must be used with care in any case, as Rajagopalan and Wagner (2013) explain.

Constitutional political economy entails Buchanan's many efforts to explain how the framework of rules by which a governing regime is constituted influences a regime's properties. Normatively, Buchanan was a democrat who embraced the democratic ideology of self-governance. His orientation in this respect was like that which Vincent Ostrom (1997) expressed toward democracy as simultaneously desirable and subject to a degradation that required conscious effort to resist. Recognition of the potential for democratic degradation was present at the American constitutional founding when Benjamin Franklin responded "a republic, if you can keep it" to a woman who asked him what form of government the Constitutional Convention had created. Establishing a democratic government entails both normative and positive presuppositions, and constitutional political economy was Buchanan's intellectual creation through which he explored his normative interest in self-governing republics while simultaneously recognizing that the qualities of democratic governance depended upon the institutional arrangements by which a regime was constituted. Constitutional political economy is the term that bears witness to Buchanan's effort to relate the outcomes of group deliberations to the underlying desires and beliefs of the people who established that group in the first place. Central to Buchanan's theorizing was his recognition, traceable to Wicksell, that the degree of correspondence between the actions that emerge from a parliamentary assembly and those outcomes that might reasonably have been imagined to have emerged from the underlying population depends on both the rules by which a parliamentary assembly does its business and the rules by which membership in that assembly is determined. Through his construction of constitutional political economy, Buchanan sought to combine the legacies he received from Wicksell and de Viti with his own creative imagination in developing an alternative approach to a theory of public finance that speaks to the situation that confronts self-governing republics.

THE CALCULUS OF CONSENT:
UR-TEXT OF VIRGINIA POLITICAL ECONOMY

James Buchanan and Gordon Tullock's (1962) *The Calculus of Consent* is undoubtedly the Ur-text of Virginia political economy. Yet several forms of political economy are in play, with those forms pointing in different analytical directions. In recognition of this situation, Blankart and Koester (2006) distinguished between public choice and political economics as alternative forms of political economy. Yet the opening line of the Preface to *The Calculus of Consent* reads: "This is a book about the *political* organization of a society of free men" (italics in original). It's clear that there are different ways of bringing economic theory to bear on politics just as there are different ways of constructing economic theories. Any such act of construction will start with some pre-analytical cognitive vision (Schumpeter 1954, 41) which the scholar then seeks to articulate to make it intelligible to others. The articulation of that vision will occur through some ordered string of units of thought. How those units are strung together and how they are conceptualized will depend on the tools of thought that an author has available to work with. Vriend (2002) explains that agent-based computational modeling offers a good platform for working with some of Hayek's ideas about knowledge that is fragmented and distributed and nowhere possessed by one person or scholar. Yet such tools of thought weren't available to Hayek, so he had to resort to literary reasoning that was easily reducible to a statement of equilibrium conditions, the incoherence of which was subsequently illustrated by Grossman and Stiglitz's (1976; 1980) claiming to have explained that Hayek erred when they ignored Hayek and did not contest his formulation. Where Hayek reasoned about emergent dynamics over some interval of time using plausible reasoning, Grossman and Stiglitz eliminated action through time by working with comparative statics at some instant using demonstrative reasoning. The ability to extract implications from a pre-analytical cognitive vision depends on the tools of thought the author possesses. Hayek lacked some tools that could have facilitated his construction; Grossman and Stiglitz worked with tools that denied by assumption Hayek's cognitive vision.

The interpretation of *The Calculus of Consent* and its significance for Virginia political economy and public choice is likewise influenced by tools of thought. Ideas about complex systems and agent-based computational modeling were not available to Buchanan and Tullock, though some game theoretic models were then available. What resulted was an effort at articulation that had a mixed-metaphor quality about it that is subject to misinterpretation, as Wagner (2013; 2015a) explains. *The Calculus of Consent* was conceived as an effort to explain that the complex constitutional arrangement that was founded in 1789 reflected a coherent economic logic of governance through divided and separated powers. Indeed, Vincent Ostrom's (2008) *Political Theory of a Compound Republic*, first published in 1971, is effectively a flying buttress to *The Calculus of Consent*. Where Buchanan and Tullock took recourse to some of the simple equilibrium models that were then used by economists to illustrate some of their arguments, Ostrom maintained contact with the complex constitutional arrangements that were established in 1789.

The Calculus of Consent was published in 1962, and used tools of thought and modes of expression that were in play at that time. This situation creates problems in understanding past scholarship when the tools of thought in play between then and now have changed, and when scholarly contestation at any moment often yields work with a mixed-metaphor quality because the existing tools of thought are not fully suitable for illuminating the intuitions behind that thought. *The Calculus of Consent* is universally cited as one of the half-dozen or so canonical works of public choice, and is undoubtedly the Ur-text of Virginia political economy. That book reflects in spades the problem I have just mentioned. It was constructed using mostly simple neoclassical tools of thought that were in wide use at the time. Among other things, this generated a focus on representative agents and median voters.

Yet the intuition behind the book was to use economic logic to make sense of the complex construction of the American constitutional system of 1789, where power was divided in numerous ways and not concentrated in some image of a median voter. All scholars have the problem of making themselves understood while using the tools of thought that are in play among their cohorts. *The Calculus of Consent* and the vision of public choice it enables is best understood as a confluence of the liberal political economy of classical times (Robbins 1952; Samuels 1966) and the public finance orientation of the classical Italian theorists (de Viti de Marco 1888).[1] In saying this, I don't deny sensibility to the standard reading, but rather assert that the alternative reading is more consistent with the authors' intuitions and their later bodies of work, including a predilection for the classical use of plausible reasoning over the neoclassical predilection for demonstrative reasoning, which Polya (1954) explains and which Wagner (2015b) illustrates with respect to welfare economics.

The schemes of thought associated with any scholarly tradition that is a progressive research program can be likened to a river into which numerous scholars contribute. With multiple schemes of thought and research programs being in play at any moment, it is not unusual to find admixtures among schemes sometimes occurring due to strategic and competitive elements entailed in the generation of scholarship as scholars compete for attention space (Collins 1998), and with schools of thought emerging in consequence of that competition. As the Virginia tradition developed over the half-century following publication of *The Calculus of Consent* (Buchanan and Tullock 1962), the mainline currents of its thought became mixed with currents from the mainstream of economic thought, invoking Peter Boettke's (2007) distinction between the mainline and mainstream branches of economic theory.

The constitutional scheme of separated and divided powers meant that the median voter model was more a fictional construction than a reasonable model of a constitutional arrangement. A median voter model might pertain for a five-member town council that has the sole authority to allocate tax revenues among expenditure items. It would not, however, apply to complex arrangements of separated and divided powers where concurrence among different entities is required before collective action can be undertaken. In these kinds of settings, outcomes are products of interaction and negotiation and not products of choice. The American constitutional system created a complex structure of divided and separated powers that required concurrence among different sets of people. Within a bicameral legislature, for instance, the degree of concurrence that is required varies with the principles by which the two chambers are selected. Within the original constitutional setting, the federal Senate was selected by state legislatures while the House was selected directly through election. In consequence of constitutional amendment in 1913, the federal Senate also became selected directly through election. This change surely created more commonality among the electorates than had previously existed. In a two-chamber system where both chambers are staffed through at-large elections, selection is likely to operate similarly in both chambers. Quite different properties would result should one chamber be populated by property owners and the other by renters, and with legislation requiring concurrence between both chambers. In this respect, one well-cited game-theoretic exposition of fair division occurs where one person slices a cake and the other person takes the first slice. This formulation is similar to requiring concurrence between differently constituted chambers.

In any case, the prime purpose of *The Calculus of Consent* was to explain that the complex system of government that the American Constitution established and which had been under strenuous attack by Progressives at least since when Woodrow Wilson (1885) wrote *Congressional Government*, where he extolled the virtues of a strong administrative apparatus in place of continual congressional negotiation. *The Calculus of Consent* was conveyed mostly by equilibrium formulations of a relatively simple sort, even though the purpose of the book was to explain how the complex American constitutional system made sense from the perspective of economic logic and even though that sense would vanish if the system were reduced to conform to the simplicity of the logic, as Vincent Ostrom (1973; 1997; 2008) recognized with especial cogency. *The Calculus of Consent* was penned as an antidote to the call for centralization that the Progressivists had been promoting for around half a century, and to reduce collective action to a choice by a median voter is to embrace the core of Progressivism. It sought to explain how a political group constituted along the lines of the 1787 Constitution could generate reasonable collective outcomes, thus standing in sharp opposition to progressivist claims on behalf of streamlining and centralizing political power in a strong ruling cadre.

PARTICIPANTS, OBSERVERS, AND PUBLIC FINANCE THEORISTS

So long as public finance theorists worked within organicist frameworks, they had no need to confront the daunting challenge of explaining the actual processes through which fiscal outcomes emerged in societies with democratically organized polities. One could always invoke a language that spoke of "social wants" or "merit wants" to justify whatever activity one wanted to justify, knowing full well that you would not be alone in voicing such sentiments, even though you would also face opposition. Thrust and parry, after all, is a key feature of a democratic process. You have a program you favor, so you wrap language around that program that arouses favorable sentiments within a relevant population. Such sentiments invariably speak of public goodness or value, perhaps disparaging the stinginess or meanness of opponents in the process. Such activities are time-honored features of democratic processes, as Eisenstein (1961) explains with respect to taxation and as Pareto (1935) explains for democratic processes in their entirety.

Professional economists participate in these processes just like everyone else. To participate in an activity, however, is different from observing or explaining that activity. A participant requires a different language and concepts than does an observer or explainer of what is observed. An economist-consultant might think a new prison program would be a good idea and marshal supporting evidence, perhaps performing some cost-benefit analysis. An opponent might dispute that evidence by creating a different interpretation of the evidence or presenting different evidence. These activities form part of ongoing morality plays within democratic systems, and the course these plays take generates continual change within democratic systems. In this respect, democratic action is a form of improvisational drama, as Frank Knight (1960) recognized in *Intelligence and Democratic Action.* Public finance theorists have an array of concepts and categories to put them in position to participate within these morality plays, in what de Viti (1936) described as practical statecraft as distinct from explanatory science.

Explaining an activity, however, is different from participating in that activity. With respect to the proposed prison program, explanation would concern such things as trying to explain what there is about programs that marshal support relative to those that don't. Explanation is not advocacy, but economists are called upon to do both, unavoidably so Buchanan (1997) recognized due to economics being a science whose findings are of significant public interest. As a practical matter, a theorist can operate both as a participant and an observer, only not at the same instant, though one can change stances. Still, as a participant, the theorist seeks either to propel the proposed program forward or to oppose it. As an observer, the theorist would seek to account for the strength of support and opposition in terms of the standard economic categories of utility, cost, profit, and the like.

Figure 2.3 summarizes the scholarly challenge that Buchanan (1949) set in motion in calling for development of an individualist orientation toward public finance. The economic theory of markets is already firmly ensconced in trying to explain with increasing nuance and subtlety how highly complex patterns of market organization and coordination emerge out of social interactions governed by the simple legal framework of property and contract (Epstein 1995). An explanatory theory of public finance in the spirit of de Viti (1936) and Buchanan (1949) would seek to develop a similar explanation of the complex patterns of public economic activity summarized as G in figure 2.3. While progress has certainly been made since 1949, an explanatory theory of collective activity still lags far behind explanatory theories of markets. One significant problem that arises in this respect is the variation of institutional arrangements governing collective action relative to those that govern market action. Sure, specific details regarding rights of property and obligations of contract can differ across time and place; however, the range of variation among legal regimes governing private interaction is surely narrower than it is for collective interaction.

For instance, consider the effect of size on the complexity involved in explaining market and collective phenomena. For market phenomena, production and trade can be explained in the same manner regardless of whether it occurs in a small village or a large city. The principles of demand and supply, for products as well as for inputs, operate in the same fashion in towns and in cities. The only difference between the two is that the magnitudes would be larger in cities. A theory of markets looks the same when used to understand the economic organization of a town as it does when brought to bear on a city. The explanatory situation is different for collective action. For an organicist theory of public finance, the size of the collective unit is irrelevant because there is nothing to be explained. The theoretical concepts and categories are not used for explanatory purposes. They are used as inputs into argumentative strategies when theorists are acting as participants and not as observers.

For the individualist theory that de Viti and Buchanan espoused, a wholly different intellectual challenge arises. To meet this challenge requires the theorist to recognize that the size of a political unit can matter for efforts to explain the pattern of collective activity within that unit. A small town can be governed through some form of direct democracy. A large city cannot be governed in this manner. Some system of representative democracy will be needed. It is here where significant complexity enters due to the many ways a system of representation can be constructed. One familiar point of difference is between unicameral and bicameral legislative chambers. Within bicameral chambers, moreover, there are numerous ways representatives can be selected from the population. Both chambers can be selected through open voting, as is presently practiced in the United States. Alternatively, one chamber could be selected through open voting while the other one was selected through status or standing. Until 1913, the U.S. Senate was selected in this fashion through appointment by state legislatures. Historically, there have been instances where parliamentary bodies were populated according to occupational characteristics or by notions of rank within a society.

Buchanan (1967) distinguishes between political and fiscal rules. Political rules pertain to the selection of representative assemblies and to the relationships among the members of those assemblies. All such rules are elements of the institutional framework denoted as "public law" in figure 2.3, and are part of the framework that generates public output G by shaping and constraining interaction among the members of a parliamentary assembly. While fiscal outcomes emerge out of institutionally governed interaction among legislators, those legislators are selected through some voting process by which it can be claimed that democratic processes are self-governing, meaning that people govern themselves as distinct from being governed by legislators. How closely this commonplace of democratic ideology matches reality is an open question that falls within the purview of an explanatory theory of public finance.

Parliamentary action also requires fiscal rules, though Buchanan also notes that the two types of rules overlap one another. One set of fiscal rules pertains to the power to tax, which Brennan and Buchanan (1980) explore in a manner that yields several insights that run contrary to some familiar implications from organismic public finance. A significant set of rules pertains to what might be called political property rights over tax revenue. A tax generates a volume of revenue, but how is the ability to spend that revenue governed within a parliamentary assembly? There will be rules that structure relationships and interactions among the members of a parliamentary assembly, creating relationships of priority and power within the assembly.

PARETO'S CHALLENGE TO EXPLANATORY PUBLIC FINANCE

While several Italians contributed to the effort to pursue explanatory theories of public finance, they did not speak with a single voice, as Michael McLure (2007) explains in examining the thinking of Vilfredo Pareto, and with Pareto's thought also surveyed in Mauro Fasiani (1949). Where such theorists as de Viti and Pantaleoni thought in terms of a potentially smooth interface between market activity and political activity, Pareto thought in disjunctive terms due to his distinction between logical and non-logical action. This distinction is not just another pair of terms for the distinction between rational and irrational action. Pareto did not think that irrationality was a useful concept. He regarded all action as rational, only there were different environments inside of which people act. Some of those environments elicited logical action while other environments elicited non-logical action, with all action being rational in any case.

By logical action, Pareto meant that some environments pretty much forced people to act in a logical manner. These environments were mostly market environments. A person who establishes a bicycle repair shop will be pretty much forced by that action-environment to operate that shop in what would be regarded as an economically efficient manner. Should that owner buy tools and equipment that will not prove useful in repairing bicycles, the owner will bear the resulting commercial losses. Should the owner decide to close the shop in the late afternoon while most potential customers are at work rather than remaining open into the evening when most potential customers are off work, the owner will bear the resulting loss of income. And should that owner decide to stay open on some evenings, making it necessary thereby to decline some pleasant social engagements, that owner will have decided, along the lines of Buchanan (1969a), that the value he placed on those engagements was less than the value he placed on the additional business he could attract during evening hours.

Pareto recognized that market settings were environments that placed people in the position of forming and testing what are effectively scientific hypotheses. An owner can form a hypothesis of the form that by staying open I will gain so much additional business while also losing my participation in a weekly poker group. He must choose between business and poker because he cannot have both because of the limited amount of time at his disposal. A market setting does not guarantee that a person will make the superior choice. This is a guarantee that no one can make. A market setting means only that the person will bear the value consequences of whatever choice he makes, and so is likely to make this choice from within a state of sober realism.

There are, however, many choices that people make that occur outside of market environments. Politics presents one such environment, and with there being many manifestations of such environments. In an election, for instance, two candidates might compete for one seat in a winner-take-all election. This environment is not one that promotes logical action because voters do not bear the value consequences of their choice. It is unreasonable for voters to exercise the same care in casting a vote that they would exercise in buying a car or hiring an attorney (Brennan and Lomasky 1993; Caplan 2007; Somin 2013). Candidates in turn recognize that they are pitching appeals to voters who won't be responsible for their votes, and yet who want to appear responsible while participating in social relationships with friends and acquaintances. Candidates respond to this situation by advancing slogans and phrases that resonate with voter sentiments along the lines that Pareto set forth, and which Patrick and Wagner (2015) set in a public choice context.

Voters do not face cost and choice in the same way as do customers. In choosing between options, customers pay for the option they choose, and experience the results of that choice. In contrast, voters do not pay for the option for which they voted. Nor do they experience in any way the consequences of this virtual choice. In no way does voting map into Pareto's logico-experimental method by which he distinguished logical from non-logical action. Political choices outside of elections provide other environments for non-logical action. The head of a bureau or agency does not bear value consequences from organizational actions. Non-market organizations obviously make choices, but the relationship between cost and choice is different because those organizations lack market value. There are many examples of political and market organizations engaging in similar activities, but which operate under different institutional arrangements which should influence perceptions of the costs of taking different courses of action within Buchanan's scheme of thought.

Consider the economic organization of a recreational enterprise under two distinct institutional arrangements. One enterprise is organized within the purview of private property. The other is organized through public property. Both types of enterprise face problems of economic calculation in that they must make decisions regarding such things as the size of parks, the distribution of land among different uses, and the types of equipment to buy. For the market-based enterprise, economic calculation is grounded on the projected value of the enterprise. The park must attract users, which requires that land be devoted to uses that appeal to visitors and that the equipment prove attractive to those visitors. We may further expect the enterprise to monitor its activities and facilities to enable it to replace uses that generate less net revenue with those that generate more. A manager who refuses to operate the enterprise in this manner bears the cost of following the less efficient mode of operation, meaning that that manager purchases his own slothfulness as a manager. If the manager owns the enterprise, his or her net worth is reduced, which might in turn attract outside offers to take over the enterprise, and, in any case, leaves the manager as bearing the cost of operating the enterprise in this relatively slothful manner. Should the manager be an employee who is acting as agent for the owner, much the same result can be expected though with variability due to agency costs (Meckling and Jensen 1976).

When the enterprise is organized under public property, the enterprise no longer has market value. The enterprise still faces the necessity of economic calculation because the park is still going to be apportioned across different uses and some assortment of equipment will be maintained. That equipment can be of varying quality and subject to different degrees of repair and maintenance. There will, however, be no market value for the enterprise, which points to the significance of questions regarding how economic calculation occurs in public enterprises. The central theme of Buchanan (1969a) is that economic calculation is unavoidable within any organization because officials in all organizations will confront a parade of choices through time—and cost is simply a reciprocal of choice. The existence of enterprise value creates a focal point as a kind of North Star for commercial navigation, and it is that focal point that makes it reasonable to conceptualize enterprises as teams. Without enterprise value, there no longer exists a clear focal point, as Auteri and Wagner (2007) explain in their analysis of nonprofit organizations. People in managerial positions still face choices, but there is no commercial North Star to provide navigational guidance.

Much of the resulting difference would appear in various details regarding enterprise operation. In this regard, it is good to recall Mitchel Resnick's (1994) explanation of the centralized mindset. The performance of an organization is ordinarily an emergent result of interactions at lower levels within the organization, much as Gordon Tullock (1965) set forth in *The Politics of Bureaucracy*. Does a publicly owned playground keep its swings in good repair? We might recognize that swings that are not usable will reduce usage and hence revenues within a privately owned playground, which in turn will elicit incentive to maintain swings and all equipment to attract users. But the manager of a public playground loses no revenue because swings are not kept in good repair. By economizing on the time devoted to inspecting and repairing equipment, a manager releases time to pursue activities that he values more highly than inspecting and repairing equipment. Just how that time might be used depends on the desires and options the manager has. It might be spent reading magazines or watching TV. It might be spent playing video games. It might be spent searching for jobs. It might be spent flirting with attractive visitors. In whatever manner that time might be spent, it will reflect that manager's best use of his or her time when compared with the best alternative, as Buchanan (1969a) explains. Pareto's challenge for the construction of an explanatory theory of public finance doesn't deny the possibility, but rather recalls Attilio da Empoli's (1941) recognition of the need to avoid the snare of thinking that the interface between politics and markets is a smooth one. That interface isn't smooth. It is tectonic, but tectonic phenomena are also subject to theoretical articulation.

DEMOCRATIC PUBLIC FINANCE AND CONSTITUTIONAL POLITICAL ECONOMY

Buchanan's (1949) articulation of an individualistic approach to a theory of public finance created the challenge of how to create such a theory. Buchanan was aware of Knut Wicksell (1896) and Antonio de Viti de Marco (1936) as offering precursory efforts, but construction of a theoretical edifice that would be intellectually competitive with the organismic approach to public finance was mostly a dream in 1949. The organismic approach treated groups as acting in the name of the state, but made no effort to explain how this was possible. Groups can't act as groups, for only individuals can act. If action taken in the name of a group of people is to be explained, that action must be explained as a product of interaction among the members of the group (Munger and Munger 2015). The group is constituted in some fashion, so Buchanan's effort to construct an individualistic orientation toward public finance required him to theorize about constitutional political economy. How to describe budgetary policies when the state is fantasized to be an acting person, possibly as instructed by some concept of social welfare, is easy because theories of public finance would be no different from theories of consumer or producer choice. For Buchanan's individualistic public finance, however, fiscal phenomena cannot be reduced to a choice by a representative citizen because that reduction would avoid rather than confront the process of interaction among citizens through which outcomes emerge. Truly to understand democratic regimes required Buchanan to step inside what the organicist theorists had been content to treat as a black box. In doing this, much depended on the type of group that a democratic polity was thought to be.

For the most part, Buchanan thought in terms of the members of a group as differing in preferences but not much more. For instance, Buchanan (1964b) set forth a model where people desired different amounts of some collective activity due simply to differences in income. The point of this model was to describe how a flat tax on income could produce unanimity over the amount to provide. As income increased, the income effect would lead people to demand more, but the substitution effect of higher tax-price would reduce the amounts they demanded. Should the price and income elasticities of demand be unity, everyone would demand the same quantity. This model followed closely upon Buchanan and Tullock's (1962) recognition that their theory of constitutional choice reflected a presumption of strong homogeneity within a population. There could be disagreements within a population over how heavily to subsidize medical care, but there would be no disagreements about whether abortions should be eligible for subsidization.

Buchanan (1964b) served a narrow purpose under which financing government by a flat-rate tax on income would allow reduction of political explanation to that of explaining choice by a representative citizen. To be sure, this reduction was rendered possible by making assumptions about the distribution of citizen preferences along with the presumption that a flat tax on income was in place, along with a further presumption that enforcing that tax was simple. Where a set of assumptions is made to derive a set of implications, those assumptions can be changed and alternative implications derived. For instance, it would be a straightforward extension of Buchanan's scheme of analysis to posit a budgetary process inside of which a tax code is generated (Hebert and Wagner 2013). Alternatively, a revenue-collecting bureaucracy could be incorporated into a political process, perhaps challenging some long-standing norms of organismic public finance along the lines of Brennan and Buchanan (1980).

Once it is recognized that fiscal phenomena emerge out of interaction among individuals inside of groups, it becomes necessary to theorize about the formation of groups and how the structure through which groups are constituted influences the properties of group-based action. While it is a reasonable linguistic convenience to refer to action taken in the name of a group, the black box that encases that group must be removed within Buchanan's desire to construct an individualistic theory of public finance. What results from such efforts at construction is recognition that collective phenomena are as much emergent phenomena as are market phenomena. At least since the Scottish Enlightenment, and even as far back as medieval Spain for that matter (Grice-Hutchinson 1978), economists have recognized that market phenomena emerge from interaction among interested participants and are not products of some planner's choices. Buchanan's individualistic theory of public finance required that he pursue a similar orientation toward collective phenomena, wherein the properties of collective action depend on both the size of a group and the structure through which governance occurs.

A group must be *constituted* or organized before it can act; otherwise, it is just a mass. For a group to act coherently, it must have an organizational structure that enables group action to emerge through interactions among participants. Many groups arise through voluntary action, and Buchanan (1965) sets forth a theory of clubs to generate insight into voluntary group action. Political groups differ from clubs and other voluntary groups in that it is costlier to escape the jurisdiction of a political group than to escape the jurisdiction of a club. Whether a group is voluntary or political, it will entail some constitutional structure that covers the principles of membership, the rights and obligations of membership, and the procedural rules for undertaking collective action. For sufficiently small groups, governance can be handled through direct democratic action. Above that minimal size limit, groups will work with some scheme of delegation and representation whereby a relatively small number of people will undertake action on behalf of a larger number. Within voluntary groups, should the few act in ways to which the larger number object, the group is likely to find its membership shrinking. With political groups, the option to withdraw without bearing some cost of mobility is closed. Voluntary groups must strive continually to maintain membership when those members are free to abandon the group. Political groups are relieved of a good deal of that concern, especially as the territory occupied by a political group increases.

Constitutional political economy distinguishes between the framework by which a group is constituted as a polity and the activities and outcomes that emerge through the actions and interactions of participants within that framework. Buchanan (1967) distinguishes between political and fiscal rules. Political rules cover the formation of political groups and the organization of those groups. Whether a legislature contains one or two chambers is a political rule, as are the rules that govern how people achieve membership in a legislative assembly. Once a legislative assembly is selected, there will be rules regarding the organization of the legislature, along with rules government how the legislature generates legislation. These political rules provide a framework within which members of a parliamentary assembly interact with one another to generate legislation. These rules are part of the institutional framework of a public economy just as the rules of private property and freedom of contract are part of the institutional framework of a market economy.

The institutional framework of a public economy also includes what Buchanan describes as fiscal rules. These rules are also political rules, but they are addressed particularly to fiscal activity. These rules speak to the taxing and spending powers of governments. Some of these rules might be explicitly constitutional, while other are created by legislation. Perhaps the best place to see the Italianate influence on public finance is Buchanan's (1967) *Public Finance in Democratic Process*. Buchanan starts by noting the narrow scope of public finance approached within the organicist approach, where public finance is concerned only with explaining market-based reactions to exogenously imposed taxes and expenditures, along with proffering advice on good fiscal conduct. For instance, a theorist might advocate an increase in the progressivity of the income tax, and then try to appraise that measure in terms of such things as the amount of labor people supply, the amount of underground economic activity they undertake, and the amount of taxable income they earn. The same procedure could apply to public expenditure. For instance, an expanded program of highway construction might be proposed, such as accompanied the introduction of the Interstate Highway network in the United States in the 1950s. The task of fiscal analysis would be to analyze such market-based reactions to the highway as increases in land rents near highway exits because the reduction in travel time made location near exits more desirable. Whatever the topic, organicist public finance takes fiscal choices as data and focuses on explaining market-based reactions to exogenous fiscal measures, for those measures were outputs of a black box that were beyond explanation.

In treating fiscal actions as exogenous, the organicist orientation toward public finance ignores two large areas of possible inquiry, both of which Buchanan explores in *Public Finance in Democratic Process*. One ignored area is the ability of fiscal institutions and practices to influence budgetary outcomes and not just market outcomes. This topic occupies the first part of *Public Finance in Democratic Process*, and the analyses presented there were early illustrations of public choice theorizing. The second ignored area is the choice or emergence of fiscal institutions. This topic occupies the second part of *Public Finance in Democratic Process*, and the analyses presented there were harbingers to subsequent work in constitutional political economy.

Buchanan (1967) gives several illustrations of how fiscal institutions and arrangements might influence fiscal outcomes, of which I shall mention three. First, Buchanan contrasted tax earmarking and general-fund financing. A theorist working within the organicist framework would take that mix as data and explore what differences resulted from different mixes. Within Buchanan's individualist framework, the use of earmarking relative to general-fund financing should be explainable, which led him to explore whether different people might favor different practices due to differences in their positions within the budgetary process. Second, Buchanan explored whether the withholding of income taxes before a taxpayer receives his or her paycheck might influence the size of a government's budget. The central intuition here is that taxpayers will be more aware of their tax payments if they write monthly checks to government than if they never have possession of that part of their income. The theory behind this possibility is that individual perceptions about the costliness of public output can be influenced by the way tax extractions are made. Fiscal practices are not data but are generated through some process of collective choice. Third, Buchanan examined the effect of public debt on budgetary outcomes. The principle of Ricardian equivalence must hold in the aggregate as a simple matter of double-entry accounting. An aggregate, however, is not an acting entity, so a statement about aggregate equivalence is irrelevant for any effort to explain fiscal conduct. What matters for collective action is the direction of individual desires as these are mediated through political and fiscal institutions, as different people can be affected differently by public debt. This point gets to a significant feature of Buchanan's thought: his unwillingness to make statements based on aggregates without exploring the underlying structural patterns to which those aggregates pertain. Once it is recognized that aggregates are not acting entities, collective action must be explained as emerging through interaction among acting individuals, as that interaction is mediated through some institutional framework.

Consider, for instance, Buchanan's approach to progressive income taxation. Where the sacrifice theorists like Edgeworth (1897) sought to specify the degree of progressivity that some exogenous authority should impose on a society, Buchanan sought to probe the circumstances under which a set of people might choose to employ progressivity as a form of income insurance. Progressive taxation allows people to achieve some smoothing of consumption in the presence of fluctuating income, as compared with proportional taxation. The purchase of insurance, after all, is a constitutional and not a post-constitutional activity: people purchase insurance before they have had accidents and not after. To the extent such formulations have merit, what appears to be redistribution when seen from an *ex post* perspective might represent mutual gains from trade when viewed from an *ex ante* perspective.

Alternatively, consider the treatment of broad-based taxation in Buchanan and Congleton (1998). Without a constitutional requirement of uniformity in taxation, post-constitutional politics will generate increasingly complex revenue systems as tax favors are granted or removed within the political marketplace. The resulting narrowing of the tax base warps processes of collective choice. For instance, those who are favored by the resulting fiscal discrimination will support more collective activity than they would otherwise support. With the continual churning of the tax code that results, however, most participants may end up worse off than they would have been under a simple system of tax uniformity.

Buchanan credited Knut Wicksell (1896) with showing how a democratic system could be constructed that would reasonably well reflect the consent of the governed. With respect to Panel A of figure 3.1, Wicksell's scheme had a strong polycentric character. While the details of Wicksell's scheme do not correspond precisely to Panel A, they are reasonably close. Panel A shows a single parliamentary assembly among ten people in the absence of any hierarchical order. This polycentric mapping bears a close correspondence to Wicksell's scheme of proportional representation in conjunction with requiring a high degree of consent for parliament to act. In Wicksell's parliament, there was no boss who could assign positions of varying power and status, and use that ability to influence parliamentary outcomes. With rare exception enabled by the approximation to unanimity, no party within parliament would be forced to accept measures about which its members disapproved. Every expenditure proposal would be accompanied by a proposal for covering its cost. Should a proposal fail to secure sufficient consent, the sponsors of the measure could always change their proposal, as by changing how the cost would be covered or by changing some features of the program. Within parliament, the Wicksellian scheme would provide little scope for the domination through hierarchy that is possible within monocentric arrangements.

The most notable feature about the Wicksellian system and Buchanan's strong interest in it from the start of his career is that it offers a pathway into the institutional organization of public finance within democratic regimes. Paul Samuelson (1954; 1955) claimed that it is impossible for a democratic scheme of public finance to reflect the consent of the governed in any manner resembling the way market outcomes respond to the interests of consumers. In advancing his claim, Samuelson held that despotic organization of some form was a necessary feature of political outcomes regardless of regime. In contrast, Buchanan (1949) asserted the necessity of constructing an individualist approach to public finance, which would deny Samuelson's claims in the process. While Buchanan did not complete a fully articulated theory of public finance in an explanatory motif, he did make substantial progress in this direction before he shifted his attention more fully onto matters of constitutional political economy. Much of that work Buchanan presented in *Public Finance in Democratic Process* (Buchanan 1967) and *Demand and Supply of Public Goods* (Buchanan 1968b). As Buchanan shifted his interest into matters of constitutional political economy more generally, he recurred to matters regarding the constitutional foundations of public finance in such works as *The Power to Tax* (Brennan and Buchanan 1980) and *Politics by Principle, Not Interest* (Buchanan and Congleton 1998).

Figure 3.1 presents a sharp distinction between monocentric and polycentric arrangements. There is an apex to a monocentric arrangement; a polycen-

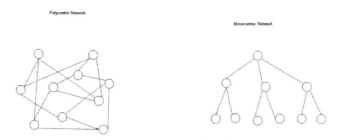

Figure 3.1.   Political Regimes as Constitutional Networks.

tric arrangement has no apex. Both types of arrangement can be represented as networks which can be described in graph-theoretic terms as constituted through some set of nodes and edges that connect those nodes in various patterns. Panel A depicts a limiting case of equality in the sense that each node has the same number of direct connections with other nodes within the system. This equality was an artifact of the constructions of Panel A. Market-based architectures, however, are not constructed by anyone. They emerge as the participants in the market choose their desired patterns of connection with other participants. Those networks could reflect random variation in the degree of connection that different nodes experience, which would still be a recognizable form of polycentricity. Alternatively, those networks could form in non-random fashion through some form of preferential attachment, in which case some nodes would stand out in their patterns of connection, as illustrated by power-law distributions rather than Gaussian distributions. With respect to the American constitutional system, the development of political parties and the creation of a joint election for president and vice president surely created a form of preferential attachment that boosted prominence of the executive within the constitutional system. The replacement of the original constitution where Senators were appointed by state legislatures with the direct election of Senators would likewise increase concentration within the network of constitutional offices.

CONSTITUTING GROUPS: THE SIGNIFICANCE OF SIZE

Buchanan recognized that the size of a group can affect significantly its democratic qualities. For small numbers of people, open discussion can occur and formal rules of procedure for making decisions might be unnecessary for reaching group decisions. With increases in size, such informality breaks down simply because of the impossibility of organizing discussion among more than a handful of people. Five people can converse among themselves without difficulty, provided only that customary principles of courtesy are followed. In contrast, five hundred people cannot carry on a conversation without first establishing a formal pattern to govern that conversation. Even for such a pattern to be created, some preceding process must exist that governs creation of the formal pattern. In any case, for there to be a genuine conversation involving 500 people requires that at any moment one person must speak and the other 499 must listen. Even if each person's statement on the topic before the group lasts only three minutes, it will take 25 hours for everyone to be heard. No one can listen to 25 hours of speech without sleep and breaks, and it would take four normal working days for all such opening statements to be delivered. We should also expect that one person's opening statement will often generate further thoughts in the other speakers. Even for this relatively small topic, small being measured by the willingness of speakers to limit their opening speech to three minutes, it could take a matter of weeks before this 500-person conversation would be concluded and summarized in the form of a vote on a motion.

Obviously, large groups cannot have truly open conversations. Democratic procedures within large groups will be inherently oligarchic, as Roberto Michels (1962) and Gaetano Mosca (1939) explained in their treatises on political sociology and as Bertrand de Jouvenel (1961) summarized in pithy fashion by setting forth the problem a truly disinterested chairman would face in trying to organize deliberation by a collective body. For there to be a conversation, most speakers must spend the bulk of their time listening and not speaking. And 500 people is a small group by contemporary standards. It is not small for a democratic legislature, but the sizes of legislatures are minuscule relative to the population from which members of the legislature are selected.

One could always retreat into the organismic mode of thinking by asserting that individual legislators are unbiased representatives of the people who elected him. This is a piece of democratic mythology or ideology whose truth value is problematic, in that it avoids facing the challenge of explanation by invoking mythology about unbiased representation. In contrast, within the framework of Buchanan's individualistic approach an analytical effort could be directed at exploring how different schemes of representation might influence the extent of disinterestedness within a parliamentary assembly. For instance, in election systems where a single representative is elected per district, roughly half of the voters in that district opposed the winning candidate. It can be different in systems of proportional representation, though how much so depends on the electoral rules that govern that system. In principle, it would be possible to develop an electoral system wherein a parliament would be selected that mirrors the population from which those members were selected. If such a parliament operated under conditions of approximate unanimity, it could be reasonably concluded that parliamentary outcomes reflected the product of disinterested deliberation. Actual systems of proportional representation are not designed with this representational precision in mind, nor do those systems operate under approximate unanimity. Hence, the size of a parliamentary assembly matters for the quality of deliberation within that assembly.

There are numerous ways a legislative assembly could be selected from among a larger population. It could be selected through elections where one candidate is selected from each electoral district, as in the United States. It could be filled through elections where multiple candidates are selected from each district, which fits the generic idea of proportional representation. Those seats could also be filled by random selection. Whatever the way in which a parliamentary assembly might be staffed, members could be allowed to continue in office as long as they win reelection, or they could be subject to mandatory replacement after serving some stipulated number of terms. Each of these possibilities, and many more, illustrate the enormous variety of ways that a parliamentary assembly could be constituted. In pursuing Buchanan's interest in developing an explanatory approach to collective action, the method by which a parliamentary assembly is constituted becomes a significant topic of analysis. Buchanan's interest in explanation would be joined with his normative interest through a line of analysis that might seek to ascertain the degree to which different parliamentary structures map into a claim that parliamentary outcomes should reflect the consent of the governed.

CONSTITUTING GROUPS: THE SIGNIFICANCE OF STRUCTURE

Any democratic political system will contain several office holders who nominally represent the underlying population. Fiscal outcomes emerge through interaction among those office holders. Interaction among those holders is shaped within an architectural arrangement among those offices and their holders. There are, however, an indefinitely large number of ways the architecture of a political system can be designed, and with those architectures generally differing in their performance properties.

Figure 3.1 illustrates two different architectures for connecting ten people within a parliamentary assembly. To simplify the exposition, it is assumed that legislators are selected within single-member election districts. The legislators are denoted by nodes in figure 3.1. Those legislators are not an unorganized mass. To the contrary, the legislature has organization. Panel A reflects a different form of organization from Panel B, but the legislators are organized within the parliamentary assembly in either case. Buchanan's approach to constitutional political economy and explanatory public finance maintains that different forms of political organization will generate different fiscal patterns even if the underlying populations are identical. Fiscal and collective phenomena arise within a specific constitutional architecture, and the challenge for Buchanan's political economy is to explain how different architectures are able to generate different collective outcomes.

Panel A shows a legislative assembly organized in polycentric fashion. This polycentric arrangement of legislators means that there are no relationships of domination and subordination within the legislature. Panel A shows that each legislator has direct relationships with three other members of the legislature. These groups of four members might be thought of as primary coalitions or committees. There is no boss of the entire parliament; there is no position of Speaker or Prime Minister within the parliament described by Panel A. The four members of any committee might agree among themselves, but they will need to obtain support from other members to get their motions enacted. No mention has been made of how decisions about parliamentary business might be made. Many voting rules are possible. With parliament having ten members, the majority principle would hold that any proposed project receive approval of at least six members. The Wicksellian scheme would require support of eight or nine members. What is of central interest for now, however, is recognition that the actions that emerge from a parliamentary assembly depend on how that assembly is constituted. Thus, we have the two-stage analytical framework central to Buchanan's thinking: (1) there are rules by which a group is constituted and (2) outcomes emerge through interaction among participants as those interactions are channeled and shaped by the constitutive rules.

Panel B illustrates a monocentric manner of arranging the ten members of the parliamentary assembly. With this arrangement, there is a boss of the parliament, a form of speaker of the house, so to speak. Panel B conveys the idea that the boss of the assembly can assign the other nine members to positions or stations within the assembly. In Panel B, the assembly is divided into three committees of three members each, with one member designated as chairing the committee and thus holding some position of authority not held by the other two members. To be sure, this monocentric structure is just a shell, as is the polycentric structure. Much of significance depends on the rules by which the participants relate to one another. The monocentric structure implies some relationship of superior to inferior that is not part of the polycentric arrangement.

It would be reasonable to expect these different parliamentary architectures to differ in their performance properties. There is a concentration of power within the monocentric network, whereas power is diffused within the polycentric network. Within the monocentric network, the chairman of a committee would generally have some bargaining advantage relative to the other two members. Even should the two committee members agree against the chairman, the Speaker might side with the chairman. By contrast, within the polycentric arrangement no one of the four members of a committee has any organized superiority relative to the other three. Coalitions can still form among the four, but they will surely be more fluid than within the monocentric arrangement where the chairman has an organizationally based advantage. No such organizational basis exists within the polycentric arrangement.

Within the spirit of Buchanan's desire to develop an individualistic orientation toward public finance within a democratic political setting, the organizational architecture of parliamentary assemblies is a topic of significance because different architectures carry different implications regarding the possible correspondence between architecture and outcome. All democratic ideology invokes the consent of the governed as conveyed by claims that within democracies people govern themselves, in contrast to being governed by rulers in other systems. Yet there is strong reason for recognizing that the architecture by which a parliamentary assembly is created and staffed can influence the correspondence between parliamentary outcomes and what would have reasonably reflected consent among the governed. While Buchanan pretty much limited his consideration of parliamentary architecture to a generic comparison of monocentric and polycentric arrangements, the making of generic comparisons invites the refinement of such comparisons to incorporate the many organizational subtleties and nuances that are missed with purely generic comparisons. For instance, one monocentric system could operate with effective tenure for people in leadership positions, whereas an alternative system could impose term limits on holding leadership positions. Wide analytical territory is available for pursuing the explanatory theory of public finance that Buchanan (1949) advanced.

CONSTITUTIONS AS FILTERS

Buchanan often treated constitutions in terms of the image of a contract, recalling notions of social contract in the process. To be sure, invoking notions of social contract is to replace explanation with mythology. Without doubt, mythology is an important force in social organization, but to invoke constitutions as social contracts, while probably conveying a significant insight, runs afoul of Buchanan's desire to develop explanatory theories of public finance and collective action. In this respect, Buchanan also treated constitutions as entailing structured patterns of offices and powers, and this treatment of constitutions offers paths toward the explanation of collective action by explaining how those patterns differ according to how different constitutional arrangements change the relationships among the individuals who participate in political processes. To be sure, the images of contract and structure are not independent of one another. Contract speaks to the idea of mutual benefit. Structure speaks to the pattern of relationships and interactions through which collective action emerges. Some of those patterns are surely more likely to promote mutual benefit than other patterns.

Constitutional arrangements are types of filters through which any proposal for collective action must pass before it is enacted. In this respect, the use of Executive Orders by American presidents is a vestige of the exercise of monarchical power and prerogative. Outside of Executive Orders, collective action requires concurrence among various persons and offices. Just what persons and offices constitutes the relevant network through which desires held by some people must pass on their way to becoming collective actions. Collective action emerges through some network structure that constitutes the relevant set of participants whose agreement is necessary to convert individual desire into collective action. A constitution is thus a filter. Like any filter, it allows some measures to pass through the constitutional gauntlet while keeping other measures out. There is, however, no such thing as a perfect filter. Any filter that allows desired objects to pass through will also allow undesired objects to pass through. Likewise, the ability of a filter to prevent undesired objects from passing through will also prevent desired objects from passing through. With perfection being impossible to attain, the only option is to achieve a preferred mix of good and bad.

A lady claims she can tell whether a cup of tea was made from a tea bag or from bulk tea. If she is judged to have that ability, she will receive a coveted position as an inspector of imported tea. She will undergo some procedure, at the end of which a judgment will be made about her ability to make the distinction. There are many different procedures a judge could follow in reaching a judgment. That judgment could also be reached by a trio of judges or by a single judge. And if by a trio, a judgment could be returned by a majority or it could require concurrence among the judges. There is also a question of the standard of judgment to be used. It would be unreasonable to expect perfection, but to say this means that it becomes necessary to determine how far short of perfection the lady can fall while still being judged as being able to distinguish between the two brewing methods.

The lady might be given 10 pairs of cups to taste. A stern judge might grant her claim if she can distinguish 9 pairs correctly. A less stern judge might grant her claim so long as she can distinguish 8 or even 7 cups correctly. Yet another judge might require that the lady be given 20 pairs of cups to taste. Whatever the standard of judgment, this alternative process would be a costlier way to reach a judgment. Instead of being given all cups at the same sitting, the lady could be given one pair each day until she had tasted the required number of pairs. This procedure would be still more costly yet, which introduces questions regarding the added cost of reaching a judgment relative to the value some judging official places on the increased accuracy the costlier procedure would enable.

The situation of a lady tasting tea is but one instance of a huge number of instances where judgments must be made in the absence of any Oracle that can divine the Truth of the matter. We may grant that the judge would like to reach the Truth of the matter, but there is no Oracle to determine whether Truth has been reached. One thing we know is that the more strongly we avoid trying to grant the lady's claim when she really can't tell, the more often we will reject her claim when she really has a systematic ability to tell the difference. Errors are impossible to avoid, of either type. There is a significant problem of judgment that is governed by the relative importance that someone places on avoiding one type of error relative to the other. There is no reason for there to exist some universally agreed standard of judgment. Different judges can reach different judgments when faced with the same evidence. Furthermore, experimentation to construct the evidence on which judgments are based is costly. More refined experimentation can lead to more accurate judgment, but that increased accuracy comes at a cost that the judge might not be willing to pay. Neither might the lady be willing to pay. But if the experimental generation of evidence is financed publicly, all participants might favor more experimentation.

I raise this illustration not to explore Buchanan's interest in experimentation but to point out the similarities between experimentation and Buchanan's vision of constitutional political economy. Buchanan always distinguished between the process inside of which some decision emerged and the contents of that outcome. This distinction maps directly onto Buchanan's methodology of constitutional political economy. Within this methodology, there is no Oracle to determine the veracity of any claim on behalf of some proposed governmental project. One can always construct a benefit-cost analysis. What one person can do, anyone can do. Many such tests can be constructed by different people, typically leading to different appraisals of the project in question. Will the construction of a lighthouse pay for itself through reducing the losses of cargo and life from the prevention of ships crashing on nearby rocks? There is no way to give a historically accurate answer to this question before the necessary historical time has passed. Until then, all we have are the various conjectures people might develop and put into their various benefit-cost analyses. There is no Oracle to tell us the value of that lighthouse any more than there is an Oracle to tell us whether the lady's claim is true or false.

All that we have is a process that we think will prove beneficial over a sequence of cases even though it can lead to mistaken judgments in individual cases. Our tests and our standards will reject some true claims and will accept some false claims. There is nothing we can do about this because there is no Oracle to speak to us. What we hope, however, is that acceptable results stem from a sequence of choices. There is no way to guarantee that every publicly sponsored project will prove worthwhile. Nor can we be sure that all horrible projects will be rejected. Beneficial projects will be rejected and horrible projects will be accepted. This is just how life proceeds when we have no Oracle to guide us. Within the Wicksellian scheme, requiring unanimous consent would assure in *ex ante* terms that no public projects would be accepted on which people placed negative value. Yet unanimity would also lead to worthwhile projects being rejected because the cost of trying to put together a legislative deal that would secure unanimous approval would more than erode the perceived gains the project would offer. As the voting rule is relaxed, some of the worthwhile projects that were rejected would now be accepted. At the same time, some projects that were evaluated negatively will now be accepted.

A constitutional system operates as a filter. Any filter that keeps out undesired material will also keep out some desired material. Should the filter be redesigned to allow a greater volume of desired material to pass through the filter, a greater volume of undesired material will also flow through. It is the same with constitutional arrangements. The polycentric network depicted in Panel A of figure 3.1 might keep out undesired programs, but it will also keep out some desired programs once costs of negotiating deals are considered. The monocentric network depicted in Panel B will make it easier for desired programs to gain acceptance, but it will also make it easier for generally undesired programs to gain acceptance.

RULES, OUTCOMES, AND CONSTITUTIONAL DRIFT

While history doesn't display sharp distinctions between political groups first choosing rules and then playing by those rules, the distinction nonetheless provides a useful point of orientation for thinking about the arrangements of human governance. With respect to Buchanan's explanatory orientation toward public finance, at any moment there will exist a *de facto* set of rules that political action follows. With respect to the material of public finance, Kenneth Dam (1977) explains that fiscal actions are guided by an effective set of constitutional arrangements and requirements, even though the American Constitution has little fiscal content written in the document. At any moment, there will be a combination of explicit rules and understood conventions that channel and shape the actions of governmental entities. These rules and conventions are the actual constitution in place at that moment, and which could always be subject to codification, as Runst and Wagner (2011) explore in seeking to set forth an explanatory theory of constitutional process. Such an explanatory theory recognizes that constitutions are not set in stone, so to speak, but also recognizes that their provisions are more durable than those of ordinary legislation. They are relatively absolute absolutes.

Charles Warren (1932) provides a wonderful illustration of constitutional drift in his examination of the continuing reinterpretation of the general welfare clause over the nineteenth and into the early twentieth century. Originally, members of Congress, and doubtlessly the population in general, interpreted the general welfare clause of the Constitution to prohibit Congress from making appropriations that would advance the interests of specific individuals as distinct from appropriations that would advance the interests of people in general. Hence, Congress could appropriate money to support the construction of roads that would promote communication throughout the nation, for this would advance the general welfare of the population. In the early nineteenth century, however, Congress overwhelmingly decided it could not appropriate money to provide relief to farmers who were stricken by drought in some counties in Ohio. While rejecting that proposal for appropriation, the members of Congress also encouraged one another to make personal contributions for relief for those farmers.

Throughout the nineteenth century, similar motions were advanced within Congress, always with the same outcome: the motion was rejected because it would provide relief for a small portion of the population, which violated the general welfare clause's limitation on the Congressional power of appropriation. As the century passed, however, similar motions to provide assistance were rejected with ever narrower margins. Finally, in 1896, one such motion to provide aid to farmers in Texas passed, only to be vetoed by President Cleveland. By the 1930s, such motions passed routinely and were never vetoed. The general welfare clause was no longer thought to limit the power of Congressional appropriation, for it became commonly understood that the meaning of general welfare was defined by Congressional appropriation. The substance of the Constitution had changed without formal amendment. Yet over short intervals, there are limits on what measures will be enacted within Congress. Those limits are not written as formal amendments, but are present all the same. How those limits form and change would be part of a *de facto* theory of constitutional process.

While Buchanan favored the image of infrequently amended constitutions over the image of a constitutional process wherein the rules and conventions are subject continually to pressure for change, either perspective maps into his vision of an individualist orientation toward collective action. In either case, there are principles, conventions, and rules in play that shape and constrain political outcomes. The distinction between constitutional and post-constitutional action still pertains to societal processes and outcomes, only the distinction between the two is relatively absolute and not rigid. Constitutional provisions and understandings move more slowly than ordinary legislation, but both are influenced by the same process of economizing individuals seeking to secure what they regard as more desired states of existence.

CONSTITUTIONAL IMAGINATION AND MORAL ORDER

A political system contains a structural pattern that is filled by participants. Figure 3.1 displays two structural patterns, each of which contains ten participants. Different rules would be represented by different structural patterns. That changes in structure would generate alternative patterns of outcome is a standard claim of constitutional political economy. The obverse of that claim is that a desire to achieve different outcomes would require a change in the rules that constitute the political process.

Commonly set aside in the examination of the relation between structure and outcome is the place of the moral imaginations of those who participate within a political system. For the most part, economists ignore the moral imagination. They do so by working with a presumption that people have fixed and invariant utility functions. While this formulation counsels economists to avoid using changes in preferences as a source of explanation, that advice is rendered against a background where human action occurs through markets. If the pattern of market output changes, it would be easy to attribute this change to a change in preferences. A more challenging line of explanation is to invoke changes in prices and incomes, as Stigler and Becker (1977) advocated. Within this formulation, economics is a form of ethology in that the human animal responds to genetic programming within an environment, but does not look reflexively upon its actions.

Yet humans are reflexive creatures. They have moral imaginations. Moreover, all choice involves acting toward an objective that lies in the future, and so must be brought to life through an act of imagination. As a formal matter, individuals can have sympathy for the situations and actions of other people. But form is not substance, for many different concrete expressions of sympathy can stem from the abstract form we denote as sympathy. With respect to figure 3.1, this means that changes in just who inhabits a node can change action undertaken within that node. That change will directly affect the other nodes connected to that node, which eventually can influence the entire society. Charles Warren's (1932) treatment of *Congress as Santa Claus* in conjunction with Buchanan's (1977) treatment of the Samaritan's dilemma illustrates how changing moral imaginations can bring about changes in the effective constitution.

In *Pauperism*, Henry Fawcett (1871) illustrated a point by telling the tale of Robinson and Smith. Both men came from the same station in life and took similar jobs in a factory. Robinson was frugal, saving a good deal of his income. He also attended classes in the evening to improve his prospects for advancement at work. In contrast, Smith spent everything he made, much of it on amusement and made no effort to make himself eligible for promotion at work. By the time the men reached retirement age, Robinson had acquired a stock of wealth that allowed him to live comfortably in retirement. By contrast, Smith had accumulated nothing and had to rely upon public support. The question of moral imagination concerns the locus of sympathy in society. If it resides with the Robinsons of the world, different measures will receive collective support than if it resides with the Smiths.

The moral imagination is at play in notions pertaining to the rule of law, as Rajagopalan and Wagner (2013) explain. The rule of law is universally contrasted with the rule of men. The contrast conveys the idea that the rule of men has a significant arbitrary element because what law is determined to be or to require depends on who does the judging. In contrast, rule of law advances the notion that it is the law and not individual men who rule. All democratic regimes espouse an official ideology that they are governed by a rule of law. Yet law can't articulate and enforce itself. Only people can do that. Again, we return to Buchanan's embrace of Knut Wicksell, who advanced a blueprint for a political regime that he thought would give substan-

Chapter Four

Federalism and the Constitution of Collective Action

Buchanan's (1949) individualist orientation toward public finance was expressed within the context of a unitary and not a federal republic. Doing this allowed Buchanan to focus on his contrast between the individualist and organicist orientations without confounding his analysis with any of the additional issues that arise with federal forms of government. Within Buchanan's individualist orientation, questions concerning the constitution of governmental power came into the analytical foreground regardless of whether that constitution was unitary or federalist in character. Questions of constitutional political economy, however, pertain to any state when pursuing individualist public finance, though Buchanan held especial interest in federal constitutional arrangements. Buchanan's doctoral dissertation, partially published as Buchanan (1950), probed some problems inherent in federal systems of government due to the presence of two distinct governments with independent taxing authority. Buchanan was particularly interested in problems associated with regional variations in fiscal capacity, the tendencies toward governmental concentration those variations created, and how a robust federal system might be maintained despite economic forces that were working to concentrate the regional distribution of income and wealth.

In raising his concerns, Buchanan accepted the proposition that a federal form of government could be a generally beneficial social arrangement, provided the system promoted competition among governments. The properties of a federalist system of governments thus depended on how that system was constituted. Buchanan's interest in constitutional political economy described in chapter 3 extends naturally and seamlessly into his interest in federalism. With respect to federalism, Jonathan Rodden (2006) explains that the conventional distinction between unitary and federal forms of government gives little insight into the actual operating properties of different governmental arrangements because those properties depend on numerous institutional details through which those governments are constituted. On this point, Buchanan would surely agree. As a matter of form alone, a unitary state means that a single government is the sole locus of constitutional authority over a relevant territory, whereas that authority is divided between governments within a federal system of government. Just how it is divided is both subject to much variety and can influence actual operating properties. Form does not dictate substance, though it does influence substance.

FEDERALISM, PROMISE, AND PERIL

Under the Articles of Confederation, the United States was constituted as 13 simple republics. Citizens of those republics were taxed and regulated only by their states of residence. There was a small national government, but its budget came from contributions the states made in response to requests from the national government. In debates over ratification of the federalist Constitution proposed in 1787 and ratified by the states in 1789, federalist proponents of the Constitution argued that the failure of the national government to have an independent source of revenue was a serious weakness of the confederation. It was widely though not universally thought that 13 independent states would have difficulty staving off invasion from the British, French, or Spanish because invasion could be directed at individual states and not at the entire 13 states. Without an independent government at the national level, it was also widely thought that competition among the states could take a destructive turn. One type of destructiveness would be a growing protectionism that could eliminate the potential advantages of a free trade zone among the states. Another potential source of destructiveness could be competition among states in their efforts to extend their boundaries westward.

While a system of numerous small governments offered many advantages, it also entailed some dangers that federalists claimed could be alleviated by replacing the Articles of Confederation with a federal system of government. The federal government, moreover, would operate with few and precisely enumerated powers. It would provide protection against foreign invasion, would prevent warfare between states, and would maintain a free trade zone among the states. In other words, the federal constitution held the promise of supporting and maintaining the liberal framework of peaceful competition set forth in the Declaration of Independence's promise of life, liberty, and the pursuit of happiness. To be sure, the new constitution did not have universal approval. Intense debates transpired between federalists and antifederalists, with the latter wanting to continue under the Articles of Confederation, though with amendments to address some recognized defects.

About one-third of the delegates assembled in Philadelphia in 1787 refused to approve the Constitution. Moreover, a two-year struggle between federalists and antifederalists ensued before the Constitution secured ratification. With ratification, the United States transmuted from a confederation of 13 simple republics into a compound republic where a federal government shared jurisdiction with 13 states. With tariffs as the primary source of revenue, the federal government ran a lean fiscal operation until Constitutional amendment in 1913 gave the federal government the authority to tax individual incomes.

What does it matter whether someone can be taxed and regulated by one government or by two? Despite intense debates between federalists and antifederalists, both sides agreed about the conjunction of promise and peril that government represented. Vincent Ostrom (1984; 1996) expresses that conjunction beautifully by invoking the image of the establishment of a government as making a Faustian bargain. Throughout the myriad versions of the legend of Faust, someone accepts a bargain that offers immediate gain with significant cost to come later. When the bargain pertains to government, it entails the use of an instrument of evil in the form of force over people, hoping that the resulting gain will exceed the evil that force unavoidably brings. In contrast to government's insertion of force into society, commercial interaction along with the offices and practices of civil society operate through consensus among willing participants. There can be many reasons why someone might think some modicum of force might be necessary to maintain good civil order. It is impossible, however, to guarantee that force will be limited to maintaining good civil order. Force will be deployed as its holders choose to deploy it. This is a basic, irremediable quality of human nature. While this quality cannot be abolished, its operation can be limited through instituting such auxiliary precautions as separating and dividing governmental powers in such a manner that one holder of power is neutralized by another holder, as against the two holders colluding.

The debates between the federalists and the antifederalists were intense, as Herbert Storing (1981) surveys, and yet they reflected concurrence regarding the proposition that government entailed the injection of a Faustian bargain into society. That bargain can't be avoided, but neither should it be enthusiastically embraced. Some means must be found to limit the damage the bargain causes while obtaining the beneficial properties it can sometimes enable. Within the framework of statistical decision theory, this is the problem of designing an appropriate constitutional filter. The debates between federalists and antifederalists did not dispute the Faustian character of government, but rather entailed alternative judgments about the properties of different constitutional filters. Where the federalists argued for the advantages of creating a compound republic, the antifederalists argued that such a large republic would undermine the republican virtues that bloom more fully in small and simple republics. Both sides agreed that government entailed a Faustian bargain whose reach into society might be limited by constitutional design.

Within the spirit of the organicist public finance to which Buchanan (1949) objected, the organization of government was not an object of theoretical interest because organization was irrelevant. Governments just did what they were instructed to do, perhaps by a monarch or perhaps by a social welfare function. In any case, the operating properties of governments stood outside the purview of the theory of public finance when pursued in the organicist motif. The Faustian bargain can come to life only within the spirit of Buchanan's individualist orientation, for only within this orientation is the constitutional organization of government a matter of theoretical interest. To be sure, until early in the twentieth century, governments were a small part of economic activity. Within the United States, governments accounted for less than ten percent of national output; moreover, the bulk of governmental activity was undertaken by state and local governments. Federal activity became significant only after the federal government acquired the power to tax personal incomes in 1913.

When governments accounted for less than ten percent of total output, there was little for a theory of public finance to explain even if someone had thought of constructing an individualist theory of public finance. An economic theory of market organization would account for something on the order of 90 percent of aggregate economic activity. By leaving government out of the explanatory account, not much was left aside in those earlier times. Furthermore, regulation was narrow in those earlier times as compared with its ubiquity today. In those earlier times, government was a small black box set in a large field of market interactions and transactions. Today, that box is gigantic, nearly rivaling the volume of market interactions and transactions. In contemporary times, an organicist theory of public finance would miss much of significance for explaining and understanding the place of collective activity within society. With the continual expansion in the relative volume of collectively supported economic activity, the significance of Buchanan's (1949) individualist orientation toward public finance has surely grown as a means of understanding the processes generating the social organization of economic activity.

FEDERALIZING TIEBOUT'S MODEL OF COMPETITION

Economists often use federalism as synonymous with decentralization, as Wallace Oates (1972; 1999) illustrates. While a federal system of government necessarily entails some measure of decentralization, Eusepi and Wagner (2010) explain that federalism means more than decentralization in advancing a distinction between genuine and spurious forms of federalism. Decentralization pertains to the extent to which responsibility for budgetary and regulatory activities resides at the apex of a governmental pyramid or is parceled out to places lower in that pyramid. A unitary state can centralize its administrative tasks in the national capital or it can grant a good deal of administrative autonomy to venues in the hinterlands. A national bureau of education might centralize all staffing decisions for schools throughout the nation. Alternatively, it might issue some general guidelines and allow administrators at local schools to make their own staffing decisions within the framework of those guidelines. That decentralization could proceed even further if the national bureau were to abolish guidelines and allow local administrators to conduct their schools as they chose. A national bureau can operate in highly centralized fashion or it can allow much local autonomy. Either way, the degree of autonomy would be an administrative decision for the head of the national bureau to make. Managers of local schools might have some range of autonomy, but the width or scope of that autonomy would be determined by the head of the national bureau.

Within a system of genuine federalism, both federal and local governments have spheres of autonomy that are constitutionally established. Charles Tiebout's (1956) model of competition among local governments is one-half of a model of federalism. Tiebout described an urban area that was divided into multiple independent jurisdictions, each having to compete for residents by offering packages of taxes and services that would attract residents. Just as business firms could thrive or fail in a market economy, so could localities thrive or fail in a public economy within Tiebout's framework, especially as adumbrated by Ostrom, Tiebout, and Warren (1961). By itself, the Tiebout framework mirrors the United States under the Articles of Confederation, save that distances separating jurisdictions are much smaller in metropolitan areas than were the distances separating states in 1787. Still, local governments must attract residents, they can't force them to come nor can they compel them to remain. Tiebout (1956) described a competitive system of local governments by reasoning analogously to the theory of market competition. He did not describe a federal system of governments. Suppose a federal government is added to Tiebout's framework. Would this additional layer of government provide mutual gains for the residents of the various localities, or might the federal government become an instrument of cartelization?

Two types of conceptual experiment can be performed on Tiebout's framework. One would be to convert the competitive system of local governments into a monopoly by consolidating the individual localities. Monopoly in the public economy would have similar properties to monopoly in the private economy, as Bish (1971) and Bish and Ostrom (1973) explain. The more interesting and complex experiment would be for the localities to estab-

lish a federal level of government with independent power to tax and regulate
individual activity. It is reasonable to claim that this constitutional change
would facilitate area-wide coordination where it was desirable. For instance,
local police departments might be able effectively to handle traffic and mis-
demeanors, while having difficulty with criminal investigation. While the
various localities could work out cooperative arrangements regarding criminal investigation, transferring that activity to the metropolitan level might be
judged more effective by all participants. This is the positive side of creating
a higher-level government. But there is also a negative side, which is the
ability of the higher-level government to act as a cartelizing agent to restrict
competition among localities.

In "Federalism as Ideal Political Order," Buchanan (1995) described a
system of competitive federalism as occupying an intermediate position between a system of autonomous separate states on the one hand and a centralized unitary polity on the other. Buchanan's image of autonomous separate
states corresponded to the United States under the Articles of Confederation,
with each state being able to determine the extent of governmental decentralization within its territory. Buchanan's image of a centralized unitary polity
was an organizational arrangement that Alexander Hamilton favored (Rodden 2006), but there was little support for creation of a national form of
government at the time. It is not really accurate to characterize the constitution of 1787 as creating some intermediate arrangement between the two
extremes. Rather, it represented a different organizational arrangement en-
tirely, neither national nor confederal. While Buchanan's image does not
truly fit the options, it does allow Buchanan to pose significant questions
regarding the historical dynamics of a federal system. At the time of its
creation, the powers of the federal government were limited to a few explicitly enumerated powers, with everything not enumerated being left to individuals and state governments. That has changed, partly through explicit constitutional change and partly through changing notions about desired practice.

Systems undergo transformation because interactions among participants
within those systems generate transformation. In some cases, systemic transformation can be an unintentional by-product of the efforts of some people
within that system to secure situations they desire more highly, as illustrated
by the growing opposition to slavery throughout the first half of the nineteenth century. In other cases, that systemic transformation can be a product
of intentional action, as illustrated in the early twentieth century by constitutional amendments to allow the federal government to tax income and to
select senators by direct election rather than by having state legislatures
appoint senators. Whether systemic transformation is intentional or is an
unintentional by-product of action aimed elsewhere, we should expect the
constitutive arrangements of governance to experience change through the
same competitive processes as drive in-period political competition.

To be sure, Buchanan tended to think in terms of constitutional frameworks as being relatively durable, and subject to change only through explicit amendment. This is an image that fits with his commonly made distinction between choosing the rules by which a game will be played and then actually playing the game. That image is reasonable for the playing of sporting and parlor games, but it is not adequate for playing the game of life, to recall the title of Bernard Suits' (1967) "Is Life a Game We Are Playing?" Life can't be stopped while discussion occurs about possible changes in the rules. Such discussions are part of life. In 1787, governance under the Articles of Confederation continued until the new Constitution was ratified; moreover, competition over different approaches to amendment was an activity that continued as one of the activities of social life at the time. Buchanan often expressed his admiration for Frank Knight's invocation of "relatively absolute absolutes." With this invocation in mind, one can recognize that there are regions of life that are relatively durable while other regions are fluid. In this respect, there was no disjunction between a time where slavery was accepted and when it was not. Nor was there a time when common usage referred to the United States in the plural, as in "these United States," and in the singular as in "the United States." While slavery was officially abolished in 1863, its acceptability had been challenged and disputed with increasing intensity throughout the early history of the republic. The shift in referring to these United States to referring to the United States reflected changes in common usage and was not an act of government. Both instances, however, point to recognition that Buchanan's distinction between constitutional and post-constitutional politics is not a distinction to be absolutized so much as it reminds us that some things are more absolute than others.

Within a genuinely federal system, local governments would have areas of autonomous action. A city that wanted to shift support from parks to police could do so without securing approval from a higher level of government. Indeed, within a genuine federal system, the distinction between higher and lower levels of government is misleading. A genuinely federalist system entails a polycentric arrangement of governments, in contrast to the monocentric arrangement of unitary states. The image of one government occupying a higher level than another implies that the higher government can intervene into the activities of lower levels of government. For a genuinely federal system of government, different governmental entities exist but they don't occupy positions of higher and lower. For instance, an individual might secure traffic control services from a town while receiving assistance in recovering stolen property from an area-wide unit of government. Within an idealized system of competitive federalism, both types of relationship between individuals and governmental entities would be contractual within Buchanan's scheme of analysis. Within a federal form of government, the federal government cannot dictate to the lower levels of government that comprise the federation. Within the American system, both the federal government and the state governments have independent constitutional standing. The federal government can influence state action, but cannot issue orders to state governments.

To be sure, the line that separates "dictating" from "influencing" can be wafer thin. This thinness is due in significant measure to the superior taxing ability the federal government has. In imposing taxes, state governments have reason to be concerned about the willingness of taxpayers to bear the taxes the state imposes because taxpayers can always choose to locate in other states. For most taxpayers, there is a fixed cost of moving to a different state, which creates a margin of tax extraction that states can impose on current residents before they consider moving. Other things the same, increases in one state's tax extractions relative to other states will reduce the relative attractiveness of that state as a place of residence. In contrast, the national government, especially in such a large continental nation as the United States, faces less intense competition to maintain residents so it faces larger margins over which taxes can be extracted without inducing emigration. Emigration from California to Arizona is considerably cheaper under most circumstances than is emigration from the United States to Panama.

Just as economists have worked with the idealized notion of an openly competitive economy, so is it possible for them to think about the notion of an openly competitive federal system of governance. Within that type of idealized system, all governments would compete freely and openly to attract residents, and in this competitiveness governments would be no different from ordinary businesses. There would be no protected spheres of governmental activity, just as there would be no sheltered positions where private firms were protected from competition. Policing might originate as a local activity. Within a system of open competition, local police enterprises could face competition from two directions: from below they could face competition from private citizens who were not pleased with the service they were supplying at the price they were paying; from above they might face competition also from dissatisfied citizens but who sought remedy by creating higher levels of government. In the first instance, some citizens might be dissatisfied with the ability of local police to locate missing persons and so organize a private firm to do that. In the second instance, some citizens might recognize that a town or city is not an efficient jurisdiction within which to search for missing persons, and so propose that a higher-level government establish a bureau of missing persons to do that. In any case, the organizational map of enterprises would be subject continually to modification as people seek for new organizational arrangements for meeting their wants and desires.

While it is possible as an intellectual matter to conceptualize a truly competitive organization of governments, the reality of the matter is that the unavoidable presence of political power is unlikely to destroy itself through free and open competition. Power will be present in all political systems, and power will be used to create sheltered positions by restricting competition. Indeed, much of the history of American constitutional development has been the replacement of competition among governments with collusion with the national government serving as the principal organizing agent (Epstein 2014; Greve 2012; Kenyon and Kincaid 1991). The transformation from competition to collusion began with the establishment of political parties which created a hierarchical chain of political offices that induced collusion across political offices at different levels of government. It was boosted with the Constitutional amendments of the early twentieth century that established the direct election of senators and allowed the federal government to tax personal incomes.

CAN COMPETITION AMONG GOVERNMENTS WORK PERVERSELY?

It is easy, almost natural, for economists to applaud the virtues of competition. And they are right most of the time, but not always. When relationships among people are governed by the principles and conventions of private property and freedom of contract, competition is synonymous with liberty inside that institutional arrangement. This means that people are free to trade with one another provided only that they don't violate the property rights of other people in the process. To speak of competition among governments, however, is not identical to speaking of competition among private persons and businesses. Business firms have market value, which means that the success of firms can be appraised in terms of changes in market value. Even closely held businesses have market value because someone can always offer to buy the firm from the owner, and that owner can respond to that offer, and with market value being established or at least approximated in the process.

In contrast, cities, states, and other units of government do not have market value. For a city financed exclusively by a tax on real estate located in the city, the value of real estate is a combination of the value of owned real estate and a share of ownership of the city that is tied with the real estate. But cities are not financed exclusively by taxes on real estate and voting rights within cities are not distributed in proportion to the value of real estate that people own. A single town that exists in a metropolitan area populated with a number of other towns does operate in a competitive environment, more so than a city whose territory is coterminous with the county in which it sits. The categories of competition and monopoly are reasonable to apply to governments, only institutional differences between commercial and political entities are also relevant and must be taken into account. References to competition among governments in metropolitan areas reflect a reality that can evaporate as governments consolidate into ever larger areas (Bish 1971; Bish and Ostrom 1973). So, competition among governments is a reasonable notion, as Tiebout (1956) recognized. But the capital accounts of governmental entities lack positions of residual claimancy (Moberg and Wagner 2014). The absence of residual claimancy may matter little when people face options to choose in Tiebout fashion among multiple governments. But what if those options are restricted? Can a system based on competitive localities be transformed into a cartel along the lines of Greve (2012)?

Suppose a system of local governments now takes on a federal government, much as characterized the American constitutional transformation. Is the resulting federal system likely to maintain and even strengthen the competitive pressures that characterized the system of local government? Besides periodic elections for local officials, there are now also elections for federal officials. In all competitive endeavors, advantage belongs to the skillful and the energetic. What does this simple recognition imply for political competition within a federal system? In the first place, we must remember that it's not governments that compete, despite our conventional usage to the contrary. It is people who compete, politicians in this case. As a general principle, we may reasonably assume that whatever office one holds, it will be necessary to continue to compete to keep that office, as well as to advance to some more preferred office.

Local officials must compete to maintain their positions by satisfying citizen desires more effectively than a majority of voters think could be better satisfied by some other politician. With a federal level of government now in place, does the competitive process stay unchanged? The adage that all politics is local politics conveys an important truth that is fraught with implications about competition among governments within a federal system. Within the founding American system, the federal government's enumerated powers broached subjects of comparatively modest interest to most citizens, in comparison to the topics with which local politicians dealt. One would surely expect ambitious politicians at the federal level to compete for prominence against local politicians. There are many ways this competition can take place, all of which would move away from restricting the federal government to its enumerated powers.

So long as the federal government was limited to revenue from tariffs and not much more, the scope for federal expansion was limited. Most of the activities of interest were conducted at the local level, but federal politicians had little scope for getting involved in those activities. This situation changed with the coming of the federal income tax in 1913 (Holcombe 2002; Holcombe and Castillo 2013). The competitive situation facing local governments was the same after 1913 as it was before. Federal politicians, however, were always in a monopolistic position with respect to other governments, but starting in 1913 they had access to a bountiful source of revenue. There is nothing surprising in the resulting ten-fold explosion in the size of the federal government relative to the market economy. The federal government was established with four cabinet departments, with that total rising to six by 1913. It now stands at 15.

So, can competition among governments work perversely within a compound republic? Within Buchanan's mode of thinking, perversity denotes some practice that could not be conceivably agreeable to the affected parties. Perversity violates the mutuality of contractual relationships in Buchanan's scheme of thought. Buchanan and Tullock (1962) explain that a simple republic could enact legislation that would have the support of as little as one-quarter of the population. To illustrate this possibility, suppose the population of an isolated locality is about evenly divided between those who live in urban and rural areas. Further suppose that a measure is proposed to enact subsidies for high-density housing within urban areas, financed by a uniform tax imposed on the population. This measure would impose cost without benefit on about three-quarters of the population. The remaining one-quarter would receive housing subsidies that on average would be worth around four times the taxes that were extracted from the recipients of subsidies. This measure would thus appeal to about half of the urban population and to none of the rural population, or to about one-quarter of the total population. The probable resolution of this situation depends on the exact numbers of the two types of citizens and their distribution across electoral districts. Buchanan and Tullock (1962) explained that this situation could lead to enactment with the support of as little as one-quarter of the population who would be able to be the dominant voice for a bare majority of legislators. This type of measure would be rejected by three-quarters of the population if the measure were subject to a referendum.

This model of an isolated locality would pertain after consolidation of a system of competitive localities. So long as that competitive system was in place, however, enactment of this type of measure would be unlikely, and for two types of reasons. First, the presence of adjacent localities where this kind of tax-subsidy program is not being considered would provide information and sharpen taxpayer awareness that weakens when easily comparable options don't exist. Second, a locality that practices such tax-subsidy operations might prove attractive to those who expect to receive subsidies, but it won't be attractive to those who would be required to supply those subsidies through paying higher taxes. In other words, the survival prospects of non-contractual programs will be weak within an openly competitive system of local governments, as MacCallum (1970), Boudreaux and Holcombe (1989), and Wagner (2011) explore from different but complementary orientations. Creation of a federal government can strengthen those survival prospects,

especially if the federal government has access to a prolific source of revenue.

If faction is a natural product of a simple republic, how would creating a
compound republic by adding a second government with independent authority to tax and regulate do anything other than to create double jeopardy? The
answer Buchanan (1950) gave, and which Ostrom (2008) amplified is that
the outcome depends on the institutional arrangements by which a compound
republic is constituted. To the extent those arrangements promote genuine
competition among governments, the outcome is likely to be mutual protection, with competition among governments working to weaken the force of
the Faustian bargain. By contrast, should those arrangements facilitate the
formation of governmental cartels, double jeopardy is a likely outcome. A
federal system could entail competition among governments that protects
liberty, but it could also operate in cartel-like fashion whereby liberty suffers
for the benefit of subgroups within the population who control political offices (Greve 2012; Wagner 2014a). Either way, Buchanan's interest in federalism follows immediately from his interest in constitutional political economy and individualistic or explanatory public finance.

Buchanan and Faith (1987) explain that secession is an important option
for creating and maintaining a system of competitive federalism. Secession is
implied by the contractual principles in terms of which Buchanan thought. In
this respect, Thomas Jefferson is famously noted to have asserted that constitutions should be renewed every twenty or so years, as against running indefinitely. The contractual principle applied to the constitutional level of analysis requires that constitutional bargains be mutually agreeable. Secession,
Buchanan and Faith recognize, is a possible remedy to a failure of post-
constitutional politics to meet the anticipations that were present at the time
of constitutional formation. An option to secede, moreover, can be effective
even if it is not used.

ASSIGNMENT VS. EMERGENCE IN A THEORY OF COMPETITIVE FEDERALISM

It is common to approach federalism through the notion of an assignment of
functions and activities to different levels of government. This approach
comports with common intuitions about geography. Some services cover
small territory; others cover large territory. Services can differ in their geographical range. A small playground might be used by people who live in the
neighborhood. In contrast, a park containing a thousand acres and enabling
many types of activity might attract people from miles away. Albert Breton
(1965) developed the concept of "perfect mapping" to denote a situation
where the geographical range of a service coincides with the set of people

who supply taxes to support that service. Where the small park might be provided by a town, the large park would be the domain of a large city, a county, or even a special district that cuts across several counties. The approach to federalism through assignment does fit some observations and conform to some intuitions. Cities provide police departments and not armies; the reverse holds for the federal government.

Yet common observation and intuition are incomplete in several respects. At any instant, there is some observed distribution of activities across retail establishments. This distribution could be described as a market assignment of activities to enterprises. But no one has made that assignment. Indeed, it is not truly an assignment. It is rather an emergent result of numerous entrepreneurs seeking to create and maintain profitable enterprises in the face of continual competition from other enterprises. At some instant, some stores will be large while others will be small. Some stores will stock tools while others stock groceries. At some later instant, observation will show a different scene. Some of those large firms will have gone out of business, while some of the small firms will have become large. New firms will have appeared, and with some of them becoming large. What the stores stock will often have changed. The store that stocks tools may now offer a consulting service for people wanting to do home repairing and remodeling. The store that stocks groceries might have reduced severely the space it provides for canned fruits and vegetables, using that released space to stock prepared meals. What looks at some instant to be some assignment of activities is actually a momentary observation that emerges out of continual competition among market enterprises.

Buchanan recognized that to speak of assignment in the standard fashion left unaddressed the identity of who makes those assignments. Buchanan's answer was that, within a system of competitive federalism, the observed distribution of activities among units of government would be emergent products of a competitive process where all political figures, just like commercial figures, are seeking to expand their reach, but must meet competition from other people seeking to do the same. Within an idealized framework of free and open competition among governments, there would be no sheltered positions where rents can be captured indefinitely. All producers, public as well as private, must continually stave off the competitive efforts of other producers. A city that establishes a municipal bus service might find much initial success. Being successful now, however, does not guarantee being successful tomorrow. Within a genuinely competitive federalism, a municipal bus service that was failing to generate sufficient revenues to pay its suppliers would not be able to obtain a subsidy from a higher-level government. Whether a city continues to provide bus service depends on its ability to attract sufficient patronage to continue in business.

There is, however, an ambiguity in the very notion of a competitive federalism that revolves around the near-universal ability to advance rationalizations for subsidies based on claims of uncompensated externalities. In this respect, Albert Breton (1965) rationalizes grants from higher to lower governments as means of internalizing external effects stemming from actions undertaken by the lower government. Suppose the municipal bus service is financed 50 percent from fares and 50 percent from budgetary appropriation, and with that appropriation rationalized as being warranted to reflect the option demand that residents secure from the availability of the option to use the bus. Further suppose that half the ridership come from residents of adjacent jurisdictions. Someone who wants to marshal support for the bus service could advance a claim for support from a higher-level government as such support being approximate compensation for the services it supplies to non-residents without sufficient compensation.

FEDERALISM AND THE PROBLEM OF UNCOMPENSATED EXTERNALITIES

In reasoning about federalist systems of government, most theorists think in organicist fashion in terms of governments as acting, goal-seeking entities. For some theorists, this treatment is given a veneer of an individualistic appearance by positing that governments are driven by the median voter within their boundaries, as illustrated by Albert Breton's (1965) model of "perfect mapping" to justify grants-in-aid from higher to lower governments based on migration and median voters within jurisdictions. Within this common analytical framework, a local jurisdiction would support public education up to the point where the marginal gain the median voter placed on another unit of education equaled the marginal cost. This outcome would conform to the efficient system of local government that Charles Tiebout (1956) sketched in opposing Paul Samuelson's (1954; 1955) claims that efficient governmental action was impossible without the imposition of some social welfare function because there were no market-like mechanisms or processes through which people would reveal their preferences for collective activity. Tiebout (1956) supplemented by Ostrom, Tiebout, and Warren (1961) sought to explain how a competitive system of local governments could operate to reveal the preferences of citizens through competition for residents.

The Tiebout-like framework pertains to Breton's notion of perfect mapping, for the consequences of choices made by median voters remain within the boundaries of local jurisdictions. By contrast, imperfect mapping describes a situation where consequences of choices made within one jurisdiction spill over into other jurisdictions. The supply of education by local governments has long served to illustrate the problems for Tiebout-like efficiency claims because many of the recipients of local education move to other jurisdictions after receiving their educations. In this case, some of the education supplied within one jurisdiction spills over to residents of other jurisdictions, just as surely as air polluted within one jurisdiction can blow into neighboring and even far-away jurisdictions. A jurisdiction that provides education provides an external benefit to other jurisdictions, which lowers the benefit received by the median voter within the original jurisdiction. Faced with this Pigou-like situation, numerous arguments have been advanced in support of grants and regulations by higher-level governments to induce median voters in lower-level governments to choose socially efficient levels of the activity in question. This type of analysis illustrates the straightforward application of the Pigouvian framework that Coase (1960), Buchanan (1962), and Buchanan and Stubblebine (1962) showed to be incomplete because it didn't pursue fully the implications of a model that began with the assumption that there were unexploited gains from trade in the initial situation.

Figure 4.1 illustrates the potential problems for Tiebout-like efficiency claims that are created by spillovers of costs or benefits across jurisdictions. Shown in figure 4.1 is the situation faced by a median voter in a typical local jurisdiction. Without spillovers, the median voter would face the budget constraint described by $I_0 S_0$, where I denotes income and S denotes the voter's receipt of value from local education. The slope of $I_0 S_0$ denotes the price of local education to the median voters. To construct a model of choice for a median voter requires some concept of price to be built into the model. In this respect, figure 4.1 operates at the purely formal level; it conveys the form of a model of constrained maximization applied to a hypothesized median voter as the most prevalent of all public choice models. And yet Buchanan, and even more so Vincent Ostrom (1997) disputed the usefulness of ordinary median voter models because such models represented an elevation of form over substance. Within the model depicted by figure 4.1, the local jurisdiction, reflecting the desire of the median voter, chooses the quantity of elementary schooling associated with B_0 in the absence of spillovers across jurisdictions.

But spillovers do exist, and of two types. One type is due to exist from the jurisdiction of students who take their human capital with them when they leave. This migration raises the price to the median voter of buying education through the local budget. As shown in figure 4.1, the post-spillout price rises to $I_0 S_1$. On average across local jurisdictions, however, spillouts are matched by spillins. While the locality loses when pupils take their educations with them when they migrate, the locality gains when immigrants bring with them the educations they received elsewhere. When aggregated over the national territory, spillins offset spillouts in magnitude but not in effect. The income

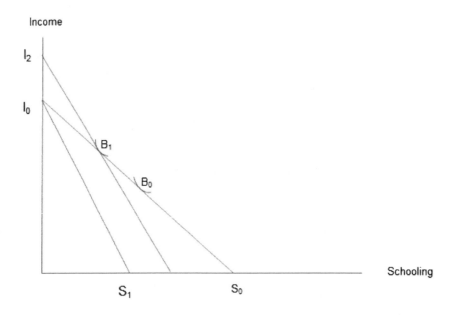

Figure 4.1.   Spillovers and Efficiency in a System of Local Government.

effects from local choices cancel but the substitution effects remain, as the alternative budget constraint I_2S_2 illustrates. The amount I_0I_2 illustrates the uncompensated gain in educational value the median voter receives by virtue of immigration. This income effect, however, is independent and hence uninfluenced by actions the median voter takes. The tax-price the median voter pays is higher in the presence of spillins and spillouts than if there were no movement among jurisdictions. In this situation, the median voter will choose the amount of schooling associated with B_1 in figure 4.1. Within the standard Pigovian framework, support from a higher-level government could be warranted as a means of restoring systemic efficiency in the presence of spillovers among individual localities. What results from this and several related lines of analysis is that Tiebout-like competition among jurisdictions can have socially beneficial properties, but it will also be plagued by external costs that require action by higher-level governments to correct, as several of the essays collected in Zodrow (1983) explain.

In contrast to conventional, Pigovian thinking, Buchanan (1962), Buchanan and Stubblebine (1962), and Coase (1960) recognized that no satisfactory model can be created that starts by positing uncompensated externalities because the presence of uncompensated externalities implies also the presence of unexploited gains from trade. A system of locally supplied schooling might feature uncompensated externalities along the lines that figure 4.1

depicts. But that same depiction implies that the median voters to which the depiction pertains would simultaneously recognize that they could gain from undertaking collective action of some sort. That action could be a program of grants from a higher-level government, but it need not be that type of program. For instance, it could that the form of some set of peering arrangements whereby compensating payments would be made in response to migration. In this manner, a jurisdiction that loses a resident would receive compensation from the receiving jurisdiction.

Within Buchanan's orientation toward explanatory public finance, it is not sufficient to assert that fiscal outcomes reflect median voter preferences in light of prevailing tax prices. These types of assertions keep the theory within the organismic motif because they don't offer a genuine path from individual desire to collective outcome. Numerous steps are left out of crossing the bridge from individual desire to collective outcome, of which Buchanan explored several and many of which remain to be explored. A referendum on a school budget could be described as selecting the outcome preferred by the median voter, but this isn't the only possible outcome. In this case, much depends on the process by which a ballot is constructed. In figure 4.1 the median voter chose the preferred outcome B_0; however, the ability for the median voter to do this is based on auxiliary assumptions that might not pertain. For instance, the ballot might be constructed by a committee that places only two options on the ballot. One might be much higher than B_0 while the other is well below it. With this procedure, the outcome will still be that desired by the median voter, only the median voter's most preferred outcome will not be an option for choice. Within this alternative two-step procedure where a committee selects the options about which a larger group decides, the median voter could select something well above B_0 if the option was inferior (Levine and Plott 1977; Plott and Levine 1978).

Figure 4.1 depicts a tax-rise to a median voter. Yet public output is not typically priced through direct pricing where people can choose how much they pay by choosing how much to buy. There are cases where public finance proceeds in this manner, as when a public park charges admission fees. Yet most politically sponsored activity is financed by taxes that are not direct charges for services used but are parasitical attachments to market transactions (Pantaleoni 1911). A personal income tax, for instance, is an attachment made to market transactions that generate income. A retail sales tax is an attachment to transactions where consumers make purchases. Furthermore, not all transactions within these generic categories are subject to tax. Some transactions may be exempt from tax. Also, multiple tax rates can apply to the same category of transaction, as exemplified by personal income taxation. Antonio de Viti de Marco (1888; 1936) posited the concept of a tax-price in seeking to pursue an explanatory theory of public finance, which Buchanan (1967; 1968) carried forward and which Eusepi and Wagner

(2013) explored. Figure 4.1 depicts a purely formal notion of fiscal catallactics which can be useful for organizing thought but which is insufficient for truly explaining the operation of the public finances. As Buchanan recognized, to move public finance in an explanatory direction requires development of ideas about the processes and procedures by which collective options emerge within some democratic system of political economy. To undertake such development requires schemes of thought suitable to the challenge. Buchanan's (1969a) treatment of the theory of cost was central to pursuing that line of development.

EXTERNAL COSTS, PUBLIC GOODS, AND THE SOCIAL ORGANIZATION OF LIGHTHOUSES

Lighthouses have long served to illustrate claims about public goods and market failures, with those claims subsiding only modestly since Ronald Coase's (1974) description of the supply of lighthouses in England through market arrangements. The situation Coase described entailed ships paying tolls to support lighthouses upon entering a harbor. The tolls were collected by a public official and paid to the owners of lighthouses. Coase argued that this historical experience showed that the use of lighthouses to illustrate claims about public goods and market failure were wrong because market arrangements were able to accommodate the supply of lighthouses.

Yet public officers and agencies were clearly involved in the provision of lighthouses even if those lighthouses were built and owned by private individuals. Rather than denying the usefulness of claims about market failure and public goods, the organization of lighthouses during the period Coase examined illustrates how the public utility concept can be refined to unite public and private elements of an activity. Lighthouses were built and operated by private businesses. Public collection of tolls, however, was necessary for this arrangement to work. Should a public agency not collect tolls and distribute the revenues to lighthouse operators, what appears to be a market-based system would collapse. When viewed from this point of view, the market-based provision of lighthouses does not deny claims about government involvement in the presence of public goods, but illustrates that that involvement can take many forms.

That provision could proceed through a public establishment of a Bureau of Lighthouses that would build and operate lighthouses. That Bureau could be financed by budgetary appropriations or by tolls collected from ships that dock at harbors in the Bureau's jurisdiction. Either way would appear to support standard claims about collective support for the provision of public goods. Note, however, that this entire conceptual discussion takes place against a background of a prefabricated world. The social entities with which the theory deals are already in place. Those entities don't emerge or become assembled through human efforts aimed at securing ends that people desire. Within this prefabricated world, cost appears to be separate from utility or demand. Shippers want lighthouses whose protective beams will keep them from danger. That desire for protection must overcome the obstacle represented by the cost of producing lighthouses. The cost of production appears to be distinct from the value the produced service would provide, and the standard claim on behalf of externality and public goods theory is that public supply can overcome an inability of private supply to meet the demand for lighthouse protection.

While Buchanan often opined that we must start from where we are because there is no option, he also recognized that that opinion pertained to a limited and certainly not a universal domain. In many cases it is necessary to know how something has been put together before its operation can be properly understood. Buchanan clearly thought that the social world could not be assembled by mere summation over the individuals who constituted that world, due to the presence of phenomena that arose and emerged through interaction among those individuals. An individual Robinson Crusoe alone on an island will surely develop habits, patterns, and customs, but he will not quarrel with neighbors nor will he be able to call on them for support or to engage in joint ventures. Property rights will not exist, nor will procedures have been created to adjudicate conflicts among neighbors. Organizations to undertake cooperative ventures will not have been established, nor will coalitions have formed to foment controversy among neighbors. To understand the source and operation of such social phenomena requires a scheme of analysis where social practices and conventions emerge out of interaction among individuals. Buchanan's analysis in *Cost and Choice* provides a path toward doing this.

We may reasonably posit that people formed the idea of traveling by ship before they formed the idea of building lighthouses. As people and merchandise began to travel by ship, it does not take much of a stretch of the imagination to recognize that occasions will arise when a ship runs aground or crashes on rocks near shore. These accidents are pure losses to all persons involved, running from the owners of the ships to the sailors and owners of the merchandise carried on the ships. Some ship owners might respond to these dangers by having their ships sail only during daylight hours. Someone else might develop the idea that a strong light placed on a tall building near dangerous rocks could provide warning for approaching ships.

This person faces the entrepreneurial problem of converting that idea into a product with commercial value. There are numerous ways through which this could be done within a social system grounded in private ordering. Obviously, the potential customers for the entrepreneurial idea are the owners of ships most of all. But there would be others who could potentially gain from lighthouses. These might include sailors, though increased safety would doubtlessly reduce their compensation as more people became willing to become sailors. The owners of shipped merchandise would also gain through a decline in expected loss. And there could be investors who would see opportunity for gain in supporting the entrepreneur's idea, either by lending to the corporation the entrepreneur establishes or by becoming shareholders in the corporation.

The final step necessary to commercialize the idea of the lighthouse would be to develop a way of collecting revenue from shippers or ship owners (Krause 2015). The entrepreneur would surely find collecting revenue from ship owners to be less costly than trying to collect revenue from shippers. Among other things, the ship owners are small in number and readily identifiable, and have a strong portion of their livelihood wrapped up in their ships. The entrepreneur might think of asking ship owners to make contributions when their ships arrived safely in port. Perhaps some owners would make modest contributions, but the predicted undersupply offered by the standard theory of public goods would be in play in this situation. In response, the entrepreneur might have decided to drop the project.

At this point, there arises one of those forks in the analytical road. Down one branch, the entrepreneur could have approached a politician to provide help with his venture. The outcome of traveling down this branch would resemble the situation Coase (1974) described. To be sure, that individual politician operates within some collective process in which he must sell his legislative idea to other legislators, the result of which might be the establishment of a Ministry of Lighthouses, or perhaps Ministry of Shipping. In any case, political involvement in the operation of lighthouses is a plausible outcome of a situation that started with an entrepreneur's idea. This entrepreneur faces the problem of commercializing his idea, and perhaps determined that using his political connections provided the least cost or most profitable means of doing that.

It is also easy to imagine an alternative outcome. The entrepreneur, either as an individual or through a corporation he organized, gains control of dockage at relevant harbors. Institutionally, there are several ways this control could be attained. It could be achieved through a purchase of land. It could also be achieved through acquiring rights to the docks without acquiring the adjacent land. In one form or another, the entrepreneur would be able to organize the collection of revenue, and would do so in what he regarded was the least cost fashion. That least cost fashion might entail the entrepreneur's corporation owning docks as well as lighthouses. It could also entail public operation of docks with tolls being transferred to the entrepreneur's corporate entity. Whichever organizational form would be established, the entrepreneur's effort to maximize his net worth would lead him to the same destination as would his effort to minimize his cost. Buchanan's treatment of the reciprocal relationship between cost and choice offers insight into the assembly of the commercial world.

There is no reason for the analysis to end with the establishment of a lighthouse enterprise, however it collects revenues. The comparative statics of equilibrium theory would end the analysis here, but the emergent dynamics of creativity and emergence that Buchanan embraced would allow the situation to evolve. Should the alternative of a Bureau of Lighthouses be the means by which the lighthouse is commercialized, we can reasonably expect controversy to arise from time to time over the size of tolls, both on average and perhaps even more on their distribution across ships of different size. We can also expect controversy to arise over the return that accrues to the lighthouse corporation. We might also expect that a politically organized lighthouse bureau won't operate in the same manner as a private corporation would operate. Just as a quota creates different dynamics of political economy than does a tariff even if the effect on the aggregate volume of imports is the same, so would a politically supplied Bureau of Lighthouses operate differently than would a consortium of ship owners aiming to accomplish much the same thing. In any case, Buchanan's treatment of the reciprocal relationship between cost and choice opens an analytical door into the continual reconstitution of the social world, in sharp contrast to the closed analytical door presented by the Marshallian cross of independent forces of utility and cost.

ATTENUATED PROPERTY RIGHTS AND STRATEGIC INTERACTION

Buchanan (1950) was concerned with interaction among units of government within a federal system, and the ability of that interaction to undermine the promise of a competitive federal system. Jonathan Rodden (2006) explored similar problems that arise because of the attenuated character of ownership rights within governmental entities. At base, a federal government faces less competitive pressure than do the individual states which must attract residents in the presence of competition from other states. A competitive system of local governments will generate spillover effects among the entities. It is an easy act of imagination to describe how a higher-level government could act to internalize those spillovers. Doing this is standard welfare economics where knowledge is presumed to be complete and motivation is pristine pure.

The situation is different once reality is confronted. Knowledge is invariably far from complete. People, moreover, respond to the incentives they confront within their situations. One can characterize a system of local governments as a form of competitive equilibrium, and yet the institutional differences between private ordering with its residual claimancy and public ordering with its absence of residual claimancy can be a significant source of difference in comparative performance properties. Some units of local government might become heavily indebted and perhaps even enter bankruptcy. This situation happens to private businesses as well. Insolvency and bankruptcy play out differently for governments than for private individuals, due to the attenuation of property rights within governments, as Moberg and Wagner (2014) explain.

Differences in institutional frameworks between firms and governments generate significant differences in both the causes and consequences of insolvency. Within a regime of private law, insolvency is a problem for those creditors alone, and the principles of private ordering generally operate to concentrate liability for choices on those who make them. It is different with public ordering. Normally, governments act within some scheme of common ownership where liability for entering insolvent states is diffused in large measure among property owners within a jurisdiction. A private executive who supports a project that turns out badly will generally bear cost in a way that a public executive does not. In large measure, this is because residual claimacy makes it relatively easy to know when a project turns out badly. By contrast, this determination is not so simple to make under public ownership where enterprises have no market value.

One can imagine a system of governments held together in contractual fashion along the image of a network of hotels, as originally sketched by Spencer MacCallum (1970). Hotels offer a tied package of commonly available and privately organized services and activities. While most hotels have small territorial footprints, there is no necessity that those footprints must be small. A network of hotels, moreover, could be organized as a federation, perhaps as a form of city state with both urban centers and hinterlands. Within this organizational scheme, a higher-level government would handle matters of common interest, and would have a governing structure that aims at maximizing the value of the constituent units. As Buchanan and Lee (1994) explain in the context of the European Union, this situation would play out differently depending on whether the higher government could gather its own revenue or had to rely on contributions from the lower, member governments. In the latter case, the willingness of the lower governments to support the higher government would depend on the value of the services the higher government is thought to provide, as evaluated by lower-level officials.

Buchanan (1950; 1995) recognized that the operating properties of a federal system of government depended on the social organization of political competition within the federation. State and local governments are unavoidably in a competitive situation, more so as their boundaries shrink, reducing the time it takes to travel from one state to another. Local units must remain competitive with their neighbors. A federal government does not encounter this problem with anything resembling the intensity of local governments. While the United States remained a federal republic after adoption of the federal income tax in 1913, this change in the ability to tax created a substantial change in the distribution of political power, as the federal government moved from having what was surely a weaker power to tax than the states possessed to having by far the stronger power to tax.

In this respect, Buchanan and Lee (1994) examined the European Union with respect to different arrangements for distributing the power to tax. Their central point can be conveyed with a simple model of two forms of revenue sharing, one form called normal revenue sharing and the other form called reverse revenue sharing. Normal revenue sharing refers to the idea, which gained currency in the United States late in the 1960s, that the federal government would transfer some of its income tax revenues to the states. At the time when this idea surfaced, it was also noted that federal revenues grew more rapidly than aggregate income while state revenues grew roughly in proportion to aggregate income. Where states would have to make conscious efforts to increase tax rates if they were to increase spending on programs beyond what normal economic growth would allow, the federal government continually obtained increasing revenues without having to enact explicit changes in tax rates. The idea behind revenue sharing was that the federal government could transfer some of the superior ability of its income tax to raise revenue to state governments, where more of the demand for publicly provided services resided. In contrast to conditional grants in aid which provided support for explicit programs, revenue sharing would be given free of conditions. What happened since the idea of revenue sharing surfaced was a combination of increased conditional grants and a greater amount of federal funding of what had traditionally been state and local programs.

The idea of reverse revenue sharing is that revenues originate with the member governments within a federation, and those governments determine how much revenue to transfer to the federal government. Where regular revenue sharing works in a top-down manner, reverse revenue sharing would work in a bottom-up fashion. With reverse revenue sharing, federal politicians would have to attract support from the lower-level governments where the revenues arise. While a political realist might be understandably skeptical about the prospect for the adoption of reverse revenue sharing, consideration of that prospect is an easy way to show that the operating properties of any federal system of government depend on the institutional details through which it is constituted. One can speak of a system of competitive federalism, for competition is prevalent throughout political life, but there are different institutional arrangements through which competition can occur, each with its own performance properties, as Buchanan sensed when he embarked on his journey to pursue collective economic action within an explanatory motif.

Chapter Five

Public Debt, Time, and Democratic Action

Within Buchanan's contractarian orientation toward public finance and political economy, the treatment of action through time acquires central importance because most contractual relationships extend through some duration of time. In the textbooks, exchanges are usually treated as spot transactions. Someone exchanges some cash for a sack of grapefruit, and any obligation between the parties is extinguished at the instant the exchange takes place. The textbook focus on spot transactions makes it possible for the instructor to focus on ideas about prices and gains from trade without verging into the complex territory associated with credit transactions where contractual obligations are not extinguished until some interval of time has passed. During that interval, moreover, events can happen and situations can arise that lead the initial contractual arrangement to unravel to some extent, or even collapse. While credit transactions create problems that spot transactions don't have even in market settings, credit relationships create especial problems when governmental entities are involved, due mostly to the absence of transferable ownership rights when governmental entities undertake transactions.

Buchanan's focus on constitutional political economy brought topics regarding the passage of time into his analytical foreground, beginning with Buchanan's (1958) analysis of public debt. All action occupies time between the initiation and the completion of the action. Sometimes the length is relatively long, and this length can create difficulties and challenges for democratic regimes due to differences in property rights within private and political settings. A person who is 80 years old can reasonably plant a grove of trees to be harvested in 30 years while knowing he will almost certainly be dead when those trees are ready for harvesting. What makes this act reasonable is private ownership of the trees, which means that the owner can sell the trees before they are ready for harvesting. Private property gives the owner strong incentive to avoid harvesting trees prematurely because he typically will be able to raise more cash by selling ownership shares in the forest than by harvesting the trees prematurely.

Political action presents a different setting for human action because political action is not governed by private property. A politically held forest does not have market value because there is no person who can sell ownership shares in the forest. Leaseholds can be offered with political forests, but these establish only rental values. The duration of those leases is usually relatively short, as in a few years and not a century or more. The present value of a perpetual ownership that returns $100 annually is $2,000 when valued at a five percent rate of discount. Should a leasehold run four years, the present value will be but $350. The duration of a leasehold can matter greatly with respect to the strength of incentive a leaseholder has. Leaseholds entail incentives for waste because the leaseholder lacks the responsibility that residual claimancy creates. To mitigate the losses from such understandable incentives toward waste, leaseholds are often accompanied by such auxiliary precautions as security deposits and damage clauses. The owner of a private forest will have strong reason to manage the forest in a value-maximizing manner even if he is unlikely to be alive when the trees are ready to harvest. In contrast, a public forest has no owners, as distinct from having encumbered lease holders. The manager of a public forest can capture whatever gain his office allows him to capture only while he holds office.

Recall from Buchanan (1969a) that the cost of any action is the actor's evaluation of an alternative action that was rejected in favor of the chosen action. The cost of any action that requires some interval of time to pass before it is completed will differ to the actor, depending on the institutional environment in which that action is undertaken. Someone who owns the trees in a forest but can't sell them will face a different cost for harvesting trees than will an owner who can sell the trees. Questions regarding property rights and their impact on actions that entail a significant passing of time are ubiquitous phenomena for the construction of explanatory approaches to public finance. Early in his career, Buchanan (1958) explored how the ability of governments to borrow led governments to increase their borrowing, imposing costs on future generations in the process. While this is a theme to which Buchanan returned on several occasions during his career, the underlying principles about how different institutional arrangements influence the course of actions that occupy significant intervals of time is a general facet of Buchanan's effort to pursue collective action within an explanatory motif.

PUBLIC DEBT AND FUTURE GENERATIONS

Buchanan (1958) claimed that financing government by issuing public debt rather than imposing taxes enabled the present generation of taxpayers to shift the cost of government onto future taxpayers, recognizing that in some cases those future taxpayers might be older versions of themselves. This book attracted reviews by several notable scholars. While the reviews were generally respectful, most of them rejected Buchanan's claim. To the contrary, the critics claimed that cost can never be transferred forward; instead, cost must always reside in the present. In this regard, several critics noted that the resources used in producing a battleship for the recently concluded war were used up when the ships were produced, so cost must manifest when production occurs. In this setting, whether the battleship was financed by taxing or by borrowing was irrelevant. With respect to the aggregate production function portrayed in figure 2.3, an increased output of battleships requires reduction in the output of private consumption, and that ends the matter. Buchanan, however, thought the comparative static method of thinking was inadequate because it ignored relationships among the individuals who implicitly reside inside figure 2.3. To bring these relationships to life, moreover, requires a scheme of thought that accounts for the passing of time, in contrast to the a-temporal character of comparative statics.

Buchanan opened *Public Principles of Public Debt* by listing the three main claims of what he described as the "new orthodoxy" (1958, 5) that he wanted to dispute:

1. The creation of public debt does not involve any transfer of the primary real burden to future generations.
2. The analogy between individual or private debt and public debt is fallacious in all essential respects.
3. There is a sharp and important distinction between an internal and an external public debt.

After he summarized the new orthodoxy and offered some methodological remarks, Buchanan (1958, 26) set forth his contrary theme about public debt:

1. The primary real burden of a public debt is shifted to future generations.
2. The analogy between public debt and private debt is fundamentally correct.
3. The external debt and the internal debt are fundamentally equivalent.

Since publication of *Public Principles*, Buchanan (1958) has been associated with the proposition that the financing of government programs through borrowing rather than taxing is a method that transfers the cost of those programs from present taxpayers to future taxpayers. In staking out this position, Buchanan voiced support for the presuppositions of classical public finance against the new economic thinking associated with John Maynard Keynes (1936) that was associated with the claim that public debt should create no concern because "we owe it to ourselves." *Public Principles* was published but 12 years after the Employment Act of 1946 was enacted, and with this Act pledging the federal government to use its budgetary powers, including budget deficits, to maintain full employment, including increasing public spending if private spending was insufficient to establish full employment. Buchanan's theme in *Public Principles* was surely anathema to those economists who favored government management of the macro economy.

While in 1958 Buchanan's *Cost and Choice* was 11 years away from being published, his explanation of his thesis about the ability of public debt to shift cost forward in time previewed his 1969 book. If a battleship is financed by taxation, it is clearly taxpayers who turn over the resources necessary to build the battleship. But what if bondholders provide those resources by buying government bonds? It's not reasonable to claim that the bondholders bear the cost of the battleship. Indeed, they have gained personal advantage by buying bonds. The voluntary purchase of bonds means that bondholders have traded opportunities they value less highly today for opportunities they value more highly tomorrow. Buying debt enables the bondholders to achieve a superior intertemporal pattern of consumption opportunities. Bondholders rearrange their temporal pattern of consumption, consuming less today and more tomorrow, and experience an increase in their present valuation of their intertemporal pattern of opportunities. Present taxpayers, moreover, don't pay higher taxes to finance the battleship, as the purchase of bonds by bondholders replaces the higher taxes that taxpayers would otherwise have paid. The only option is that it is future taxpayers who now face smaller consumption opportunities due to the burden they will bear to retire public debt. Hence, public debt allows the cost of public spending to be transferred forward in time.

To claim that public debt entails shifting the burden of public expenditure from one generation to another requires treating generations as acting entities. This is a treatment that does not sit well with Buchanan's methodological individualism. To be sure, macro theorists work with models of overlapping generations all the time, but Buchanan repeatedly rejected macro-style modeling and its holistic methodology. When a large family gets together for a festive occasion, it is meaningful to speak of a gathering of different generations because speech about generations has real meaning in this case. But to speak of a nation as comprised of younger and older generations, or something similar, is an artificial and abstract use of concepts, the only use for which seems to be its ability to accommodate some mathematical modeling.

A generation within the formal modeling, moreover, is a representative agent. A representative agent, however, can't engage in transactions. The issuance of public debt requires transactions that create debtors and creditors, which can't happen with a representative agent or a homogeneous generation. For transactions to occur, it is necessary for people to start from different positions and desires.

Had Buchanan maintained contact with methodological individualism, both as conveyed in his initial paper on the theory of government finance (Buchanan 1949) and his subsequent explanation that cost is a concept that pertains only to and is inseparable from making a choice among options (Buchanan 1969a), he surely would have avoided using generations as action-taking entities. Public debt, as all credit transactions, creates obligations that bridge present and future. Those obligations, however, are established among the people alive at the time the debt is created. Hence, someone would support debt over taxation only because that person perceived debt to entail lower cost as compared with taxation. Here, it is necessary to be clear that lower cost refers to the perception of an action-taking entity, and not to some such aggregate construction as a nation. As an alternative to taxation, the use of public debt will entail some rearrangement of liabilities for financing governmental activity.

This recognition should perhaps have shifted Buchanan's attention away from generations as acting entities to interactions and relationships among the individuals present at any slice of time. It is possible to imagine an approach to public debt where debt finance would be identical to tax finance. This would be an arrangement where liability for public debt is assigned to individual taxpayers at the time the debt is created. Public debt in this case would be no different from mortgage debt. A budget deficit would now be accompanied by an assignment of future tax liabilities necessary to amortize the debt, in contrast to the present arrangement where future liabilities remain to be assigned in future years. In this manner, public debt would be placed on more of a contractual setting. One consequence of issuing public debt in this manner would surely be an increase in the interest rate on political loans because failures by some taxpayers to pay their assigned liabilities would not be offset by higher taxes on remaining taxpayers. Hence, bondholders would bear a higher risk of default when liability was assigned to individual taxpayers rather than being left for future assignment.

In this regard, it is often claimed that the lower interest rate at which governments can borrow indicates a genuine cost saving from organizing political loans. This common claim is surely wrong. Among other things, it assumes that institutional arrangements are irrelevant for human action. To the contrary, the absence of residual claimancy for political entities reverberates throughout the gamut of economic interaction. A well-known motif of political action is to accompany projects with cost estimates that are lower than what cost turns out to be. Doing this is surely part of the public relations strategy of gaining support for projects. A project that might gain support when cost is projected at $1 billion might be rejected if cost were projected at $2 billion. Hence, a prudent strategy for a political entity is to project cost at $1 billion, knowing that it can request additional appropriations later. With $1 billion sunk into a partially completed project, the odds are good that the legislature will grant additional support, particularly when plausible sounding excuses for being over budget can always be advanced. The lower interest rate on public loans does not reflect some lower riskiness for public loans. That lower interest rate reflects a shift of the risk of default away from bondholders onto taxpayers, for bondholders receive their payments regardless of how over budget the project is. The lower interest rate on government bonds attests not to some type of governmental efficiency but to the transfer of risk from bondholders to taxpayers when liabilities for amortizing debt are not assigned at the time debt is created.

DEBT DEFAULT AND THE CONTRACTUAL IMAGINATION

Nearly all promises create debtor-creditor relationships even though people rarely think in such formal terms. Whether a relationship is formalized or left informal, the essence of the relationship is a tying together of two or more people in some common activity over some interval of time. Only a small subset of those instances will entail financial indebtedness between or among the participants. The character of this tied relationship is summarized nicely by the title of Charles Fried (1982): *Contract as Promise: A Theory of Contractual Obligation*. That book is about private law and the sentiments that tie people together during the life of some contractual relationship. While personal indebtedness forms a good portion of the material of contractual obligation, contractual obligation reaches beyond usual notions about indebtedness.

Regardless of the range of that contractual reach, public debt enters altogether different analytical and emotional material than does personal debt. In this difference in reaches, personal and public debt resemble the two parabolas X^2 and $-X^2$, in that they share a common origin but point in opposing directions. All debt entails some relationship that extends over some duration of time. Personal debt, however, is mostly incurred through explicit agreement among the participants, though it is possible to imagine cases where one party has accepted a position of indebtedness under duress or even force. Where duress and force might be relatively rare in personal debt, it is common in public debt, especially with increases in the size of political units.

Vilfredo Pareto's (1916) distinction between logical and non-logical action has significant analytical work to do with respect to the distinction between personal and public debt. Personal debt falls within Pareto's category of logical action, as is typical of market choices. The choice between paying cash for something now and borrowing now and paying cash later leads readily and easily to Pareto's logico-scientific mode of thought. With public debt, however, the action is removed from the logico-scientific mode and shifted to the ideological mode because the individual cannot act directly on the object. Pareto's category of non-logical action has often been described as a form of irrationality. This is a severe misunderstanding of Pareto's analytical scheme, as Patrick and Wagner (2015) explain. Pareto always has people acting to achieve objectives. It's only that what they can achieve and how they can achieve it differs between the logical settings of market action and the non-logical settings of political and religious action. Pareto's distinction between alternative environments within which people act is similar to Gerd Gigerenzer's (2008) treatment of rationality as something that reflects interaction between environment and calculation, as against being a matter of simple calculation.

At any moment, a person can pay personal debt in part or in whole, and can form a judgment about the experience of being indebted. In contrast, no individual can undertake action with respect to public debt. One might embrace one of several ideological sentiments that political figures and associated interest groups advance, but that is all. How one might view public debt, along with the prospect for default, is more a matter of the strength of various ideological sentiments than of some logical calculation of individual costs and gains because no basis exists for logico-experimental calculation under most conditions of public indebtedness. Buchanan's (1958) analysis of public debt can be brought into the same analytical frame of reference as Gaetano Mosca's (1896 [1939]) and Vilfredo Pareto's (1916 [1935]) analyses of democratic oligarchy and ideological competition. In this respect, Buchanan (1985; 1987b) mused about the possibly positive moral value of debt default. Throughout his career, Buchanan advocated a contractarian orientation toward the material of political economy, with the exemplary reference being Buchanan (1975a). Buchanan, though, had no truck with the ruling class theories that Gaetano Mosca and Vilfredo Pareto did so much to promote, though Wagner (2014b) presents a rational reconstruction of Buchanan's public debt theory that makes some modest effort to reconcile Buchanan with Mosca and Pareto.

TRANSFORMING PUBLIC DEBT INTO PERSONAL DEBT

Whether individual appraisal of public debt is logical or non-logical depends on the institutional framework under which public debt is created and amortized. Under typical democratic frameworks, public debt belongs to the category of non-logical action because people cannot choose among and compare potential courses of action with and without public debt. It is possible, however, to create institutional circumstances under which decisions regarding public debt can be transformed into the same category of logical action that pertains to personal debt.

Along lines that Antonio de Viti de Marco (1936) set forth, suppose an isolated town has traditionally financed its activities with a balanced budget with revenues collected from a flat-rate tax on income. The town is presumed to be isolated to focus on Buchanan's claim that it is irrelevant whether public debt is held internally or externally. This year, the town council has decided to build an arena to host various types of events and activities. The town could finance the arena by doubling the tax rate for two years, after which the tax would return to its traditional level. If the town did this, individual taxpayers would have to determine how to finance their doubled tax payments for the next two years. We may reasonably surmise that some taxpayers would pay the increased tax in cash, possibly selling some assets to raise the cash. We can also reasonably surmise that a good number of taxpayers would secure loans to pay their taxes. To the extent taxpayers seek loans, a set of debtor-creditor relationships will be established to finance the arena, but there will be no public indebtedness. Provision of the arena will have led to an increase in the aggregate amount of indebtedness within the town, but the town itself will not have become indebted.

With all debtor-creditor relationships being internal to the town, those residents who borrow to pay their tax bill will borrow from other town residents to obtain the proceeds with which to pay their tax bills. The town's construction of the arena creates a set of debtor-creditor relationships, with some of the town's residents lending to other residents. The lenders will be compensated in future years by payment of principal and interest from the borrowers, and the entire operation will fall within the domain of logical action, given the two-year doubling of each person's tax liability. Should individual borrowers move away from the town prior to discharging their liability to their creditor, that liability will nonetheless remain in force under the principles of private law until the debt is discharged. A lender might have difficulty in securing payment in some cases, but this possibility is entailed in any debtor-creditor relationship, with the risk of borrower default being one element of the price of credit.

As an empirical matter, there is good basis for thinking that there will be a skewed distribution of responses to the doubling of the tax bill, with more people choosing to borrow than to pay cash. The majority of the residents would thus borrow to finance their extraordinary tax payments. While the resulting individual indebtedness could be accomplished through a set of personal loans, it is easy to understand how pragmatic political considerations might lead the town to borrow on behalf of that majority of taxpayers.

A member of the town council proposes a motion to finance the arena by selling bonds. The motion passes, and the town's bonds are bought by the same people who would have otherwise have lent to individual taxpayers. The town bundles a large set of what would have been private loans into a single public loan, which the town sells to that subset of the population willing to act as creditors. The town can place the bonds at a lower rate of interest than would have been charged for the private loans, due in large measure to the shifting of default risk from creditors to taxpayers. By shifting from a set of private loans to a public loan, the debtor-creditor relationship shifts from the logical into the non-logical category.

It would, however, be a relatively simple matter to keep the relationship in the logical category. All that would be necessary would be for the town to assign liabilities for debt amortization to individual residents in proportion to their assigned extraordinary payments which they did not make at the time. In this case, the town council would organize the debt issue by distributing liability for that debt among those town's residents who did not make extraordinary tax payments. Those liabilities, moreover, would be permanent for those individual taxpayers just as items like mortgage debt are permanent. Neither movement from the town nor death would erase a borrower's liability because that liability would remain to be settled as part of the decedent's estate. To be sure, lenders would face greater risk of default under this scheme than if the town were to service the debt or even just to guarantee it.

Perhaps the most notable feature of this institutional arrangement is that individual liabilities for debt amortization are established at the time the debt is created. The town itself, however, is not a participant in the credit market, but rather only establishes the pattern of liabilities that leads some residents of the town to become debtors and other residents to become creditors. Of central analytical significance is the existence of a set of institutional circumstances under which public debt is indistinguishable from personal debt. Even though public debt is created by some governmental entity, it could operate in all relevant respects like personal debt. Among other things, allowances for bad debts would be part of the accounting scheme. Any person's nominal level of debt could not be boosted upward in subsequent periods, regardless of whether some taxpayers had defaulted on their payments or because some taxpayer's income had declined, which normally would have increased tax liability on those whose incomes had not declined. Public debt would fall clearly within the rubric of the promise of contract even though the debt originated with a public entity. Public law would meld perfectly and seamlessly with private law and the principles of contractual obligation.

DEMOCRATIC GOVERNMENTS AS INDEBTED ENTITIES:
A CATEGORICAL MISTAKE

It is reasonable to describe the various feudal monarchs of times past as being indebted. Those monarchs would often borrow from subjects, and they also owned assets that might have given those subjects some modicum of hope of having their loans retired. Monarchs in feudal times operated inside a society's market economy, while also serving as Big Players (Koppl 2002). Having Big Player status meant that monarchs were not subject to the ordinary principles of property and contract that held for ordinary market participants. Lending to a monarch was not identical to lending to other citizens. Still, it was meaningful to describe a monarch as being indebted, for indebtedness refers to a relationship between identifiably distinct entities, even if duress was sometimes involved when people lent to monarchs.

Democratic governments obviously accumulate debts in their name. This is a fact of direct observation. That fact, however, is a superficial fact that does not withstand closer observation. To describe democratic governments as indebted involves a category mistake. Indebtedness describes a relationship between a debtor and a creditor. That relationship, moreover, is explicit. In feudal times, a king might have been indebted to some nobles. That relationship was explicit; each party knew who was indebted to whom, and by how much. In democratic regimes, however, there is no such explicit relationship, though there could be if liability for amortizing debt was assigned at the time debt was created. Without explicit assignment of liability, public debt replaces debtor-creditor relationships with a vague relationship of collective intermediation where the only explicit relationship is between bondholders and a parliamentary assembly. Even this relationship is not fully explicit because members of the parliamentary assembly do not act on their own accounts. Members of parliament do not own the value consequences of their actions, positively or negatively. A democratic polity is not an entity that can become indebted to other entities within that society, unlike the ability of a monarch to become indebted to some of his subjects.

Democratic governments are financial intermediaries when it comes to public debt. They intermediate between people who want to save currently, which they can do by buying public debt, and the rest of society who are in an ambiguous position. It would be easy to describe these people as people who do not want to reduce their spending now, and so borrow to postpone paying taxes. But this would not necessarily be accurate. To put the matter this way is to presume that these people support the added spending, but would prefer to pay for that spending at some later date. Perhaps some do, but it's also possible that some don't and would rather have less spending and less future taxation. For ordinary credit-market relationships, the debtor-creditor relationship is mutually agreeable to the participants. To be sure, there can be instances where borrowers borrow under some sense of duress, but this is mostly in consequence of the emergence of adverse circumstances for which borrowing subsequently is superior to the alternative. Public debt, however, would be voluntary only within the framework of de Viti's cooperative state. Outside that limiting case, public debt is agreeable to some people but not to others.

Furthermore, public debt cannot be examined independently of the processes that generate the public spending that public debt supports. While public debt represents a substitution of future taxation for present taxation, any appraisal of that margin of taxation must consider the political processes through which spending is increased. In the case at hand, it's the choice to build an arena that brings about public borrowing as an alternative to increased taxation. Some people might support the arena, but others might not. Moreover, the presence of a possible arena on the public agenda does not simply emerge in mysterious fashion. Rather it is created through concerted entrepreneurial action from somewhere within the society. It is here where Buchanan's treatment of debt could gain much from integration with Mosca's and Pareto's recognition that democratic processes typically entail relatively small numbers of people pursuing their desires and promoting those desires by constructing and offering ideological images that resonate favorably with significant parts of the larger population. In his examination of some implications of Pareto's analysis for public choice, Jürgen Backhaus (1978) explains that Pareto thought that clever ideological articulation could induce people to support programs they would have opposed had the action environment in which they operated been one open to logical rather than non-logical action.

The offering of ideological images is the form that competition for leadership takes in non-logical environments. The competitive challenge is to offer an ideological image that will resonate more strongly with desires held among subsets of the society than do other images. This situation is the reverse of the logico-experimental method that pertains to market settings where scientific-like tests can be performed. In Pareto's scheme, non-logical environments pertain particularly strongly to politics and religion. Politicians compete for voter support by articulating images as points of attraction. We may be sure that a politician who wants to see an arena built will support debt finance in place of a balanced budget, and the challenge the politician faces is to offer an ideological image that secures more support than do images that would operate within the balanced budget framework. For instance, a belief in contractual obligation entails a presumption that people should pay their own way, which is roughly accomplished with a balanced budget. Someone who wanted the arena would have to counteract that contractual image. One way to do that while supporting the contractual image is to invoke notions from capital budgeting. Hence, debt financing would be limited to the services the arena provides in future years while tax financing would support current services. This competitive process, it should be noted, occurs within the non-logical and not the logical arena. Individuals have no ability to compare their experiences with alternative products or promises and to select what they judge to be superior. Such comparisons reside outside the pale of the logico-experimental method. If the capital budgeting rationale resonates with a person's sentiments, public debt can be supported. If, instead, it is fiscal sobriety that resonates, one can support the balanced budget option.

Public debt is a form of promise, as is debt in general. With personal debt, however, it is generally quite clear who promises what to whom. With public debt, and hence with debt default, it is necessary to examine who promises what to whom. Such questions regarding public debt cannot be examined independently of the budgetary and political systems inside of which public debt emerges as an instrument to finance public expenditure. Within the framework of de Viti de Marco's (1936) contrast between cooperative and monopolistic states, promising would characterize a cooperative state. To be sure, de Viti recognized the cooperative state to be a limiting model and not a miniature replica of actual societies. Indeed, the essays in de Viti (1930) are dominated by the monopolistic orientation toward political action. Monopolistic states would operate with some variable admixture of promise and imposition. Where along a monopolistic-cooperative spectrum actual democratic arrangements might reside depends on the performance properties of the institutional arrangements under which a democratic regime is constituted, which is the central theme of Buchanan's entire body of work.

CONTRACTUAL OBLIGATION AND DEFAULT WITH FORCED INDEBTEDNESS

A theory of public debt within the spirit of de Viti's model of the cooperative state is straightforward. With respect to the preceding illustration of building an arena, consensus would exist within the relevant financing entity to make the change. The only issue would be how to finance the arena. We may suppose that the polity sells bonds to some of its residents, with the bonds to be amortized over ten years by a flat tax on income. Debt finance in this case is agreeable to all taxpayers, so public debt fits within the sentiment of contractual obligation that accompanies the making of promises (Fried 1982). To be sure, de Viti's model was a limiting model and, moreover, was not even his preferred model of collective action judging from de Viti (1930). In real democracies, and we should keep in mind that de Viti had 20 years of experience as a member of the Italian parliament, public debt will entail some mixture of forced and voluntary indebtedness.

It is easy to claim that forced indebtedness vitiates what otherwise might have been a sense of contractual obligation. As is often the case with easy answers, reality might be more complex than a situation that would allow ready embrace of the easy answer. For one thing, it might not be easy to distinguish between forced and voluntary debtors. If claiming to be a forced debtor allows the claimant to secure tax relief, we can be sure that many people will claim to be forced debtors when they were pleased to see the arena built. Obviously, self-identification can't be relied upon in this situation because incentives will exist for free-rider types of activity. Yet if the possibility of being a forced debtor is recognized even though self-identification is not allowed, one is left wondering how that distinction might be made. The theory of statistical decision making offers some clues. The central feature of that theory is the impossibility of giving a definitive answer to this type of question. Someone's claim to be a forced debtor might be granted even if it is false. That claim could also be granted even though it is true. Perfection is impossible. All that is possible is to live with the post-constitutional result of the previously constituted decision process (Buchanan 1975a; Brennan and Buchanan 1985).

As an explanatory matter, one can plausibly assert some positive relationship between the extent of forced indebtedness and the degree of support for debt default, though there is no reason to assume that this relationship is linear and independent of the identities of those who support and oppose default. For instance, in the United States municipal pension funds are notoriously underfunded. These funds typically are of the defined benefit category, and actuarial soundness requires that they be pre-funded. But they typically are only partially funded, as Adrian Moore and Anthony Randazzo (2016) explain. While those funds operate with several rules and principles to keep them solvent, those rules have weak ability to withstand collusive action between labor unions and city councils or managers. Such coalitions of interests typically can exert more political force than ordinary people.

Ideological articulation operating on human sentimentality is also at work in this setting. One facet of that articulation is the claim that democracy entails an obligation to accept all democratically decided actions, as conveyed by the standard distinction between the rules of a game and the choice of strategies for playing the game. There is nothing in the logic of democratic governance that compels one to accept this claim under all circumstances. That claim is rather something that supporters of particular democratic practices advance through ideological articulation, with the hope that it becomes widely embraced within the population. It is reasonable to think that support for default will grow with increases in the share of the population that perceive themselves to be forced debtors, though there no good reason to think that there is any obvious linear relationship behind this proposition.

Contracts are promises, and it is understandable that public debt would be linked to personal debt to take hold of the promise-making character of personal debt. But public debt is not the same thing as personal debt, though the distance between personal and public debt is a variable and is not fixed. De Viti captured some of that variable quality in his distinction between cooperative and monopolistic states. There is surely nothing inherent in the nature of democratic regimes to provide a moral bar against supporting debt default because public debt is not *ipso facto* implicated in the same network of promises as is personal debt. It is easy enough to understand why supporters of expanded public spending financed by debt would support ideological formulations that wrap public debt inside the promise-making and promise-keeping ideology that pertains to private ordering of human activity. But public ordering carries forward only some of those qualities that accompany private ordering. Indeed, the long-standing aphorism that "eternal vigilance is the price of liberty" reminds us that such vigilance might well countenance episodes of default as a corrective measure for excessive drift into destructively collectivist territory, as Buchanan (1985a; 1987b) explains.

PUBLIC DEBT AND THE CORRUPTION OF PROMISING

Debtor-creditor relationships entail the making and keeping of promises (Fried 1982). These relationships typically operate within the province of private ordering, and these relationships surely help to promote trustfulness within society. Public debt, however, operates by principles of public law and not private law. Within private law, promising has clear meaning because it pertains to identifiable promisors and promisees. With public debt and public law, however, taxpayers are treated formally as promisors even if they opposed the creation of debt. In relationships governed by private law, the legal principle of contract can be restated in moral terms as the injunction to keep your promises unless the promisee releases you from your commitment. The operation of private law surely serves as an instructional device to the effect that contractual commitments are trustworthy.

With public law and public debt, however, promising can become corrupted because personal liability for promises has been eliminated from the public square. A significant question that arises with respect to public ordering is just who is promising what to whom? There are good reasons to think private and public ordering will differ in the types of promises they promote. Suppose the purchasing agent for a private firm economizes on the time he spends searching and negotiating better deals, so commits the firm to paying more than is necessary. There are good reasons to think that private ordering will operate to limit such possibilities. The purchasing agent might have an ownership interest in the firm, which might induce him to pay greater attention to his commercial duties. His activities might be subject to inspection and audit, which will work to concentrate his attention. Furthermore, the purchasing agent may have internalized values that promote success of the firm as an ethic of workmanship. The situation is different with public ordering. For one thing, the purchasing agent can't have an ownership interest in the firm because such ownership interests don't exist. Auditing might turn up the submission of fraudulent invoices, but it won't reveal variations in the intensity with which the purchasing agent pursued his activities rather than spending time taking on-the-job leisure.

Private ordering creates a form of dyadic exchange while public ordering creates a form of triadic exchange (Podemska-Mikluch and Wagner 2013). This distinction, it should be noted, is not between two-person and three-person trades. A dyadic exchange can involve many participants, just as can a triadic exchange. The distinction is between wholly voluntary trades and incompletely voluntary trades. No matter how many people participate in a dyadic exchange, that participation is voluntary. By contrast, a good number of participants in triadic exchanges are involuntary or forced participants. The treatment of triadic exchange recalls the post-constitutional analysis of political processes in Buchanan and Tullock (1962) and William Riker's (1962) theory of majority voting and political coalitions. For private ordering, mutual gain from trade applies just as well to multi-person dealings of immense complexity as it applies to a simple trade at flea market (Epstein 1995). The central point of the theory of exchange is to explain how voluntary exchange promotes mutual gains from all participants, and at all sizes of transactional nexus. The particular number of those participants is immaterial. It is the voluntary nature of the interaction and participation that is of material interest.

By contrast, triadic exchange pertains to properties of public ordering and not to the number of participants. The simplest way to illustrate triadic exchange is with three participants because this allows a coalition of two winners and one loser. A general theory of democratic political economy can be developed around three persons but not around two. To be sure, the unanimity of Wicksell (1896) and Buchanan and Tullock (1962) along with de Viti's (1936) cooperative state can be reduced to dyadic exchange. Nonetheless, normal democratic procedure and practice creates winners and losers at the relevant margins of action even if the democratic process in its entirety is positive sum. Most democratic polities entail some form of majority rule, though such polities also often entail constitutional restrictions on the abilities of winning majorities to impose costs on losing minorities. Typically, however, those restrictions, while present, are also relatively modest in preventing intense majorities from getting their way. Suppose that trust is in part a prudential habit that is validated through good experience and undermined through bad experience. It is easy to understand how private ordering promotes trust regarding social arrangements. The institutional framework of private property, freedom of contract, and personal liability channels personal conduct in this manner. Within this institutional framework, the economic world is organized in largely voluntary fashion, and that world is one that promotes mutual flourishing. For instance, the owner of a business might hire several people to perform various activities. That owner is free to dismiss people who don't perform as they were expected to perform. Hence, someone who is not punctual or is rude to customers or co-workers undermines the value of the firm and can be dismissed. While such dismissal will be costly to the person who was dismissed, it also sets in motion a learning experience, both on the part of the person dismissed and on the part of external observers who also might seek to gain employment.

Public ordering under the principle of consensus or unanimity, as described by de Viti's cooperative state, operates in the same manner. It is different, however, with the ordinary democratic framework of majority rule. Politically established relationships have less durability and persistence than market-established relationships. This lowered durability and persistence is a prime operating feature of majority rule processes where the composition of coalitions is subject to continual margins of change as currently excluded persons seek to gain political inclusion while presently included persons must be wary of being excluded. In this setting, public ordering lowers the level of trust people can reasonably hold about social institutions and practices. The simple reason for this is that promises have less durability within public ordering than within private ordering. The private ordering of promising is consistent with the promotion of trust in social arrangements and practices. The public ordering of promising can be, but as a general matter would work to corrupt the meaningfulness of promising. The further public ordering moves away from the framework of a cooperative state, the more it would seem to contribute to some degrading of trust.

KEYNESIAN FOLLIES AND THE PRETENSE OF MACROECONOMIC CONTROL

If political activity were congruent with the principles of private ordering, publicly supported indebtedness would operate in conformity with the same contractual principles as private indebtedness. Indeed, this was pretty much the scheme of classical budgetary practice until the aftermath of the Keynesian revolution. As Buchanan and Wagner (1977) explain, prior to the Keynesian revolution American budgetary practice was to run surpluses during normal times, reserving deficits to times of war and depression. Public debt accumulated during those periods of war and depression, moreover, would be reduced through budget surpluses during normal times. This pattern followed the classical theory of political economy, as reflected in the notion that prudent conduct for a nation was the same as prudent conduct for a family. While publication of Keynes's (1936) *General Theory* was greeted by negative reviews from several prominent economists, Keynes quickly achieved general professional conversion to his macro-theoretic orientation. As the eminent historian of economics, Mark Blaug (1996, 642) put it: "never before had the economics profession been won over so rapidly and so massively to a new economic theory." Buchanan, however, was not won over, as such early work on public debt as Buchanan (1958) and later work on the Keynesian follies (Buchanan 1987a) show.

The Employment Act of 1946, which established the Council of Economic Advisors, pledged the federal government to a posture of exercising active control over economic activity and organization. No longer was economic life thought to be self-regulating within a legal framework of private ordering. To the contrary, an activity program of public ordering was necessary to keep afloat an inherently unstable ship of state. To promote such stability, a government's budgetary powers were thought to be a significant tool. To the contrary, Buchanan (1986b) called for elimination of the 1946 Act and the Council of Economic Advisors on the grounds that the Act could never accomplish what it was established to do. For Buchanan, economists were not mechanics, nor even aides to politicians who might think of themselves as mechanics. The 1946 Act construed economists as mechanics who had the responsibility and the talent for keeping the economic engine running smoothly. To construe economists as mechanics who respond to the desires to politicians to keep the economic engine running smoothly is to create an image that propels politicians onto center stage of the human drama, for they are the ones responsible for keeping economic life working well. It's easy enough to understand how this image flatters the political class and helps to project political action throughout society. All the same, that image is false. It is false theoretically and it is false historically, as Buchanan (1987a) recognized.

Historically, this image stems from the progressivist period of Woodrow Wilson's presidency. That image brightened in the aftermath of the Great Depression that occupied the presidencies of Herbert Hoover and Franklin Roosevelt. The resulting New Deal created a massive social and economic earthquake, equivalent to around 9.5 on the Richter scale, and the American economy has never been the same. The standard narrative of American economic history is that the Great Depression was an accident and the New Deal was a valiant effort to restore prosperity. This narrative is false, as Lawrence White (2012) explains luminously. To the contrary, the Great Depression started with the progressivist creation of the Federal Reserve Bank in 1913, which set in motion a bias toward creating money and credit that has continued to the present time. The 1920s were an inflationary period for money and credit even if prices were not rising, and that inflationary period led to the Great Depression.

Theoretically, the image of mechanics and engines is false. This image asks the listener to imagine an economy as a simple machine that isn't working properly, with that image calling for a mechanic. That image, however, is as wrong as wrong can be. Economies are not machines. They are complex webs of interacting people who pursue their objectives in imaginative and creative fashion. A truly useful economics requires recognition of the inherent complexity of economic phenomena, as Buchanan recognized. As a historical matter, the progressivist narrative needs to be reconfigured in light of the growing recognition that societies and economies are complex organisms and not simple machines. This recognition would not eliminate the need for political mechanics, but it would remove them from center stage to the periphery of the human drama. The simple fact of the matter is that politics is a business, though a peculiar one (Wagner 2016a). Many people earn their livelihoods in politics. They invest capital in supporting parties and candidates. Politicians create programs they think will gain support, just as do ordinary businesses. With ordinary business, success can be gauged largely by an enterprise's market value. It is different with political enterprises. They have no market value. Where stock markets do important work in bringing market discipline to bear on commercial enterprises, stock markets are unable to bring discipline to bear on political enterprises. All enterprises claim to offer valuable services. For commercial enterprises, those claims are tested through market transactions. Incorrect claims will lead to enterprises making losses, so they revise their commercial plans or go out of business.

For political enterprises, however, no services are sold to customers. Instead, political enterprises obtain their revenue mostly from taxation that is part of the peculiar business of politics. Political enterprises thus attach themselves parasitically to the activities of commercial enterprises. There is no possible market test for the truth claims of political enterprises. Political enterprises do face competition, largely from other politicians and the enterprises they favor. That competition, however, inhabits the world of ideology and not the world of experience. This difference makes all the difference. Any claim that an ordinary business makes can be tested by customers through their experiences. This testing resembles what goes on in a scientific laboratory. A commercial enterprise claims that customers will prefer its product to alternative products. This claim can be tested by consumer responses to different products.

No such testing is possible for the claims of political enterprises and candidates. Political enterprises operate in the world of ideology and not that of science. This is the world of persuasion when there is no genuine ability of people to test the truth-claims the persuaders offer. The world of persuasion is still competitive, but that competition cannot be brought to scientific-like testing. Instead, competition takes place through candidates seeking to develop ideological images that resonate more strongly with relevant parts of the electorate than the images that other candidates offer. Look, for instance, at the financial crisis that arose in 2008. Where some claim that the events of 2008 show the need for more regulation of credit markets, others claim that they show the need for less or at least amended regulation. Both types of claim accept the image of policy mechanics, only differ over which mechanic is better. In truth, the image of the policy mechanic is the basis of a deeper problem that speaks to the relationship between political and commercial enterprises.

Not so long ago, historically speaking, credit markets were organized largely through the private law principles of private property and freedom of contract. A creditor faced the problem of creating a portfolio of loans that generated acceptable returns to the firm's investors. In seeking to do this, firms chose among applicants for loans depending on beliefs about the reliability of debtors. A potential debtor whose reliability was questionable could offer to pay a higher interest rate or pledge collateral rather than having his application rejected. In any case, credit markets under private law operate through agreement, and with the terms of those agreements emerging out of the search for mutual gains between debtors and creditors. In contemporary times, public ordering has acquired a deep presence within credit markets. No longer is agreement between borrowers and lenders sufficient for making deals. Political officials also intrude into credit markets, thereby engaging in commerce as peculiar participants. They are peculiar participants because they are not seeking to help commercial enterprises serve their customers and investors better. To the contrary, they seek to force commercial enterprises to serve the interests of political officials. For instance, creditors must now develop loan portfolios that conform to regulatory requirements regarding such things as gender, race, geography, and income. Hence, some people will receive loans who would not have done so under private law. Consequently, other people will be denied loans who otherwise would have received them. This situation means that lenders will sometimes make politically mandated loans that they would not have made if credit markets were governed by private law. It further means that there will be a greater volume of commercial failures than would otherwise have resulted, and with those failures increasing the amount of economic turbulence within a society.

The fact of the matter is that there is an incongruity between the operations of commercial and political enterprises. Commercial enterprises operate with their own money, and have strong reason to use that money to attain commercial success. The peculiar businesses that are political enterprises operate with other people's money. Political enterprises have no commercial value, so there is no objective way that success can be gauged. For commercial enterprises, one can gauge success by comparing changes in market value. For political enterprises this is impossible. All that is left is to gauge success by holding popularity contests. This is not to deny the presence of competition among political enterprises, including candidates for election. Indeed, such completion is generally intense in democratic political systems. The features of that competition, however, differ when it pertains to commercial enterprises than when political enterprises enter the competitive arena. In any field of human endeavor, open competition among contestants generally selects for superior qualities with respect to that field of competition. This does not, though, mean that political enterprises are to be judged as equivalent to commercial enterprises.

To make this claim would be to make a category mistake by treating the two forms of competition as identical when they diverge from one another. For commercial competition, successful competitors are those who are particularly good at converting capital that investors supply into products that customers desire sufficiently strongly to return a profit to those investors. By contrast, for political competition, revenues are derived through taxation rather than by selling services to buyers. Moreover, political enterprises can't engage in profit-and-loss accounting. Hence, the managers of political enterprises can't be compensated in any fashion by the profitability of the firm. Whether managers perform well or poorly cannot be revealed through changes in the attractiveness of the enterprise either to investors or to consumers.

Still, competition among political enterprises will select for quality just as will competition among commercial enterprises. Those qualities will differ, however, depending on the field of competition. For instance, there are excellent divers who are but ordinary swimmers, just as there are excellent swimmers who are only ordinary divers. Each form of competition selects for excellence within its field, but this does not mean you would select a swimming team by watching people dive. Late in the eighteenth century, Adam Smith asserted that little is required to carry a society from misery to opulence but peace, easy taxes, and a tolerable administration of justice. Opulence is surely universally preferred to misery. Moreover, it does not seem particularly challenging to keep taxes low and to administer justice in tolerable fashion. The maintenance of peace might be a bit more challenging, but still seems attainable in light of the general dislike people have for living in war zones of varying intensity.

Hence, it seems relatively easy to replace misery with opulence. But misery has not been vanquished in the 250 years since Smith puzzled about its persistence. How can the failure to attain something that is universally desired be explained? Perhaps those three conditions are not so easy to attain after all. In *Systems of Survival*, Jane Jacobs (1992) explained that a well-working society requires both commercial and guardian modes of activity. Her distinction, moreover, is not the same thing as a distinction between businesses and governments. Even business will engage in guardian activities. While a construction firm will earn its livelihood from its construction activities, it will also engage in some guardian activities. One such activity will entail inventory management and auditing, which are necessary to ensure that employees don't convert company materials to personal use.

In reflecting on what happens when commercial and guardian moral syndromes commingle, Jacobs coined the term "monstrous moral hybrids." For instance, an auditor who covers over a theft for a fee is commingling commercial and guardian roles. As businesses become increasingly involved in politics and political enterprises come increasingly to participate in business, monstrous moral hybrids grow within a system of entangled political economy. The human drama in which we all participate is improvisational and not scripted. There are, however, some time-honored principles that speak to the qualities of various possible dramas. Those principles were recognized by Adam Smith and later by Jane Jacobs, among many other thinkers through the centuries. These principles place commercial and industrial activity in the foreground of the human drama, while putting political action mostly in the background.

Over the past century or so, however, foreground and background have largely reversed. It is now widely believed that politicians bear primary responsibility for the extent of flourishing within a society. This situation generates a simple but dynamic template that encapsulates the contemporary world. A problem arises. Say an earthquake or fire destroys a good part of a city. In earlier times, recovery would have occurred quickly through the offices of private law. These days, recovery occurs more slowly and fitfully, due to the predominance of public law. With private law you have many businesses seeking opportunities for mutual gain. With public law, you have contending political officials who are using the disaster to project themselves onto society's center stage. Save for dreaded diseases, the human body has a natural ability to recover from sickness. It is the same with societies and economies. Indeed, the prime teaching of economics until the arrival on the intellectual scene of Marxism and Keynesianism has been that societies have natural abilities to recover from economic distress.

In a similar vein, a propeller-driven aircraft has natural stability properties. An aircraft that passes through a storm will be tossed up and down, but the plane will continually move toward level flight. Should the pilot react to a dip in the plane's nose by increasing the angle of attack, a stall and possibly a crash can result. Politicians are not pilots of a ship of state, and yet public rhetoric makes them appear to be just that. Actually, there is little politicians can do actively to promote human flourishing other than secure peace, keep taxes low, and administer justice tolerably well. If they stick to this recipe, they will avoid inserting harm into society. That is the best situation any society can attain. All the same, a soberly realistic person would surely be pardoned for thinking that politically induced turbulence will continue to be part of our economic experience, as will the parade of future policy mechanics offering themselves and their programs to control the turbulence their predecessors helped to create. Recognition that political action beyond the maintenance of some simple governing framework does more to promote turbulence than to calm it was a central theme in Buchanan's writings regarding the institutional arrangements governing credit and money, as exemplified by Buchanan (1961; 1983).

CENTRAL BANK PROMOTION OF THE KEYNESIAN FOLLIES

The Keynesian follies have been playing now for the better part of a century, and their popularity does not seem to be diminishing. It is reasonable to wonder whether Buchanan's orientation toward political economy offers any insight into this popularity. Consider a simple model that contains five people, and with collective decisions made by majority vote. Each person starts a new business. Two of those are successful while the other three owners liquidate their businesses. Within the institutional framework of private ordering, those three owners might start new businesses or they might hire themselves out to work for someone else. Indeed, these will be the only options people have within a system based on private ordering.

But how likely is a system of private ordering to resist intrusion of public ordering when it comes to matters concerning business failures and reorganizations? In the five-person model, a majority has experienced a disruption in their commercial plans and must now bear the cost of creating and implementing some new plan. Just as it is rare to find a losing politician admit to having offered an unattractive program, it is surely also rare to find a business person admitting to having offered an ill-conceived product. Far more likely will be explanations based on a constellation of events, as in an inability to secure credit on reasonable terms or on a sudden unavailability of essential inputs. In any case, a political program to assist in the creation of new businesses out of the shells of liquidated businesses might secure majority support. The simplest way to do this might be to create a government credit program to support such businesses. The proponents of the program doubtlessly would claim that the initial subsidies would be self-financing due to tax revenues generated in future years when those businesses come into maturity. This will undoubtedly happen to some of those subsidized businesses, but not to all of them. As time passes, more businesses will fail and more subsidies will be supplied. Those subsidies will be provided by taxes imposed on successful businesses. It is reasonable to think that the central bank will on occasion buy these government bonds, thereby releasing additional funds to use in subsidizing more new businesses.

Buchanan (1961; 1983; 1986b) recognized that without central banking the Keynesian follies would cease, for reasons George Selgin (1996) and Lawrence White (1999) set forth in their examinations of monetary arrangements and processes. Within the American Constitution, the monetary power of the federal government is the fifth of the 18 enumerated powers, and it appears as an instance of the power of Congress to fix standards of weights and measures. Among the standards of weights and measures, a dollar had the same fixed measure as the other weights and measures. Originally, the dollar was defined as a weight of silver, which was expressed alternatively as about 1/25th ounce of gold. Someone who promised to pay you $25 would have to pay you one ounce of gold. The sixth of the enumerated powers pledged the federal government to combat counterfeiting. With respect to money, counterfeiting occurs when coins are reminted and reissued with less gold content. Buchanan's (1961) advocacy of a brick standard recurs to the original treatment of the monetary power as part of the certification of weights and measures. In conjunction with the creation of the Federal Reserve in 1913, the Keynesian follies (Buchanan 1987a) has entailed continuous counterfeiting as the dollar has been redefined continually downward. It is as if a pound has become an ounce and a foot has become an inch, only the original names are still used. Where the original Constitution called upon the federal government to prevent counterfeiting, creation of the Federal Reserve created counterfeiting as an instrument of public policy that is played out through the Keynesian follies.

Placing the monetary power within the rubric of certifying standards of weights and measures reflected the operation of rule of law principles within the liberal constitutional order that was established, and whose underlying logic rooted in economizing action Buchanan and Tullock (1962) set forth. The classical political philosophers thought that democracies would face difficulties in sustaining themselves against internal forces that were always latent and often active, whereby people could try to live at other people's expense, though would invoke ideologies of justice and public good in doing so. Some of this process of disintegration of the moral toughness required for democratic governance Buchanan (2005) described as a fearfulness of being free. A good number of Buchanan's later papers explored problems and difficulties of maintaining liberal institutions and arrangements, and Buchanan's efforts in this regard were amplified marvelously by Vincent Ostrom's (1997) *The Meaning of Democracy and the Vulnerability of Societies*, where he explains that living freely is not some natural function like respiration or bodily elimination, and instead is a costly practice that can be done with variable quality and with concomitantly variable effect for the living together in close proximity that we all necessarily experience.

Chapter Six

Entitlement, Liberty, and Responsibility

The Declaration of Independence was the founding constitutional document of the United States, or at least it was in Abraham Lincoln's judgment in 1864 when he opened his address on the Gettysburg battlefield by noting: "Four score and seven years ago." Aside from slaves and the natives who preceded the arrival of immigrants from Europe, the United States was founded as a form of liberal republic. The Declaration promised to Americans "life, liberty, and the pursuit of happiness," and nothing more. These three qualities denoted what Americans were entitled to in the late eighteenth century. That list has expanded greatly in the ensuing 250 or so years. Often, starting in 1976, I recall hearing James Buchanan remark at addresses he made at conferences sponsored by Liberty Fund, the publisher of his Collected Works, that "Liberty Fund's program is my program; my program is Liberty Fund's program." At those same conferences, a representative from Liberty Fund would invariably explain that Liberty Fund was dedicated to exploring the requisites for a society of *free and responsible individuals* to establish itself and to maintain itself once established.

To live in a regime based on liberty requires responsible action on the part of individuals, much as Benjamin Franklin recognized in responding "a republic if you can keep it" to the lady who asked him what kind of Constitution the Constitutional Convention had established. A regime grounded on individual liberty will not automatically renew itself as time passes. Renewal requires that people act responsibly to maintain that free republic. In this respect, Franklin was aware that the classical political theorists thought that a liberal democracy could be only a temporary form of government that would dissolve into some form of servility and tyranny as people came to exchange their liberal birthright for the proverbial mess of pottage. Like Franklin,

Buchanan was aware of the concerns of the classical political philosophers, and of the need to explore the relationship between liberty and responsibility.

In this regard, the relationship between liberty and responsibility is like the relationship between product markets and factor markets in general equilibrium theory. Any action on a product market requires a supporting action on a factor market. Herbert Hoover's promise of a chicken in every pot pertains to the product market, but fulfillment of that promise requires that people be compelled on the factor market to supply those chickens. Liberty is a quality of life that people can consume, but to consume it requires that it be produced. Liberty is not a natural quality of social life; it is not like respiration or bodily elimination. It is a social practice, like dancing or singing, so can be undertaken to better or worse effect. The enjoyment of liberty requires the supply of responsible activity to maintain liberty, and responsibility is a costly activity. Liberty is easy to accept, as would be the offer of a chicken for your pot. By contrast, responsibility is a form of work which can be onerous. People might judge the price of liberty to be higher than they are willing to pay. If so, a regime based on liberty can transmute into one based on servility or tyranny of some form, as explored in such places as Belloc (1912), Ostrom (1997), Buchanan (2005), and Buchanan and Yoon (2015).

COMPLEMENTARITY BETWEEN LIBERTY AND RESPONSIBILITY

It is widely thought that just as a market economy is an expression of economic freedom, so is a democratic polity an expression of political freedom. A market economy and a political democracy would thus seem to combine to form a constitution of liberty for a free society. In this respect, the renowned constitutional scholar Charles McIlwain once noted that "constitutional government is by definition limited government" (McIlwain 1947, 21). Without some explanation as to how it is possible truly to limit government, this common formulation is perhaps more sentimental than realistic. The task of grounding that sentiment in a reasonable sense of reality raises some knotty issues regarding the institutional framework of a free society that contains within it a democratic polity.

The very idea of limited government implies that people create government, which means that government is limited by the prior and superior rights of the people who form it. Buchanan and Tullock (1962) and Buchanan (1975a) explain the economic rationality of this movement from private property to the establishment of a government. It is commonly presumed that without government to preserve and protect person and property, people would be subject to predatory attack, both from each other and from outsiders. This common presumption has been challenged by Edward Stringham (2005; 2015), who advances evidence both that people have been able to preserve and protect rights of person and property without government and that government has regularly been an instrument of predation and confiscation. Stringham's two pieces of evidence do not mean that social life can proceed without what we recognize as government. Power and force have ubiquitous presence within and among societies, as Carl Schmitt (1932) explains in his analysis of the autonomy of the political. What Stringham's evidence really means is that people will often take recourse to Paretian derivations to put a courteous face on their uses of political power.

It is easy to illustrate the problem of limiting government. If two people acting privately cannot rightfully take the property of a third person, neither should they be able to do so simply because they comprise a political majority. Suppose Primo, Secunda, and Terzo comprise a town. Primo's property contains some marshland which he plans to drain and fill to create a shopping center. Secunda and Terzo each prefer to see the land remain as marshland, even if it means they must go elsewhere to do their shopping. Within the liberal framework of a market economy, Secunda and Terzo can easily obtain their desired marshland. All they must do is convince Primo to maintain the land in its marshy condition. There are several ways they could do this. The simplest would be for them to buy the land from Primo. Another would be to secure a long-term lease on the land. Yet a third would be to convince Primo to join with them in creating a conservation trust to hold the land. And other methods can also be imagined, all of which would entail agreement among Primo, Secunda, and Terzo that leaving the land in its marshy state was superior to converting it into a shopping center.

Primo might value the land at $100,000 if left in its marshy condition and at $1 million if converted into a shopping center. So long as Secunda and Terzo value the bird sanctuary they would put on the marshland at more than $900,000, there is a bargaining range inside of which they can convince Primo to leave the land in its marshy state. The prime difficulty Secunda and Terzo would confront in proceeding in this manner is that they would have to pay Primo around $900,000 to keep the land in its marshy state. Yet Secunda and Terzo comprise a majority in this simple republic. With Primo having no recourse to call upon some other government to offer protection within a federalist system, Secunda and Terzo would have the power to take Primo's land in some manner. And there are different manners this could be done. We may reasonably assume that Secunda and Terzo do not want to think of themselves as engaging in simple banditry, for this wouldn't comport with democratic ideology. They can overcome this obstacle by wrapping their use of force with an ideological sentiment of higher public value being served by keeping birds in their natural habitat than by building a shopping center. They might create an Ornithological Protection Act that prohibits destruction of land where birds live. This Act won't change Primo's opposition, but it will enable Secunda and Terzo to feel better about their use of political power.

In short, government is not necessary to create programs that create public benefits, but the crooked timber of humanity (Berlin 1991) is unlikely to follow the austere rules and requirements that the principles and conventions of property and contract put in the way of political power (Schmitt 1932). The use of political power to take desired objects is unlikely to be held in check by its holders. In democratic regimes, the deployment of power is likely to be accompanied by ideological formulations that resonate with sentiments resident within the population. Playing on such sentiments might convert some opponents into supporters. Not to be ignored, though, is the ability of such ideological formulations to enable supporters to feel better about themselves and their actions than they would have felt had they engaged in simple banditry. So, yes, Buchanan (1975a) and Ostrom (1996; 1997) are right about the necessity of government, even if that explanation is incomplete.

The Fifth Amendment to the American Constitution allows governments to take private property through eminent domain, but also places restrictions on the use of this power. One restriction is that any taking must be to advance some legitimate public purpose. Another restriction is that the owners of property be justly compensated for any taking. As Richard Epstein (1985) explains, the history of eminent domain over the past century or so has increasingly run in the direction of governments taking property for what are private uses and paying only partial or token compensation in return. Despite its clear wording about public use and just compensation, the Fifth Amendment does not seem to create a strong bar against governments taking private property for private use while failing to pay just compensation. The Fifth Amendment, along with any constitutional document, is just a piece of parchment. While parchment paper is stronger than ordinary writing paper, it is not sufficiently strong to deter rapacious governments and interest groups from using government as an instrument of predation.

In *Federalist* No. 48, James Madison observed that legislatures in Virginia and Pennsylvania had repeatedly violated their state constitutions by acting as instruments of predation on behalf of some people at the expense of others. Madison concluded his examination by noting "that a mere demarcation on parchment is not a sufficient guard against those encroachments which lead to a tyrannical concentration of all the powers of government in the same hands." The articulation on parchment of a declaration of limited government to protect and preserve is not by itself sufficient to generate protection and preservation as the core activity of government.

There is a tenuous balance between liberalism as social philosophy on the one hand and democracy as political system on the other, as the American Founders recognized. A system of economic organization based on private property might not require some measure of government activity, but prosperous economic activity will attract political actors all the same (Wagner 2016b). Liberalism is grounded in individual freedom and private property. In this liberal scheme, government itself is simply a reflection of people's use of their rights of person and property, and is not a source of those rights. Even though there may be general agreement about the proper principles of governmental activity, that agreement often dissolves in the specifics of practice. Primo, Secunda, and Terzo might all affirm the principle of limited government, and yet Secunda and Terzo will participate willingly and even eagerly in taking Primo's property when doing so allows them to promote a favored project at lower cost to themselves, provided only that they can invent public-sounding rationalization for doing so to ease their moral qualms about using political power to circumvent the market in building their bird sanctuary. To subdue such qualms, they might also invoke such doctrines as strategic holdouts and free riders as a kind of therapy to ease their minds. This would allow Secunda and Terzo to convince themselves into believing that Primo really valued the bird sanctuary, only refused to say so because he was holding out to get a higher price.

As Vincent Ostrom (1984) explains, government entails a Faustian bargain. While that bargain can't be avoided, its terms can perhaps be influenced. There are two principal approaches to securing more favorable terms. One approach looks primarily to education and related processes for cultivating virtue and wisdom within a population (Walker 1990). The claim here is that the wiser people are about the dangers of the Faustian bargain, the less eagerly they will embrace it. Parchment will serve as a stronger barrier to predatory uses of government as people become wiser in their understanding about such predatory uses of government. The other approach looks primarily to an of opposition of interests to limit government predation. Metaphorically speaking, this alternative approach looks to guns more than to parchment (Wagner 1987; 1993). The basic principle behind this approach is for governmental action to require some concurrence among different participants with opposed interests and powers. Such concurrence, it should be noted is exactly what market exchange promotes. Within the frameworks of property and contract, Primo, Secunda, and Terzo will all concur in the market-generated outcome concerning the use of Primo's marshland.

Both approaches reflect a presumption that self-interest is predominant in all human activity, in government as well as in commerce. The justification for government resides in the need to control the darker side of self-interest. With self-interest being ineradicable, the problem of constitutional control becomes one of how to control, not abolish, the operation of self-interest within government while allowing government the ability to perform those governing tasks that its justification requires. Ultimately, the task would seem to require both parchment and guns, that is, both knowledge pertinent

to the task and rightly aligned incentives to act consistently with that knowledge. Knowledge and incentive, moreover, do not act in separable fashion,
for knowledge is generated through practice and practice is shaped by incentive, as Charles Warren's (1932) examination of the changing interpretation
of the general welfare clause illustrates. The process Warren describes is
clearly one of a continuing spiral involving both belief or knowledge and
incentive or interest. One of the central themes of the classical approach to
moral education was that morality was simply good conduct that was reduced to habit through practice. The ability successfully to take property
through politics instead of relying upon market transactions is to engage in a
contrary form of practice. This alternative form of practice, where legislative
takings replace market transactions, may, if repeated sufficiently, become
sufficiently habitual to promote alternative beliefs as to what comprises just
conduct.

BUCHANAN, MUSGRAVE, AND SOME
AGONISTICS OF SOCIAL JUSTICE

James Buchanan (1999–2002) and Richard Musgrave (1959) were the dominant figures in American public finance in the second half of the twentieth
century. Buchanan was an American whose approach to public finance was
strongly influenced by continental approaches to public finance. Musgrave
emigrated from Germany to the United States, and his approach to public
finance reflected more of the Anglo-Saxon orientation that Buchanan rejected. Yet Musgrave and Buchanan both gave Knut Wicksell the seat of
primacy in their Pantheon of public finance theorists. Despite their conver-
gence on Wicksell as a source of inspiration, they differed sharply in what
they took from Wicksell, as Marianne Johnson (2006) explains.

For Buchanan, Wicksell was one of the two inspirations for his individualist orientation toward public finance, the other being de Viti de Marco.
From Wicksell, Buchanan took unanimity and not majority rule as the bench-
mark for theorizing about political processes. As Wicksell recognized and
Buchanan elaborated, agreement among participants is the only meaningful
test of whether a proposed political program is worth more than its cost. So
long as the sum of the valuations held by the different participants exceeded
the payments they would have to make, the program would be superior to the
alternative state without the program. Buchanan also recognized the difficulties that might arise in securing unanimity among people who might be
trying to hold out for more favorable terms. This recognition led Wicksell to
relax his support for unanimity by advancing a pragmatic rule of approximate unanimity, which he illustrated by referring to such possibilities as
three-quarters, five-sixths, and nine-tenths majorities.

Musgrave did not dispute Buchanan's emphasis on approximate unanimity that he took from Wicksell, for the plain text of Wicksell was clear in this respect. Musgrave claimed that Buchanan conveyed only part of Wicksell. Yes, Wicksell supported approximate unanimity; however, Wicksell also thought a just distribution of income must first be achieved: "It is clear that justice in taxation tacitly presupposes justice in the existing distribution of property and income" (Wicksell 1958, 108). Musgrave (1939) brought Wicksell and Erik Lindahl to the attention of English readers by describing them as formulating a voluntary exchange theory, which is the line of approach to public finance that Buchanan pursued. The dispute between Musgrave and Buchanan, set forth in Buchanan and Musgrave (1999), was set in motion when Musgrave (1939) rejected the voluntary exchange approach in favor of the planning approach that characterized Anglo-Saxon public finance. That approach follows standard welfare economics and its formulation in terms of its so-called two theorems. One theorem is that competitive equilibriums are Pareto efficient. On this, Musgrave and Buchanan agreed that Wicksellian approximate unanimity accomplished for public finance what competitive equilibrium accomplished for a market economy.

The second theorem of welfare economics holds that one Pareto-efficient allocation can be transformed into a different Pareto-efficient allocation through some set of lump sum transfers. Within orthodox welfare economics, a social welfare function is invoked to select among the Pareto-efficient allocations. A competitive process generates Pareto efficiency, but the point at which that competitive process starts must be normatively just, according to the second theorem. Musgrave claimed that Buchanan ignored this facet of Wicksell. It's true that Buchanan set this facet of Wicksell aside, but it's not true that he ignored the associated matters of justice, which Buchanan (1971; 1972) explored particularly in light of his interest in John Rawls' approach to justice.

Buchanan showed interest in matters of justice but didn't accept Musgrave's desire to incorporate Wicksell into the spirit and framework of welfare economics. To do that would have violated Buchanan's central theoretical concern to develop explanatory theories of collective action in democratic environments of self-governance. The two theorems of welfare economics do not characterize democratic processes. The first theorem can, with approximate unanimity being the political complement to market organization. The second theorem, however, requires there to be some outside position of power that can insert its desires into society. That outside source is a vestige of monarchical or feudal control. For Buchanan, however, there was no such source of control. Sure, there can exist power in society, plenty of it. But that power is generated internally through constituted processes of interaction. This is what it means to theorize about the ways in which people govern themselves, in contrast to Musgrave's willingness to insert some position of outside authority. In this respect, Musgrave advanced the notion of merit wants as wants that were particularly meritorious and should not be restricted by ordinary notions of willingness to pay. In contrast, Buchanan would have claimed that there was no outside position from which merit wants could receive special consideration. If some people thought that some activities were under-appreciated, there were various steps they could take to increase that appreciation. In Buchanan's framework, internal processes of political entrepreneurship would do the work that Musgrave wanted to impose through planning. Following Musgrave along this path, however, would take Buchanan away from his desire to pursue public finance and collective activity in an explanatory manner.

THE SAMARITAN'S DILEMMA: SENTIMENTAL AND MUSCULAR LIBERALISM

Buchanan's (1975a) articulation of the Samaritan's dilemma illustrates some difficult matters concerning the relationship between liberty and responsibility. In doing this, it also brings into play the distinction between sentimental and muscular versions of liberalism. Buchanan's articulation starts with the original Biblical story where a Samaritan comes across a beaten traveler and supplies aid to the traveler. That story can be read as containing a message about personal responsibility. In this case, a person's responsibility would be to supply assistance to people who have encountered misfortune. Examples of providing this kind of assistance are common, as readers can surely see by introspection. Buchanan did not present the Samaritan's dilemma to offer moral instruction to individuals; however, he presented it to probe some problematical features of liberal regimes that place personal liberty in the foreground and relegate responsibility to the background.

The Samaritan who encounters the beaten traveler can either stop and offer aid or can continue to his destination without stopping. This situation describes a simple choice that the Samaritan faces. The Samaritan will respond to this situation depending on his or her scheme of values along, perhaps, with some sense of the cost that might accompany tardiness in arriving at the destination. A Samaritan for whom tardiness means arriving late to join some friends at a pub might stop to offer aid, but a Samaritan for whom stopping to offer aid means failing to arrive for an interview for a desired job might continue without offering aid, as Philip Wicksteed (1910) explains with charming brilliance. As a theory about choice, the Samaritan's dilemma lacks economic content within Buchanan's (1964a) theoretical framework where economics is about social interaction and not personal choice.

To convert a setting of choice into a setting of interaction requires that there be multiple instances of potential Samaritans coming across beaten travelers. By typical moral conventions, the burden of action is thought to rest with the Samaritans because they are the ones who face an immediate choice whether to aid the traveler. The Biblical story extols the Samaritan for choosing to aid the traveler. But it is the Samaritan who faces the choice and not some abstract ethical standard. From the choice-theoretic point of view, what the Samaritan does depends on the cost the Samaritan perceives will arise from stopping to offer aid. That cost can be highly variable. The more severely the traveler appears to be injured, the greater the amount of time it will require for the Samaritan to offer aid. One element of cost to the Samaritan is the value of the displaced options that are entailed in different amounts of time spent in offering aid. Another element of cost consists in the characteristics of the traveler. For instance, the Samaritan is surely more likely to offer aid to a traveler the Samaritan finds visually attractive. No doubt, numerous illustrations could be created to characterize details of interactions between Samaritans and travelers. Samaritans could offer aid in some cases, while not offering aid in other cases. The provision of aid, moreover, could be of various qualities. Preachers and moral philosophers might exhort people on their duties to care for injured people they come across, and observation of historical experience would surely show a variety of responses to this set of situations. Suppose through concerted preaching and philosophizing there is an increase in the willingness of people to act as Samaritans when they come across beaten travelers.

Should this be judged a good outcome? If the number of beaten travelers was a piece of data, the increased willingness to provide aid would surely be a good outcome. Buchanan's exposition of the Samaritan's dilemma leads in a different dilemma. What makes the situation a dilemma is recognition that the presence of Samaritans can increase the number of beaten travelers. If so, offering aid can lead conceivably to an inferior social state where the number of beaten travelers has increased and the amount of time Samaritans devote to offering aid rather than undertaking other activities has increased. In aggregate terms, this situation could be described as an inward shift in a utility-possibility frontier.

Buchanan's point in advancing the Samaritan's dilemma was not to engage in moral philosophy but to contrast relatively sentimental with relatively muscular versions of liberalism. The sentimental version counsels people to do what is regarded as good without considering consequences that might be set in motion. This version opens Samaritans to exploitation by parasitical elements within society, once it is recognized that travelers can to some extent take precautions against being beaten, though they must bear a cost in doing so. The muscular version of liberalism would recognize that offering aid can serve as a substitute for the costly exercise of responsibility by travelers. Hence, a muscular liberalism would not embrace an open-ended injunction of offer aid, but would ration offers of aid. This rationing of aid would not be out of stinginess but from recognition that misfortune can often be instructive. A traveler is beaten, and returns home in battered condition. The traveler's condition will be instructive to friends and neighbors who might thereby exercise more care when traveling. Misery can have positive didactic value, not just for the traveler but for people who later hear the traveler's tale of woe, as a reflection of the muscular version of liberalism James Fitzjames Stephen (1873) set forth in contesting John Stuart Mill's (1859) presentation of a more sentimental version of liberalism. It can't be pleasant to ignore someone's plight, but if that plight could have been prevented by the subject of that condition it can be socially beneficial to avoid offering aid, but doing so requires ignoring moral injunctions to the contrary, as Buchanan explained in closing his paper on the Samaritan's dilemma.

SAMARITANS AND THE AVOIDANCE OF ACCIDENTS

It seems often to be assumed that people are naturally provident and hard-working, so being in positions of need is a result of chance or limited capacity, and not a product of choice (Friedman 1953). The offer of aid, however, can increase the number of people who are in a position that elicits offers of aid. There is a well-developed economic theory of accidents that is directly relevant for relating the Samaritan's dilemma to questions of aid and charity. This theory notes that there are not only direct costs to accidents, but also costs to avoiding accidents (Landes and Posner 1987). While there is controversy over whether automobile accidents rise with increases in vehicle speed *per se* or rise with increases in the variance of the speed at which cars are traveling (Lave 1985), there is no doubt that automobile fatalities could be nearly avoided if everyone were to drive at no speed higher than, say, 20 miles per hour. That no one wants to drive so slowly involves an acceptance of risk to arrive at destinations more quickly. Regardless of the relation between speed and accidents, there are also various actions drivers and car-makers can take that would increase or reduce the risk of accidents. A manufacturer can produce a car with such features as air bags and shatter-resistant windshields. Highways can be built in various ways with different safety qualities engineered into their construction. For instance, four lane roads are safer than two lane roads, though they are also more expensive. Whatever forms of safety is embedded in those cars and highways, safety is nonetheless a matter of interaction between drivers and the builders of cars and highways. It is well recognized that the construction of cars with more safety features will reduce the care that drivers take because these features allow people to feel safer when they are driving more recklessly (Peltzman 1975). Cars do not harm people; people driving recklessly in cars harm people. If the incentives are appropriately aligned to encourage people to drive more safely, fewer accidents will result. The extent of safety is a matter of interaction between or among people and is not a matter of simple choice.

Being in a position of need is similar to being in an accident. While both destitution and accidents may be partially attributable to unforeseeable, random circumstances, they are also to a significant extent outcomes of choice. Henry Fawcett's (1871) tale of Robinson and Smith in *Pauperism* helps to illustrate this point. In Fawcett's story, both gentlemen were blue-collar workers who entered adulthood with similar skills and in similar occupations. From that common point of departure, their lives diverged due to different choices they made and actions they took. Robinson performed his job conscientiously, was frugal in his spending, and spent time studying to become eligible for higher-paying positions. In contrast, Smith performed his job in so-so fashion, did not devote time to preparing to secure higher-paying positions, and instead spent all of his earnings, much of it on amusement. By the time both reached retirement age, Robinson was well-to-do and had accumulated a good sum of capital through his saving during his working years. Smith had accumulated no capital through saving, and retired at a similar earnings level to where he began.

Though Fawcett's story focuses on the life choices each man makes, it is possible to incorporate some degree of chance into the narrative. We can imagine a scenario in which an economic downturn hits and both men lose their jobs due to layoffs unrelated to their performance. However, as with the literature on the economic theory of accidents, there are steps that each man can take to minimize the chance that serious economic harm befalls him in this circumstance. For example, immediately after being laid off, we can imagine Robinson actively trying to find a new job, perhaps studying for a new certification so he can shift into another, less-vulnerable occupation. We can imagine Smith taking the job hunt less seriously, sending out a few resumes, but spending much of his time enjoying his newly found leisure. Though both men were laid off through no fault of their own, it is highly likely that the steps Robinson takes will allow him to find a new job before Smith.

An outside observer, or a strict follower of the orthodox approach to public finance, who is unfamiliar with these details may conclude that Smith was a candidate for aid and that Robinson was someone who reasonably could provide such aid. To be sure, Smith's utility could have been raised by reallocating some of Robinson's earnings to him. Yet by the very structure of the story, Smith could have achieved a similar outcome had he been willing to act similarly to Robinson. To be entitled to life, liberty, and the pursuit of happiness entitles the Robinsons and Smiths of the world to use their wealth as they see fit and to live with the value consequences of their actions. The

Samaritan's dilemma tells us that if Smith is offered aid, which must be financed by a tax on Robinson, Smith will take even less care to look after his future and Robinson will create less wealth as well. To avoid this outcome requires employment of the muscular liberalism of the Samaritan's dilemma

This story of Robinson and Smith illustrates why Buchanan's Samaritan's dilemma offers challenging insight into the extent of entitlements in society. Robinson can support himself in old age due to his exercise of providence in earlier years. Smith can't do this because he has exercised no providence. For him to be supported requires that he be entitled to support through a tax imposed on Robinson. In this respect, entitlements are not earned but are legislatively dispensed largesse. In the United States, social security is the largest entitlement program. It is commonly described as "social insurance," but this is an ideological formulation that undoubtedly increases support from the program than if it were presented as a welfare or tax-subsidy program. Social security is not an insurance program. If it were, people could choose their carriers. Their benefits, moreover, would vary directly with the sizes of their contributions compounded by interest earned on those contributions. To the contrary, social security, as entitlement programs generally, are largesse dispensed through democratic legislation. The degree of support for entitlement programs can be subject to explanation, as illustrated by Carolyn Weaver's (1982) explanation of the emergence and growth of social security. For the most part, so-called social insurance programs operate by giving what are effectively gifts to recipients. It is easy for governments to spend money. This is something they do well, meaning that account balances are emptied by the end of the fiscal year.

NEXUS, EMERGENCE, AND POLICY-INDUCED REGIME DRIFT

A political enterprise might announce a course of action, but the effect of this announcement on the political economy will depend on the various patterns of interaction that are set in motion. Once this emergent feature of so-called policy measures is recognized, it becomes possible to explore the relationship between institutionally supported practice and the emergent quality of the nexus of economic interaction. The connections that comprise the nexus of economic interaction are crafted through various forms of activity, and the substantive content of those activities can plausibly influence the moral imaginations of participants (Schlicht 1998).

Dyadic relationships between market-based participants are framed by the legal principles of property and contract. Those principles, moreover, reflect a concomitant moral imagination: property reflects a moral injunction to avoid taking what is not yours; contract reflects a moral injunction to keep your commitments (or repair the damage if you don't). These moral princi-ples, moreover, are reinforced continually through commercial transactions among market-based participants, and these surely play out differently in the presence of political enterprises, as illustrated previously by the ability of Secunda and Terzo to use political power to obtain a bird sanctuary at Pri-mo's expense.

The relative volume of market and political nodes in the transactional nexus within a society may have significant implications for moral belief within a society. An expansion in politically generated nodes and connec-tions might promote drift in the character of a regime, due to systematic differences in the types of moral instruction that are embedded in the institu-tions and practices of different regimes. Rectitude would seem to be a casual-ty of an expansion in the relative significance of political enterprises within a society. To the extent property shifts from the private to the communal domain, the injunction to avoid taking what is not yours becomes vacuous. With communal property, there can be no taking but only temporary appro-priations countenanced by the legislature; moreover, the legislature may be petitioned about anything and whatever determination it makes ends the matter for the moment. That any such change modifies rights in a large number of ways for many people is irrelevant, for the state is *ipso facto* the proper arena for such activities (Murphy and Nagel 2002). There is no right and wrong, as demarcated by the distinction between mine and thine. There are simply contending desires over how to use communal property. For in-stance, zoning that prevents the development of undeveloped land is not a taking of property, even if it provides a playground for the residents of adjacent developed land, because it is simply one among many possible outcomes under communal property. Rather than buying the land to create a park, it is proper to petition the legislature to declare the land a park under the communal property. A proposal to steal is transformed into a proposal for social reform when it is placed before the legislature.

On what grounds can a person legitimately complain about his position in life, and to whom? When relationships are ordered through private property, people are presumed to be responsible for their own situations in life. People may make bad choices, in many ways and along many dimensions. Still, the responsibility, for good as well as for bad, rests with those who make the choices. Everyone occupies the position of residual claimant with respect to the uses of their talents and property. Someone else can be held accountable for one's bad fortune only if that person can be shown to have violated some right of the complainant. A failure to achieve some desired commercial out-come may be a signal to try harder or to try something different, but it calls for no redress from someone else, unless that other person can be shown to have violated some right of the complainant.

It is different when relationships are ordered through communal property (Wagner 1992a; 1992b). It now becomes possible to use the legislature as an arena for securing gains by imposing disabilities on other people. The security of property rights is governed not by principle but by the pragmatic operation of the market for legislation. Dissatisfaction with one's situation can now be blamed on everyone else, anonymously, as with society in general, and not upon particular abridgers of rights. As such, legislation teaches that other people's property need not be respected in the search for personal gain, provided only that abridgements of those rights are channeled through the legislature, or through the regulatory agencies to which the legislature has delegated authority. The moral rectitude that predominates in the presence of private property weakens as the domain of communal property expands, as there is no principled limit to infringements upon the rights of others. Any infringement of rights is permissible, provided only that it is mediated through the legislature or one of its organizational delegates.

The moral imagination that accompanies private property and market ordering is one wherein people who are discontent with facets of their life will look first to themselves for betterment, unless they can point to some person who has violated a right of property. This is a stern morality. Among other things, it says that if you are drinking coffee while driving, spill it and burn yourself, and in your distraction crash, it is you and not the vendor who is responsible for your condition. That morality surely weakens as property takes on communal attributes. Consider, for instance, a few famous cases in the economic analysis of torts, where Landes and Posner (1987) argue that the Hand Formula can be seen at work to promote economic efficiency. Recall that this formula defines liability for an accident as arising when the cost of preventing the accident is less than the expected cost of the accident, where the latter is the product of the damage caused by the accident and its probability of occurrence. Consider two illustrations that have been widely used to illustrate the power of the Hand formula to convey the economic efficiency of tort law. In *Hendricks v. Peabody Coal*, a boy (age 16) was injured when he dove into a lake that had formed in an abandoned mine. The plaintiff argued that the injury could have been prevented had the coal company fenced the property, and the cost of fencing was low relative to the damage. The plaintiff won. In *Adams v. Bullock*, a boy (age 12) was walking across a bridge while swinging a wire. The wire struck the trolley wire below, and the boy was burned. The boy lost this case, with the Hand-like gloss on the case being that the cost of fencing overpasses would be too high relative to expected damage.

To be sure, no explicit remarks were made about costs of fencing in either case. Nor were notions advanced about probabilities. Someone who wanted to believe the Hand formula as a kind of metaphysical principle for separating court decisions between those that the plaintiff won and those that the defendant won could probably refer to the Hand categories in doing so without fear of outright contradiction. But this isn't the only possible explanation. *Adams* was decided in 1919, some 50 years before *Hendricks*. Perhaps these cases illustrate that the moral sentiments were sterner in 1919. It's doubtful back then if someone would have received a favorable judgment for a coffee burn; or, alternatively, for being burned as a result of pouring cognac over a lit candle; or thirdly, from being wounded by bursting metal after you stuck a wet, hot-air balloon into a clothes dryer.

Perhaps there is a kind of paradox at work here. A stern morality may be conducive to progress, at least so long as it is of the market-generating type. Yet the progress that results undermines the requisite sternness, as the increasing wealth allows people to reward conduct that formerly would have been condemned. So long as the legal system is relatively clumsy and cumbersome, however, this may end up being but a relatively minor nuisance. Very few disputes go to courts, and this is perhaps a good thing in many respects. Perhaps rather than seeking to expand court capacity to reduce queues and bring more business into court, even more rationing by waiting might be better for economic progress. Schumpeter might even have been right about the eclipse of capitalism, except that he grossly overestimated the capacity of governmentally related processes and institutions. Or perhaps he was right, only we don't recognize the evolutionary change, so that what started as a game of rugby has morphed sequentially into a game of American-style football, and without the transformation being much noted.

CHARITY, FUTURITY, AND REDISTRIBUTION

The Samaritan and his dilemma can be generalized or universalized by recognizing that it speaks to a widespread quality of human nature to render assistance when coming across instances of need. While need is typically objectified through such measures as percentages of median income and poverty indexes, it ultimately resides in the affective sentiments held by some people toward the observed situation of others in society. A needy person is thus someone whose observed situation activates sympathetic feelings from other people in society. This does not, however, mean that charity is an apt description of those feelings because it pertains to the instant of observation and does not extend to possibilities beyond the moment of observation. These possibilities are expressed by the notion of futurity. While purely charitable impulses may certainly exist, in which the donor gives aid without any expectation of a behavioral change on the part of the recipient, generally donors prefer that their assistance help the recipient achieve a better trajectory for his or her life. That is to say, the donor wants to enhance the recipient's future prospects illustrates the notion of "futurity."

Without doubt, life outcomes are determined partly by skill and effort and partly by luck. With the right set of incentives in place, a minimal safety net can indeed encourage individuals to rely on aid only when needed, and for only as long as needed. Yet this set of incentives is difficult to design. While donors may want to assist those who are temporarily disadvantaged due to an unfortunate set of circumstances, it is nearly impossible *ex ante* to distinguish between those individuals who will use the extension of aid to improve their future prospects and those who will use it to support a slothful lifestyle. Few donors would want to help the latter for any extended period of time, but many would be willing to assist the former. Though the distinction between the deserving poor and the undeserving poor is seldom publicly acknowledged in modern times, the notion still exists that some individuals are more deserving of our sympathies than are others. Even if the actual distribution of empathy in society varies widely, it is undeniable that the sight of people in need often invokes sympathetic responses to render comfort and assistance in some degree.

Though donors typically expect recipients to have a different future in response to receiving aid, our public redistribution system has created a situation whereby the donors are totally removed from the recipients. In the United States, as in most developed nations, social welfare programs are funded through taxes. Specialized bureaucracies are then allocated a specified amount of money to spend on their respective aid programs. While there may be a great many people working in these bureaucracies who are genuinely concerned about the futures of the individuals they are assisting, they are trapped in a situation where by law they must provide assistance to all individuals who meet a specified set of criteria. Indeed, because a large bureaucracy lacks the knowledge necessary to understand the particular situation of each aid recipient, the only set of criteria they can use when doling out aid is the simple set of one-size-fits-all benchmarks they are given. It is thought worse to commit a type I error than a type II error, so aid ends up in the hands of those who will squander it, in addition to those who will use it to get back on their feet. Consequently, our modern-day system of social assistance has almost completely divorced the achievement of specific life outcomes from the provision of aid.

Donors have not always been so far removed from the recipients of aid. As Olasky (1992) documents, the early American model of compassion held that giving indiscriminate aid was as damaging as was turning a blind eye toward the poor. Indeed, prior to the late-1800s the very word "compassion" had a different meaning than it does today; originally, compassion meant "suffering with," and required that any person trying to help the poor must be acquainted with the particulars of that person's condition. These early providers of relief believed that the key to helping people out of destitution required an examination of the whole person; moral shortcomings needed to be addressed along with physical and economic shortcomings. This theme is explored by Gertrude Himmelfarb (1983; 1992). Without using the term, the narratives both Olasky and Himmelfarb tell about early forms of relief provision entail recognition that the successful provision of aid requires some level of participation by recipients of aid. The avoidance of accidents, economic theory tells us, requires appropriate action by both Samaritans and travelers.

VOTES AS PROPERTY RIGHTS IN A WELFARE STATE

The earlier comparison of Buchanan and Musgrave (1999) over the uses they made of Wicksell's principle of approximate unanimity stressed the difference between Musgrave's organicist approach to public finance and Buchanan's individualist approach. Within his organicist approach, Musgrave could refer without contradiction to some black-box notion of the state as generating a just distribution of income because he was not concerned to pursue public finance in an explanatory direction. The generation of that just distribution was not something capable of being explained, but it made the appraisal of approximate unanimity a contingent value and not an absolute value, whereas Buchanan's repeated mentions of the necessity of starting from here rendered approximate unanimity a relatively absolute value, as reflected in his repeated invocations of relatively absolute absolutes.

Musgrave's willingness to take recourse to some black box type of non-explanation was a source of uneasiness to Harold Hochman and James Rogers (1969), who attempted to address that uneasiness by trying to advance an explanatory theory of income redistribution. Hochman and Rogers explained redistribution as a form of collective charity. The reasonableness of this characterization depends on whether it is the act of giving that is the source of benefit to a donor or the extent to which some aggregate reduction in destitution is accomplished. If the former, charity is an ordinary private good. If the latter, it is a public good within the theoretical frameworks in use at the time. In this case, ordinary free-riding sentiments are in play, and charity falls in the rubric of being a public good. The title of Hochman and Rogers' (1969) article was "Pareto Optimal Redistribution." The authors' intention was to peer some distance into the black box that Musgrave (1959) created in creating his distinction between allocation and distribution branches within his theory of public finance. Where the allocation branch could work by approximate unanimity, the distribution could not do so as it had to create the proper initial conditions within which the allocation branch could work in Wicksellian fashion. Hochman and Rogers sought to break apart Musgrave's black box by importing the Wicksellian scheme into the distribution branch.

To do this, they distinguished between market-generated distribution and subsequent redistribution of market incomes through collectively undertaken charitable activity. Two points are notable about this formulation. One is that the extent of redistribution was the province of those who chose to make transfers to those with lower incomes. It is as if there was a club of donors who decided collectively to transfer some quantity of income to those with lower incomes. The second, and related point is that this formulation did not truly address the justice of the initial position. To the contrary, it accepted the market distribution, and from that point of departure potential donors could determine collectively how much charity they wished to purchase. Hochman and Rogers avoided addressing issues pertaining to the initial conditions from which economic interaction proceeded. On this point, Buchanan often asserted that there is no option in these matters but to start from where we are, as against pretending that we can do something else.

Buchanan (1975b) noted that redistribution in Hochman and Rogers was determined wholly by those who made transfers. Recipients were recipients of transfers, but they did not participate in determining the amount of transfers. In the model of Hochman and Rogers, voting was restricted to people who paid taxes. People who received transfers could not vote and so could not influence the size of transfer spending through their votes. In "The Political Economy of Franchise in the Welfare State," Buchanan (1975b) noted the obvious point that in contemporary times the franchise is nearly universally distributed. He went on to ask what implications might follow from recognizing that the franchise is a type of property right. As a property right, it has value to its holders. As for the magnitude of that value, one plausible measure can be gauged hypothetically by comparing budgetary outcomes under present voting rules with universal franchise with budgetary outcomes under a franchise restricted to taxpayers, and possibly with votes weighted in proportion to taxes paid.

This way of putting Buchanan's question touches upon Liam Murphy and Thomas Nagel (2002), who claim that one should not speak of government as redistributing income because that speech is predicated on a presumption that property rights are privately held. Hence, market activity as a reflection of property rights generates a distribution of income. Once this has been done, government acts through taxing and spending to redistribute what were market-generated incomes. This standard way of comparing market distribution of income with a subsequent distribution after taking taxes and expenditures into account assumes that private property is the appropriate point of departure, and with government subsequently intervening into market outcomes. Hence, government is involved in taking property and redistributing it. To the contrary, Murphy and Nagel advance the notion that property rights reside with government, only government typically chooses to exercise only some of those rights.

While Murphy and Nagel's formulation obviously clashes with the assertion in the American Declaration of Independence that governments derive their just powers from the consent of the governed, Buchanan's (1975b) effort to conceptualize the right to vote as a property right points in a similar direction, even if Buchanan doesn't travel nearly as far down the collectivist analytical highway as do Murphy and Nagel. Buchanan performed some comparative statics within a median voter framework as an elaboration of Hochman and Rogers's exploration of Pareto optimal redistribution. One voting equilibrium occurred when the franchise was limited to taxpayers. The other equilibrium occurred with a universal franchise. This extension of the franchise led to a new budgetary equilibrium that included more spending on programs that were valued particularly heavily by people in the lower regions of the distribution of income.

LIBERTY AND DEMOCRACY:
NAVIGATING A CONSTITUTIONAL TENSION

What is the relationship between liberty and democracy? There is a strong ideological current running throughout contemporary society that asserts that democracy and liberty are necessarily and inescapably complementary. According to this current, a democratic form of government is the appropriate way that a self-governing people manage their public affairs. This image is taught in schools starting from early grades, and is repeated throughout the various social media. So strongly does this current run throughout our society that little skepticism is voiced when politicians and other public figures express their hope that the reach of democracy will soon extend throughout the world. According to this ideology, democracy is the political value *par excellence* for a people who aspire to excellence in the practice of self-governance. Yet democracy and liberty cannot be complementary political values, at least not without a significant effort at constitutional reconciliation. At base, democracy embraces the principle that majorities dominate minorities. In contrast, liberty is a principle of non-domination whereby interaction among people is governed by principles of private property and not by majority rule. Only to the extent that people have agreed to abide by majority voting in particular instances is democracy consistent with liberty. Such agreement is typically present when people choose to join established clubs that have procedures in place to make group decisions. To be sure, it is often noted that democracy is accompanied by restrictions on majority domination. These restrictions surely exist, but the presence of those restrictions shows that the United States has not yet become thoroughly democratic. A thorough democracy would be plebiscitary democracy. In this respect, referendums are more democratic than representative assemblies. Moreover, representative assemblies could be selected randomly through sortition, which would be more democratic than representative forms of democracy because everyone would have an equal opportunity to be a legislator, whereas only subsets of people have plausible chances of becoming legislators.

Liberty was the founding value of the American republic, as was recognized in the Declaration of Independence's assertion that governments derive their just powers from the consent of the governed. The principle of liberty holds that people use their prior rights of property to establish governments to preserve and protect those rights. In sharp contrast, the Progressivist strand of democratic ideology holds that the determination of property rights is the province of government, as Murphy and Nagel (2002) illustrate in claiming that what is called private property is nothing but a grant of temporary authority from government, as a type of usufruct that the government can bestow or remove as it chooses. Vilfredo Pareto (1935) recognized that people will tend to embrace ideological articulations that enable them to feel good about themselves. America is governed by a democratic form of government, and most Americans like to think of themselves as constituting a free people. An ideology that links democracy in the service of liberty is surely an easy product to sell, particularly when the historical experience of the past century has been dominated by various forms of totalitarian bestiality. And yet there is always a potential conflict between liberty and democracy.

Constitutions do not enforce themselves any more than law substantively rules over men. Law can't rule; only people can do that, as Rajagopalan and Wagner (2013) explain. Constitutions are what someone with authority to dominate the issue in question says it will be, as Warren (1932) explains. What keeps a liberal order from eroding or what controls the speed of that erosion is some conjunction of strong belief combined with arrangements of governance that require concurrence among different possessors of guns as it were, and with each possessor able to maintain his or her own position, leading effective governance to require concurrence among the different possessors of guns (Wagner 1993).

In this respect, Federalism is a form of government that possibly has some potential to resist the scale-free qualities of democratic polities, as Vincent Ostrom (1997) explains. The original American Constitution mostly had this kind of federalist feature. The federal government was limited to a few explicitly enumerated powers. Everything else was reserved for the states or for individual citizens. The establishment of cities and towns and their jurisdictions, moreover, was the province of states and not the federal government. It is much less costly to move from one state to another than it is to change nations of residence. It is less costly still to change localities within a state. In addition, capital market principles operate with localities to the extent those activities are financed by taxes on real estate.

Furthermore, one of the two chambers of the Federal Congress was appointed by the states. This meant that the Federal Senate sat as a kind of chamber of the states, and with individual senators subject to recall by the states they represented. The federal government, moreover, could not tax individual earnings, and federal revenues were pretty much limited to revenues from tariffs, which meant in turn that most federal spending was limited to military affairs. Furthermore, the federal government had no central bank that could accommodate an expansion in federal activity by buying federal debt as a particular way of printing money. The monetary authority of the federal government was limited to the certification of weights and measures, as illustrated by a dollar being defined as a unit of measure represented by 1/25th of an ounce of gold of a particular fineness. In other words, monetary policy at this time was directed at offering protection against counterfeiting. In sharp contrast, monetary policy became a form of legalized counterfeiting after establishment of the Federal Reserve, and with the value of a dollar having declined some thousand-fold since the Federal Reserve was established.

This federalist arrangement stayed in place pretty well until early in the twentieth century when the Constitution was amended to create direct election of Senators and the federal government granted the power to tax incomes. Also, the Federal Reserve was established. These three shifts in constitutional authority were all significant moves in the direction of democratic oligarchy, and we have been living under these oligarchic arrangements for a century now. To be sure, democratic oligarchy is not a term currently in use, but it is an accurate description of contemporary democratic processes all the same. The constitutional promise is one which holds governments accountable to the same standards of conduct as private entities in society. The Fifth Amendment to the American Constitution exemplifies this standard nicely, as Richard Epstein (1985) explains. That Amendment allows governments to take property through eminent domain, though that taking is subject to two conditions: (1) it must be for a genuine public purpose, as distinct from a purpose that advances the interests of some at the expense of others and (2) it must be accompanied by just compensation, and with just meaning that the owner of the taken property is left as well off as he or she would have been by selling that property. Where the original constitutional arrangement created what could reasonably be called a system that entailed more competition than collusion among governments, that system has been largely replaced by a system of collusive federalism over the past century or so as Michael Greve (2012) examines in his explanation of how the American Constitution has been turned upside-down.

The American republic was founded on a rejection of the European feudal heritage wherein a few within a society were born to govern and with the remainder of society born into their various stations of servility. Where the feudal regimes were governed by relationships grounded in status, the American republic was to be governed by relationships grounded in private property and freedom of contract (Maine 1864). Governments were established to preserve and protect this new order where people largely governed themselves through a variety of civic associations that they created. The robust commercial republic that emerged through this constitution of liberty clearly warranted the designation of American exceptionalism. That exceptionalism has been under assault for around a century now as the consensual principle on which the American regime was founded has come increasingly to give way to the factional principle, whereby government becomes an instrument that confers advantage on some people by imposing costs on other people, which the original American Constitution sought to resist.

The key feature of Progressivist governance is that the few govern the many. In his chapter on democratic despotism in *Democracy in America*, Alexis de Tocqueville explained that democratic despotism would feature people wearing velvet gloves and not mailed fists. It would take the form of shepherds guiding sheep. An open question concerns how much of the population truly wants to live as sheep as against living their lives on their own terms. Hillary Clinton (1996) was surely right when she claimed that it took a village to raise a child. Her conception of that village, however, was of a Health and Human Services bureaucracy and not as a republic of free and responsible people whose creative abilities to manage their affairs dwarfs the talents and capacities of any political bureaucracy. Buchanan (2005) raised the possibility that significant parts of the population are becoming afraid to be free, and so are open to politicians who promise to reduce the cares and costs of living freely by providing many of the goods and services of living that people otherwise would have to tend to. A Health and Human Services bureaucracy might not be an ideal environment to have with you in meeting the challenges of daily living, but it does alleviate some of the pressures and possibly terrors of daily living all the same for people who might be afraid to be free.

Steven Walters (2014) explains how tax limitations in California and Massachusetts changed dramatically the framework of political incentives operating in those states in the late 1970s. Before tax limits were imposed, politicians continually sought to reward supporters by increasing public spending. Some of this spending was financed by taxation, with the rest financed by borrowing, which is just deferred taxation. These political incentives, however, operated contrary to the conditions for economic flourishing which requires: (1) protecting private property by allowing its owners to reap the returns from their property and (2) maintaining public property in good order. Tax limits forced politicians in California and Massachusetts to do this more so than they had been doing, creating boom towns in the process.

What holds for the state and local governments that Walters examined holds even more strongly for the federal government. It is not difficult to set forth the contours of what would be required to reestablish a constitution of liberty. At base, it would be to put the Constitution right-side up, recurring to Michael Greve's (2012) image of an upside-down constitution. It's doubtful that the income tax could be repealed, but its exemptions and rates could be lowered, which would bring more people within the purview of the income tax. With government becoming more costly to more people, the demand for governmental activity at the federal level would decline. A significant step toward turning the Constitution right-side up would be to eliminate unfunded liabilities by requiring governments to use defined contribution plans and to operate under genuine insurance principles. A related significant step would be to require governments to assign personal liabilities for the amortization of public debt at the time that debt is created. In such manners as these, the conduct of governments would become more compatible with the central operating principles of the private property that governments are instituted to preserve and protect in a regime where no privileged status positions exist. All such movements would be movements in the direction of approximate unanimity that was central to Buchanan's scheme of thought.

Chapter Seven

Ethics, Social Philosophy, and Liberal Political Economy

When James Buchanan and Warren Nutter moved to the University of Virginia, Buchanan for the fall 1956 semester and Nutter for the spring 1957 semester, they established the Thomas Jefferson Center for Studies in Political Economy and Social Philosophy. Subsequently, Buchanan and Nutter removed social philosophy from the title because they found the full title unwieldy to work with and not because they wanted to reduce the range of concerns over which they directed their attention. Buchanan focused mostly on constructing a science of liberty growing out of his initial interest in public finance and in securing an alternative theoretical foundation for political economy. While he found inspiration for his work in Knut Wicksell and some Italian theorists from the late nineteenth century, Buchanan retained his interest in ethics and social philosophy throughout his life. In this respect, the seventeenth volume of his Collected Works is titled Moral Science and Moral Order.

While Buchanan wanted to incorporate collective action into an explanatory theory of political economy, he also recognized that any such theory must occupy an analytical position somewhere between predictive science and moral philosophy, to recur to the subtitle of Buchanan (1982a). The theorist who seeks to explain the economizing logic of collective phenomena resides within the phenomena he seeks to explain. Political economy is not just ethology applied to human societies. Political economists reside inside the objects they seek to explain. They may try to adopt the pretense that they have distanced themselves from their object of interest and so can act as pure scientists by embracing the strictures of Stigler and Becker (1977) to model individuals as if they had identical and invariant preference functions, thereby placing social explanation on the same analytical plane as ethological explanation. But this is pretention pure and simple. Prices and incomes can't be treated as data while at the same time being allowed to vary through exogenous shocks that generate economic phenomena, because exogenous shocks are nearly non-existent within human population systems. What are typically described as exogenous shocks is the unavoidable clashing of plans that results when people are free to create plans and insert them into society to see how they fare.

Buchanan is right to think that it is possible to theorize about political economy in a reasonably scientific manner, provided that the theorist recognizes that he or she is also living inside the object of that theoretical activity. Political economists carry their preferences and beliefs into their theoretical activities, and can't escape this situation. While a theorist can try to articulate those preferences and beliefs, these might not even be fully known to the theorist, and yet they can exert influence. In this respect, Arthur Lovejoy (1936, 7) explains that the nominal features of theories rest on and reflect "implicit or incompletely explicit *assumptions*, or more or less *unconscious mental habits*" (Lovejoy's italics). With respect to these mental habits, Lovejoy distinguished between two within the western philosophical tradition, both present in Plato. One is what Lovejoy labeled an other-worldly scheme of thought that appears robustly in much Enlightenment-style thinking, and which posits a vision of societal perfection toward which to strive. The other is a this-worldly scheme of thought which replaces fables about perfecting reality with an emphasis on pursuing vigorous action within this life.

These visions obviously are not disjunctive, as Lovejoy (1936) explains, and the different visions surely influence how theorists theorize about political economy. For instance, a theorist who has internalized the belief that his or her objective in life is to participate in a mission to improve society will surely be attracted to equilibrium theories and employ the method of comparative statics to convey the requirements of movements in a perfecting direction. By contrast, a theorist who is not grounded in a vision of societal perfection, as was the case with Buchanan and also Frank Knight, will be attracted to theories that contain creative and entrepreneurial action and which employ methods grounded in emergent dynamics. Buchanan grew up in the neoclassical world of comparative statics, but his cognitive vision for political economy entailed emergent dynamics, and with this vision entailing recognition that political economy necessarily resides somewhere between predictive science and moral philosophy (Buchanan 1982a).

JANE JACOBS AND BUCHANAN'S PROBLEMATIC

So far as I know, Buchanan was not familiar with the work of Jane Jacobs. I say this based on her absence from the index of names in the twentieth volume of Buchanan's *Collected Works*. This is surely unfortunate, for many of her insights complemented what Buchanan was trying to accomplish. Jacobs' (2004) warning about a *Dark Age Ahead* resonated robustly with concerns Buchanan voiced about on-going erosion of the traditional liberal constitutional order within the United States and the western world. The author who sensed that a good number of people were apparently becoming "afraid to be free" (Buchanan 2005), would have found *Dark Age Ahead* to have articulated complementary concerns. Both Buchanan and Jacobs were concerned about processes of retrogressive regime drift (Wagner 2006) due to the ability of institutionally supported practice to undermine the moral imaginations on which liberal societies are based. In *Systems of Survival*, Jacobs (1992) explained that a well-working society required a balance between commercial and guardian moral syndromes. That balance required maintenance of a tension between the commercial and guardian syndromes. Jacobs's idea of a tension between the syndromes fit seamlessly with Buchanan's distinction between the constitutional choice of rules and the post-constitutional choice of selecting strategies and actions.

For Buchanan, maintenance of a constitutional framework required that post-constitutional actions be consistent with maintaining that framework. While maintenance of that framework is often attributed to law enforcement, it is impossible for any police department or attorney general to maintain a set of rules unless the bulk of the citizenry wants to see those rules maintained. There is enough historical experience with riots to recognize that police are pretty much helpless against such surges of humanity. Sure, simple economics would tell us that for any size mass of rioting humanity, the larger and more violent police action becomes, the more quickly the riot will subside. In societies with democratic polities, however, the ability to marshal brutality to enforce law is clearly limited. Whatever the extent of that limit relative to some mass of rioting humanity, the enforcement and maintenance of rules of law is in the first degree a matter of desires residing within the general population. The moral imaginations possessed within the citizenry has much to do with maintaining a constitutional framework, or in promoting constitutional drift along the lines that Charles Warren (1932) described for changing interpretations of the general welfare clause of the Constitution. For Buchanan, maintenance of a particular constitutional arrangement required appropriate action by enforcing authorities along with a general willingness by the general population to abide by those constitutional rules and principles.

For Jacobs, carriers of the guardian syndrome were to enforce and maintain the rules of commercial interaction that was the province of carriers of the commercial syndrome. As with any relationship based on some form of tension, that relationship can go awry, and from two directions. From one direction, carriers of the commercial moral syndrome can participate in guardian-type activities. This can happen when people in commerce work with carriers of the guardian syndrome to restrict the actions of commercial competitors to enter that line of business. It can also happen when commercial competitors enjoin politicians to promote their commercial activities, which necessarily will come at the price of restricting competitive commercial activities. From the other direction, carriers of the guardian moral syndrome can act in a faux-commercial manner, warping commercial practice in the process. The provision of so-called social insurance exemplifies this penetration of the guardian syndrome into commercial activity. Insurance is a commercial activity that people organize within the framework of private property and freedom of contract and association. The very source of support for social insurance resides in the ability of politically organized power to override commercial interaction by preventing some contractual relationships from being made while also forcing faux-commercial relationships to be undertaken.

In this respect, insurers might be forced to limit their coverages and prices to conform to some logic that responds to political power rather than the commercial imperative of exploiting gains from trade. One illustration of the creation of faux-commercial relationship with insurance is requiring providers to provide coverage for pre-existing conditions. Such coverage violates the basis for the provision of insurance, which resides in uncertainty about future events and situations. It is this uncertainty that allows everyone to gain from insurance, even though most people receive less in claims than they make in payments. With respect to auto insurance, some drivers will have accidents, but most won't. Before they take to the highways, drivers can't know whether they will be involved in an accident. Most of them won't and will pay for insurance that turns out to have been unnecessary. But some will have accidents, and will recover more in payments than they paid in premiums. To force insurers to include coverage for pre-existing conditions without charging actuarial prices for that coverage is to violate the imperatives of the commercial moral syndrome, which is to give good value for money paid. To require coverage for pre-existing conditions is to force insurance providers to offer great value without payment, which is an act of charity parading as commerce.

Advocates of forcing coverage for pre-existing conditions defend this practice by advancing ethical claims on behalf of the practice. Without doubt, pre-existing medical conditions can be expensive to treat and lie beyond the means of many people. This is an indisputable fact of life. The systemic question that Jane Jacobs raises does not dispute this unfortunate fact of life. It does, however, raise the question of how to respond to that fact. The popular response is to degrade the commercial syndrome through injecting politics into commerce. The alternative response is to leave the expenses and traumas associated with pre-existing conditions within the purview of carriers of the guardian moral syndrome. Hence, carriers of the guardian syndrome could carry support for pre-existing conditions on their budgets rather than forcing that support onto private budgets. In this manner, express redistribution would be folded into the domain of collectively organized charity, as befits Musgrave's (1959) distinction between allocative and redistributive budgets. It would also fit within the scheme of thought set forth by Hochman and Rogers' (1969) treatment of Pareto optimal redistribution as supported by Buchanan's (1975b) effort to incorporate voting rights as a form of property right into an analysis of welfare-state programs.

It should be noted that Jacobs' distinction between commercial and guardian moral syndromes is not identical to the distinction between government and business, but it is close. There can be governmental entities that practice commerce, as perhaps illustrated by a city that supplies electricity to residents, and with that supply financed by charges attached to the use of electricity by residents. Should that city enterprise incorporate surcharges and subsidies into its pricing, it will have allowed the guardian syndrome to invade the commercial syndrome. Similarly, commercial entities commonly engage in guardian activities. Auditing and the accompanying record-keeping is one such illustration. A construction firm will develop records and procedures to manage its inventory of supplies and equipment to guard against pilferage by employees who might otherwise be tempted to commandeer items for their personal use.

Commercial and guardian activities are inescapably commingled, necessarily so because interaction between the two types of activity is necessary for good organizational performance. For a business to continue as a going concern, it is necessary for commercial-guardian interaction to work well. This well-working quality does not require separation between commercial and guardian activities, because points of contact will be necessary as well as being unavoidable. It does, however, require awareness and moral rectitude that recognizes that a liberal system of people living together in closed geographical spaces requires that patterns of societal governance be constituted in a manner that avoids generating desires for people in business to engage themselves in playing politics, while also avoiding situations where people in politics engage in commerce. Jacobs' (1992) problem of constructing a liberal system for societal flourishing was fully congruent with Buchanan's (1975a) problem of developing a constitution of liberty (Hayek 1960; 1973–1979). Both forms of the problem setting were also explored within the German theory of order associated with Walter Eucken (1952) as summarized by Viktor Vanberg (1988).

ORDER THEORY AS CONSTITUTIONAL POLITICAL ECONOMY

The Germanic tradition of *ordnungstheorie* reflects a similar two-stage mode of analysis with which Buchanan and Jacobs worked. For Eucken and other participants in this tradition, a sample of which includes Leipold and Pies (2000), Rath (1998), and Streit (1992), there was a two-stage conceptualization of constitutional choice. The first stage concerned whether human interactions would be governed by liberal principles of equality or by feudal-like principles of classes, privileges, and duties. Under the assumption that people would mostly choose to live within a liberal framework of a market order, the next question concerned whether the state would maintain or undermine that liberal order. Here, the constitutional principle of market conformability was articulated. Market conformability is a heuristic principle, the intention of which is to keep relatively short the gaps that will surely arise between the principle of a constitution of liberty and post-constitutional politics along the lines that Buchanan (1975a) examines.

Market conformability is an idea that is easy to express and hard to implement. It means that governmental actions should be compatible with the central operating principles of a liberal market economy. In this respect, market conformability is presumed to be a principle that would resist the ability of governmental actions to inject feudal or collectivist principles into the market order. A simple example of the distinction and the constitutional work it does can be conveyed by reconsidering the standard textbook comparison of tariffs and quotas. It is a standard textbook exercise to demonstrate the equivalence of a tariff and a quota. Suppose a tariff is imposed on the importation of sugar. As compared with the initial position without a tariff, the tariff will increase the price of sugar and reduce the amount of sugar that is imported. As a secondary matter, the increased price will induce some increase in domestic production from what it was without a tariff. As a matter of textbook demonstration, it is a simple matter to impose an import quota that would yield the same reduction in the importation of sugar that the tariff brought about, leading also to the same increase in the price of sugar. With the same effect on price and output, moreover, the quota would also have the same effect in inducing the same increase in domestic production.

The textbook analysis typically stops at this point, but more than this is involved once matters pertaining to constitutional political economy are opened for consideration. The tariff leaves ordinary commercial channels in place. Importers can choose how much sugar to purchase from which producers, just as they did before the tariff. By contrast, this is impossible with a quota. With the quota, no one can import sugar without receiving a license to do so from some governmental agency. That quota will stipulate some allowed quantity to import, and can also be accompanied by a list of permitted sources from which to import sugar. Whoever heads the quota office now holds a position of power where he or she can decide whom to favor with quotas. In such settings, it is reasonable to expect that secondary transactions of some sort will take place because the number of quotas people are seeking will exceed the number of quotas that can be supplied. Seekers of quotas will thus compete among themselves to secure higher standing with dispensers of quotas. There are many possible paths along which to achieve higher standing, some highly venal and others less so. Whatever the degree of venality, those who seek quotas will become supplicants for largesse the quota-dispensing official grants. With the non-discriminatory tariff, social relationships are governed by the private law principles of private property and freedom of contract, and with the essays in Buckley (1999) exploring the rise and fall of freedom of contract. In contrast, the introduction of quotas transforms social relationships from being grounded in ordinary business people seeking to put together mutually beneficial transactions into feudal relationships where supplicants try to secure largesse from the lord of the manor. The feudal principles of standing and status displace the liberal principle of contractual equality. The principle of market conformability seeks to provide a heuristic for resisting this displacement.

The Fifth Amendment to the American Constitution prevents government from taking private property unless that taking is for public use and is accompanied by the payment of just compensation. This Amendment likewise illustrates the principle of market conformity. The Fifth Amendment limits a government's ability to take private property to uses that entail good public purposes. It further seeks to achieve market conformability by requiring governments to pay just compensation for the property they take. To be sure, governments can probably never be placed on the same footing as market enterprises with respect to assembling property. A private person who assembles property is a residual claimant to any net increase or decrease in value resulting from the assembly. It is different with a government, for it is taxpayers and not governing officials who are residual claimants. Still, the Fifth Amendment illustrates the founding interest in achieving conformability between the operating principles of private and public law, and with such conformability helping to keep the practice of political economy in line with liberal principles of governance. Without market conformability, there would be commingling between commercial and guardian syndromes, which would inject such feudal modes of operation as status and privilege into social life.

Buchanan's distinction between constitutional and post-constitutional stages of analysis is central to game theory, where the rules of the game are first stipulated, after which people select strategies and play the game. Buchanan often illustrated the distinction by referring to familiar parlor games. A few friends gather for an evening to play poker. Before they start playing, they must agree upon the type of poker they will play along with the rules that will govern betting. This is the constitutional stage. Outcomes emerge as people play within a set of rules. In Buchanan's scheme of thought, constitutional rules were fixed for relatively long periods of time. He often illustrated this idea by invoking the notion of relatively absolute absolutes. By doing this, Buchanan recognized that some aspects of society change slowly even as other change quickly. Generally held moral beliefs change slowly, but the items that a grocery store stocks undergo continual change. The theory of markets and of political economy pertain to the organized quality of societal life at the post-constitutional stage. The theory of markets explains how generally orderly patterns of economic activity emerge without anyone creating that pattern. Buchanan's interest in developing an individualistic rather than an organismic theory of political economy seeks to do the same for politically sponsored activity. Constitutional political economy would explain the working properties of different constitutional rules, and would take the form of a comparison of systems of constitutional rules.

The principal source for Buchanan's constitutional scheme of analysis is *The Calculus of Consent,* and with that scheme further elaborated in *The Limits of Liberty.* The unifying feature of both of those works, as well as the remainder of Buchanan's writings on constitutional political economy, is the application of what Buchanan often described as conceptual unanimity to the selection of constitutional rules. Those rules might well allow post-constitutional actions to be taken without unanimity, but the constitutional stage was conceptualized as one of unanimity. This conceptualization created a point of constitutional determinism that could contain within it indeterminism at the post-constitutional stage. A set of people could agree to the rules of play; these rules would shape the contours of subsequent play without determining the outcomes. Buchanan's invocation of conceptual unanimity was an analytical point of departure that reflected his preference for models of game theory over models of constrained maximization (Buchanan 1964a). Game theory entailed interaction, and allowed a ready distinction between choosing the rules by which to play and choosing strategies within the framework of those rules. To be sure, game theory doesn't require that the participants agree to play the game. They can be forced to do so as reluctant duelists (Ellsberg 1956). To do that, however, would be to start with an aura of disagreement and turbulence, which Buchanan did not want to do. Turbulence and change was thus confined to his post-constitutional stage of analysis.

PROTECTIVE AND PRODUCTIVE STATES WITHIN A CONSTITUTION OF LIBERTY

The central concern of the mainline of economics, following Boettke's (2007; 2012) distinction between mainline and mainstream branches, has been to explain how a market economy generates an orderly pattern of economic activity even though there is no person or office that creates this order. The order that we observe emerges as if it were imposed by an invisible hand. Only there is no hand. Rather, many hands participate in the generation of orderly economic life. What promotes the coordinated patterns of our economic life is the framework of institutional rules within which people conduct their activities. This institutional framework is characterized mainly by the principles of private property and freedom of contract. Economists have traditionally sought to explain how it happens that when economic relationships among people are governed by those principles, productive patterns of economic activity emerge and societies flourish. Buchanan's (1999–2002) oeuvre mostly entails his many efforts to explore how government relates to this institutional framework. Wicksell (1896) similarly sought an institutional framework that would render government action congruent with market-generated action; the Germanic theorists of order theory with its heuristic of market conformability explored the same topic.

Buchanan (1975a) pursued this topic by advancing the conceptual distinction between protective and productive states. By protective state, which reflected the guardian moral syndrome of Jane Jacobs (1992), Buchanan referred to the state's maintenance of a framework of property and contract within which people relate to one another. The protective state denotes the state as a referee that acts impartially within the spirit of a rule of law. By productive state, which reflected Jacobs' commercial moral syndrome, Buchanan referred to the state as an organization that provides goods and services that could not be provided effectively through ordinary market transactions and arrangements. The productive state is a player in the organization of economic activity, and in principle is subject to the same operating properties as privately owned enterprises. The formation of such state enterprises as schools and subway systems, according to the logic of the productive state, follows the same principles as the formation of such private enterprises as restaurants and hardware stores. People thus buy some services from privately organized vendors and other services from publicly organized vendors.

Wicksell, Eucken, and Buchanan all recognized that it is far easier to state the vision of political activity that complements market activity within a liberal political and social order than it is to create institutional arrangements that would channel politically sponsored action in that manner. Private property creates positions of residual claimancy. Political property extinguishes such positions. To theorize as if people who interact within a system of political property rights nonetheless act as if they were interacting within a regime of private property is to ask political participants to pretend that they are something they are not. Constitutional parchment is unlikely to be sufficient to enforce this kind of pretension when other societal forces are beckoning in different directions. Market conformability might argue against quotas. Yet domestic political forces might support particular sources of foreign supply to provide imported goods, which in turn require the use of discriminatory quotas rather than non-discriminatory tariffs. The more fully political power is divided among independent offices and with collective action requiring concurrence among holders of those offices, the greater the likelihood that constitutional parchment will withstand divergent politically-expressed desires that would degrade that parchment.

Buchanan treats budgetary operations as potentially transforming private property into common property, thereby changing the governance relationships that operate within a society. At its most fundamental level, budgeting converts private property to common property, with the state serving as the arena where rules for governing the commons are made. The tax side of the budget is where obligations to stock the common stores are apportioned among the citizenry. The appropriations side is where citizens compete for access to those common stores. As a result of this competition, individual citizens differ in the amount of access they secure, just as they differ in the obligations to stock the commons that they are forced to bear. Buchanan recognizes that taxation can become a means of transforming property from private to common. The strength of this transformation is inversely related to the extent that post-constitutional politics are restricted by constitutional arrangement to consensual operation. Again, the Wicksellian system, which was of central significance to Buchanan, sought to render collective action congruent with market action. Within the Wicksellian system, the conflict between private and collective property would be eliminated through the incorporation of the state into the order of private property, much as the principle of market conformity sought to do within the framework of order theory.

TRADE, MIGRATION, AND MORAL COMMUNITY

In several writings, Buchanan explains that the social philosophy associated with liberal political economy supports the open movement of goods and services but does not support the free migration of people (Buchanan 1975a; 1978). Buchanan's position on this topic runs contrary to much market-based writing on trade and immigration which holds that free trade and open immigration are complementary practices. But they aren't, as Buchanan recognizes. To be sure, it is possible to create an abstract model of an imaginary world where free trade and open immigration would be complements. This would be an unrecognizable world anywhere other than when looking at a theorist's whiteboard. That world would have to conform to the textbook model of exclusively private goods organized through competitive markets. This model means that all consumption occurs in private spaces isolated from all contact with other people. It also means that people are just inputs into a production process, receiving the values of their marginal products. This austere world has no dancing, singing, fighting, or any other recognizable social activity. All input owners receive the values of their marginal products, products are priced at marginal cost, and free trade generates factor price equalization. In this imaginary world that is totally privatized, there are no opportunities for anyone to gain by immigration.

This imaginary world is not even a remote approximation of any reality, as Buchanan recognized and explored for its implications for social philosophy and liberal political economy. This imagined situation pertains to no one, nor could it because people are social creatures who through interaction with one another generate communities of varying qualities and characteristics. Free trade follows from liberal principles; open immigration does not, with Leland Yeager (1958) setting forth the distinction clearly and with Buchanan and Wagner (1970) and Buchanan and Goetz (1972) building upon that distinction. As between the two jurisdictions, the wealthier jurisdiction will offer services and amenities the other jurisdiction lacks. In both jurisdictions, residents consume some mixture of private and public or social goods. Some of these social goods are produced through explicit acts of production, as in building schools and roads. Many of them, however, are cultural products of societal interaction. Some examples include the customs and manners of a population, conventions about how loud and boisterous one can reasonably be in public settings, and the level of courtesy displayed when passing through congested public places.

Many of these qualities can be captured by the common recognition that there can be many places that someone might wish to visit without, however, wishing to live there. Furthermore, immigration changes the characteristics of the voting population, much as Buchanan (1975b) explores with respect to treating the franchise as a form of property right. While the more cultural type of social goods cannot be priced equivalently to those social goods that are produced, Buchanan and Goetz (1972) set forth a reasonable framework for exploring the tendencies toward excessive immigration toward wealthier communities that free migration creates. While immigrants can secure equal wages, under factor price equalization, in the two jurisdictions, they obtain higher returns through the more elaborate supply of social goods in the wealthier jurisdiction. Therefore, people in the poorer jurisdiction can gain by immigration due to their ability to capture shares of the locational rents the superior supply of social goods offers.

A familiar adage asserts that "all politics is local politics." In these days of rhetorical flourishes extolling inclusion and globalization, Buchanan wrestled with that adage and those flourishes in exploring the idea of moral community. While the technologies of communication and transportation have clearly shrunk the effective size of the globe, Buchanan recognized that most people were still rooted creatures. Many of them may roam far and wide, and yet most of them will have some place they regard as home, and for which there exists intensive and extensive limits of interaction (Buchanan 1978). Trade does not entail membership; immigration does, and can thus change the moral community.

EQUALITY AND STATUS WITHIN BUCHANAN'S LIBERAL ORDER

When people speak of equality these days, they mostly have in mind some such notion of material equality as the distribution of income or wealth. Material equality is not, however, the only notion of equality. It is probably not even the most significant notion. It is, however, the only notion that can be reduced to numbers, even if those numbers are enshrouded in ambiguity. Other notions of equality speak to moral equality and the moral imagination. The material and nonmaterial notions of equality overlap in significant ways, as Buchanan (1971) recognizes in his examination of "Equality as Fact and Norm."

What significance resides in a finding that a measure of inequality has increased between one point of observation and another? Many people seem ready to claim that this kind of observation points to some defect within the present system of political economy, for which remedies ranging from increased taxation of the rich to the awarding of free college tuition for people with low incomes are quickly advanced. These types of reactions indicate that the reactors presume that inequality is valued negatively regardless of how it comes about. Yet there are many choices that people freely make that result in an increase in measured inequality. Not everyone is provident and hard-working, as Henry Fawcett's (1871) tale of Robinson and Smith illustrated. A distribution of income or wealth is not something that someone chooses. To the contrary, it is a variable that emerges through interactions among people throughout a society. It's easy enough to imagine that different social arrangements and practices would result in the emergence of different distributions due to the ways in which those arrangements influence individual actions.

Within the liberal framework of a market economy, the sources of material inequality result from choice, luck, effort, and birth (Buchanan 1971). As Buchanan explains, it is doubtful if anyone would object to inequality that resulted from personal choice. Someone who takes on dangerous work understandably will earn more than someone who does not but who otherwise is equal in all relevant respects. Similarly, someone who takes on a second job on the weekends will earn more than someone who doesn't. An increase in the number of people who choose to undertake second jobs, moreover, will increase measured inequality. As for luck, we can all recognize its appearance in our lives, and some people seem to have more of it than others. Moreover, luck seems to be positive for some people and negative for others. While the vagaries of luck can affect personal positions within a distribution of income, it is hard to see that the operation of luck would have any systematic effect on measures of inequality.

What remains is birth, as no one has anything to do with the circumstances and conditions regarding gender, race, national origin, or numerous genetic features under which he or she enters the world. As Buchanan notes, nearly all controversy over distributional matters revolves around the treatment of accidents of birth, mostly asking whether there is anything that can or should be done to address accidents of birth. Most claims about unfairness or injustice in economic arrangements and processes center on questions of birth. Entry into the world is a piece of data about which the acting subject has no choice. What is open to choice, and all that is open to choice, are the responses people make when they confront that data. In this respect, there are two categories of response, which can be described as feudal and liberal.

In feudal systems, people were largely born into stations in life. Participation in government was the province of royal families. Merchants and peasants might hope to live under good governance, but they could not participate in that governance in any case. Someone born a peasant will stay a peasant, though such a peasant can hope to live under a kindly lord rather than under a ruthless lord. Either way, the material condition of the peasant will be the lord's business. Henry Maine (1864) advanced the thesis that the direction of movement in progressive societies had been a movement from relationships based on status to relationships based on contract. Maine voiced his thesis at about the same time as he was beginning to sense some possible reversal of that direction of movement. Starting with colonial beginnings, the American system was based largely on a rejection of the feudal trappings of status and power. That rejection was not total, and Jonathan Hughes (1977) explains that the colonial period in America had embraced *The Governmental Habit* even though European feudal duties and obligations were gone. Within the feudal mode of thinking, emphasis is placed on offering moral exhortation to the well-to-do to skew their activities in a manner that increases the material condition of those who have less. The direction of obligation is positive and directed at the well-to-do. There is no obligation attached to those who have less. In contemporary times, the feudal orientation is expressed in large measure by supporting numerous programs to redistribute income and wealth without that redistribution being limited to charitable donations.

In contrast, within Buchanan's (1971) liberal framework the direction of obligation is negative, and it is aimed at everyone in society. This liberal framework can be encapsulated by the adage of offering a helping hand and not a handout. This adage places two types obligation on the well-to-do. One type is to accept and even embrace the scheme of free and open competition that emerges from a liberal system where human relationships and interactions are governed by the principles of private property and freedom of contract. This liberal system means there are no sheltered positions in society where a prosperous enterprise can be protected from competition that would erode that wealth. The creator of a successful business cannot call upon political authorities to prevent competition from other enterprises. For a successful enterprise to continue to be successful, it will be necessary for the enterprise continually to attract support in the face of free and open competition. Similarly, within a liberal society an enterprise will not be able to secure subsidies to get started, or to keep going when otherwise it would fail because it couldn't operate as a going concern without political support.

Within a liberal society, there would be no positions of special privilege that either was established using political power or was maintained in the face of competition using political power (Tullock 1989). Such an idealized liberal society is far removed from the institutional arrangements and practices of contemporary social democracy. As for material inequality, the data on the distribution of income and wealth we observe are emergent products of the contemporary system of social democracy. To be sure, proponents of increased redistributive activity wrongly declare that observed data reflect the operating properties of the free enterprise system that accompanies a liberal polity. These days when public ordering is ubiquitous throughout society, there are no data that pertain to the distributive qualities of a free enterprise economy.

There is no doubt that negotiating life in modern times calls upon a greater variety of talents and skills than it did two centuries ago. Even such a thing as raising a child now takes a village, as Hillary Clinton (1996) explained. Many more tasks and duties are involved now in raising a child than was apparent in the Little House on the Prairie series set in the mid-nineteenth century. Those skills and talents can be secured from many places throughout a village or city. Where Hillary Clinton wanted parents to rely upon the expertise assembled within a Health and Human Services bureaucracy, they are also distributed throughout villages and cities where people can assemble their desired bundles of expertise. The modern division of labor means that people will know relatively little about many of the activities that are important to them, in that they will not be able to perform those activities, and so must rely upon expertise. But what kind of expertise provided by whom and selected how?

Within the feudalistic motif of social democracy, expertise would be assembled by the lord of the manor, operating these days as a Health and Human Services bureaucracy. This approach to the assembly of expertise carries forward the progressivist image of political authority centralized in the hands of right-thinking experts certified by similar experts. Within the feudalistic motif, ordinary people are judged to be incapable of dealing with many of the complexities of modern life, perhaps leading them understandably to be fearful of having to deal with modern life without having representatives of those Health and Human Services bureaucracy directing them (Buchanan 2005). In contrast, the liberal motif recognized that people have many sources of helpfulness in assembling what they find to be useful expertise distributed throughout the precincts of civil society as well as available for purchase through market transactions.

MOVING FORWARD WITHIN THE
VIRGINIA TRADITION IN POLITICAL ECONOMY

Peter Boettke (2012) explains that Buchanan, like Frank Knight and Henry Simons, regarded economics as a relatively simple science of great public significance. That science, moreover, could be easily manipulated and distorted in the service of special pleadings of all sorts, and with proper economics serving mostly to explain why the political promises and speeches of the day typically are more sources of problems than of solutions. Knight's generational neighbor, Vilfredo Pareto (1935), turned from economic theory in the 1890s and 1900s to sociology to understand why what he regarded as the compelling logic of economic theory and free completion found such small favor. To do this, Pareto distinguished between logical and non-logical action. Logical action was the domain of markets where prices allowed direct comparison between magnitudes. Outside of markets, however, such direct comparisons were not possible, and for which Pareto designated as the sphere of non-logical action.

In the market context, options could be reduced to a common denominator due to the existence of explicit prices. In other contexts, no such reduction was possible. Outside the market, Pareto saw competition as occurring between members of elites in society who used techniques of wit and power to gain and hold power. Success in this competitive process depended significantly upon the ability of ruling elites to articulate ideological images that resonated with sentiments that were resident within the population and which led the population to suspend any disbelief they might have, and which they couldn't check anyway because there were no prices attached to the ideological options.

Without doubt, James Buchanan's oeuvre is the fountainhead of what became recognized as a Virginia tradition in political economy. That tradition did not start from zero with Buchanan's entry onto the scholarly stage. Buchanan recurred to the classical British tradition of political economy, buttressed by contributions by Knut Wicksell and several Italian theorists of public finance. On his scholarly journey, Buchanan kept contact with Frank Knight and his ever-skeptical attitude, along with Knight's wide-ranging contributions (see, for instance, Knight (1960) on the problem of combining intelligence with democratic action). Buchanan's oeuvre contains numerous tensions. To find tensions in a research program that was developed over more than six decades and contained hundreds of items is not surprising. Furthermore, the existence of tensions points to opportunities for advancing the tradition. The main direction of potential progress, in my judgment, lies in moving ever further in the direction of subjectivism because this direction brings us ever more fully into the domain of emergent and creative social systems where open-ended human action is the vehicle for injecting change continually into society. To be sure, the continual injection of novelty along with reactions of adaptation takes place against a formal background of eternal verities. In this regard, there is truly nothing new under the sun. but we don't experience life as eternal verities, but only as shadowy reflections and manifestations of those verities. Buchanan has left behind a marvelous legacy of ideas that hold much promise for carrying forward the liberal tradition in political economy.

THE SOCIAL PHILOSOPHY TOWARD WHICH BUCHANAN'S OEUVRE LEADS

Any society will have organization about it. A social philosophy is concerned with the properties of alternative forms of social organization, as well as the processes through which social organization comes about and changes. Without doubt, Buchanan's, for whom Buchanan (1985b) is a succinct statement of his social philosophy, *bête noire* in twentieth-century political economy was John Maynard Keynes. Keynes (1936, 372–84) titled the closing chapter of his *General Theory* "Concluding Notes on the Social Philosophy towards Which the General Theory Might Lead." Keynes's social philosophy could reasonably be described as guided or controlled liberalism, in contrast to Buchanan's genuine liberalism. Keynes' model of society was bi-planar. The lower plane was occupied by ordinary people as these people and their actions are conveyed by the theory of market interaction. The upper plane was occupied by those people who lived on Harvey Road, to recur to the usage of Keynes' biographer Roy Harrod (1951, 192–93) who explained that Keynes "was strongly imbued with what I have called the presuppositions of Harvey Road. One of these presuppositions may perhaps be summarized by the idea that the government of Britain was . . . in the hands of an intellectual aristocracy using the method of persuasion." Harvey Road was the location of Keynes' family home in Cambridge. Harrod went on to explain that "Keynes tended till the end to think of the really important decisions being reached by a small group of intelligent people" (p. 193).

A ruling elite would thus allow people to pursue their desired activities within a set of market arrangements so long as that pursuit meshed with the desires and plans of the intelligentsia that proverbially resided on Harvey Road. Keynes was an elitist who preferred governance to proceed by using velvet gloves rather than mailed fists. At least this is the image Keynes presented in closing the *General Theory*. Yet Keynes also prepared a Foreword for the German edition of the *General Theory* where he states: "Nonetheless, the theory of output as a whole, which is what the following book purports to provide, is much more easily adopted to the conditions of a totalitarian state than is the theory of production and distribution . . . produced under conditions of free competition."[1] The simple logic of economizing action would suggest that the rate at which resort to velvet gloves gave way to mailed fists would vary directly with the intensity of the opposition the Harvey Road intelligentsia encountered to their plans.

Buchanan's social philosophy was sharply divergent from Keynes'. Buchanan was a genuine liberal who recognized that the living together in close geographical proximity was a continuing challenge that could easily go awry from the perspective of a liberal social philosophy. He resisted the lure of the second theorem of welfare economics to imagine a political apparatus unhampered by the requirements of consent acting in Edgeworthian fashion to redistribute wealth within a society to fit someone's distributive norms. He accepted current social arrangements as the point of departure because there was no option. For Buchanan, consent was the only reasonable standard for political action within society. Some people could still recur to higher authority in forming their normative beliefs, but they would have to follow the path of consensus if they were to insert those beliefs into society.

Buchanan's social philosophy was formed against a background recognition that claims of injustice must be addressed to identifiable individuals. This is a feature of the common law process that is part of the institutional order of a liberal political economy. Within that scheme of political economy, people bear first-order responsibility for their pursuit of happiness. This means that someone who is in an unhappy state should first of all take an internal look as a reflective creature. Civil society also contains numerous offices and resources that can provide solace and guidance to people seeking to attain more desirable states of living. In some cases, unhappiness might arise because rights of person or property have been violated by others, at least in your judgment. You might have built a house with a beautiful view of the sun setting behind a mountain in the distance. Before too long, the pleasure you obtain from watching the sunset is disrupted by recognition that a neighbor is constructing a tall building that will obstruct your view. You think the neighbor is taking some of your property, so you secure a lawyer to file a suit to obtain an injunction against the construction. Perhaps you will succeed; perhaps not. In any case, the system of liberal political economy places first-order responsibility for the pursuit of happiness on individuals, who can seek legal redress to the extent they can attribute the source of their unhappiness to the actions of other people that violates their rights of property or contract.

In contrast to common law as a liberal process for resolving conflicts, legislation mostly absolves people from responsibility in attending to their pursuit of happiness. Within the liberal framework of common law, a person unhappy with his or her material standard of living is counseled either to reduce desire or increase earnings, which, in turn, might require an expenditure of effort. In contrast, legislation, outside of a Wicksellian framework for legislation, embraces the claim that the pursuit of happiness is not a matter of individual responsibility. Instead, unhappiness is a systemic quality and so requires legislation. Instead of someone being advised to seek a higher-paying job, a systemic claim is advanced that some kinds of jobs are systematically under-compensated, and which might be contested by requiring employers to offer workers "living wages." Activities of this sort move us into the Keynesian social philosophy, where the residents of Harvey Road would determine the level of a living wage, among whatever other defects are thought to accompany a market economy.

For people to live together in close geographical proximity, it is necessary that they want to do so, which requires that they recognize advantage in doing so. The theory of a market economy explains the source of such mutual advantage that comes about when human interactions are guided by the principles and conventions of private property and freedom of contract. The social creation of mutual gains from trade is the central lesson of political economy going well beyond the time of Adam Smith to the Spanish Jesuits of Salamanca starting in the sixteenth century. Securing gains from trade through commerce and industry encounters obstacles in the autonomy of the political in society. A large part of the liberal imagination seeks to abolish the political and the Faustian bargain it brings about, but the crooked timber of humanity won't allow this to happen. Both Carl Schmitt and Walter Eucken issued calls for a "strong state" to resist the erosion of liberal arrangements through predation by predatory interest groups. The instance each of them had in mind was the collapse of the Weimar republic, which they attributed to the weakness of the state in resisting the predatory forces we now describe as rent seeking and rent extraction. There is no known recipe for accomplishing this replacement of weakness with strength, but the concerns with republican virtues and the moral imagination speak to these challenges and concerns.

Buchanan recognized that eternal vigilance was truly the price of liberty, and Buchanan (2005) voiced recognition that as increasing numbers of people came to conclude that the price of liberty was higher than they wanted to pay to maintain it, liberty would deteriorate unless other people stepped up to pay the price. Buchanan's body of work was mostly concerned with exploring and explaining the operating logic of a society of free and responsible individuals, but he also recognized that in the final analysis it is the moral imaginations that are alive within a population that determine the moral tone of a society. Those imaginations, moreover, can be influenced by institutionally governed practice because norms to some extent come from observation of what other people think and how they act—though by no means wholly, as Budziszewaki (2003) explains, and as Buchanan might have accepted.

NOTE

1. This translation comes from George Garvey (1975, 403).

Appendix

James M. Buchanan and Me:
Reminiscing about a Fifty-Year Association

This reminiscence commemorates Jim Buchanan's life and work as I reflect on my 50-year association with him. That association began in September 1963 when I entered graduate school at the University of Virginia. It ended with his death in January 2013. Of those 50 years, 34 were spent in the same university: three years at the University of Virginia (1963–1966), six years at Virginia Polytechnic Institute (1973–1979), and 25 years at George Mason University (1988–2013). By now, Buchanan's thought has been examined within a large secondary literature that treats his work from an objective point of view where the writer stands apart from the subject he or she treats. In contrast, this essay is written from a subjective point of view. It treats Jim Buchanan through reflections upon my experiences with him and observations of him over the period of our association. I seek to generate a personal portrait of Buchanan as this emerges out of those experiences and observations.

GETTING TO KNOW ONE ANOTHER

It was with great eagerness that I looked forward to Jim Buchanan's public finance course in September 1963. It was his and Gordon Tullock's (1962) *The Calculus of Consent* that had convinced me to enroll in the PhD program at the University of Virginia. During the fall semester of my final year (1962–1963) at the University of Southern California, I took a class from Richard Bilas, who had just started as an assistant professor at USC, having finished his PhD at Virginia the preceding spring. He and I got along well from the start. When he asked if I had thought about graduate school, I explained the quandary I felt: I liked the logic that I found in my economics classes, but I liked the material I found in my political science classes. Bilas suggested I look at *The Calculus of Consent*, asserting that if I did so I would see that I could study economics at Virginia while dealing with political science material. I followed his suggestion, determined he was right, was offered an attractive fellowship, and moved to Charlottesville shortly before the fall 1963 semester began.

Shortly before the mid-September start of the semester, all students had to meet with Leland Yeager, then Director of Graduate Studies, to get their programs of study approved for the coming year. First-year students who came directly from their bachelor's programs had a fixed program for the first year. This meant that for the fall semester, I would have taken history of thought with Coase, price theory with Nutter, statistics with Vining, and math econ with Ferguson. In light of my undergraduate math background, however, Yeager said I could skip math econ and take something else. Instantly, I said I wanted to take Buchanan's public finance class. Yeager said that wasn't advised for students without previous graduate study. I said I wanted to do it anyway. Yeager wished me well.

I approached that class with great enthusiasm and not a hint of trepidation. I had divided my time the preceding summer mostly between studying French to prepare for one of the two language exams that were required in those days and reading works by Buchanan, including the original, 1960 version of his public finance text. While I passed the French exam, it appears as though I did not understand the ramifications of what I had been reading from Buchanan. While sitting excitedly in class the first day, I saw Buchanan glance at his roll sheet. He looked into the room as if looking for someone, then said: "Mr. Wagner, what's wrong with the American tax system?" I felt an adrenaline rush.

After my summer's reading, that question was written for me, or so I thought. The movie *Paper Chase* had not yet been made, but if it had I would have felt like Jonathan Hart responding to Professor Charles W. Kingsfield. Instantly I began reciting things I read that summer about simplifying the tax system by reducing exemptions and deductions and such things. Buchanan seemed to be paying close attention, which pleased me hugely. When I finished, however, he responded: "Mr. Wagner, you have no business answering a question like that. We are democrats here and not autocrats." I had no idea what Buchanan meant by this, but I knew I did not answer his question well, so I slouched low in my chair until the period ended.

As the period was ending, Buchanan assigned the first of the several essays for us to write that he would assign that semester. He started his explanation of the assignment by saying he had heard that "if a grasshopper or fly (I don't recall which insect he referred to) were multiplied nine times in all dimensions, it wouldn't be able to get off the ground and might even collapse under its own weight. There is a problem of dimensionality here. The size of government has similarly multiplied several times this century. There is a problem of fiscal dimension that is surely worth exploring. For your first assignment, write an essay on 'the problem of fiscal dimension.'" Forgetting my embarrassment from earlier in the period, I raised my hand and asked: "Mr. Buchanan, could you give us some idea of what you are looking for in this essay?" Instantly, he shot back: "Mr. Wagner, if I knew what I was looking for, I wouldn't be interested in hearing what you think."

I left the classroom in silence, and went home to ponder whether graduate school was for me. By morning I had, with wonderful counsel and solace from my wife, put that class behind me and started thinking about the problem of fiscal dimension, as well as working on my other classes. The next class session opened with some discussion of the essays we wrote the preceding week, though I kept quiet and was relieved not to have been called upon. During that period, Buchanan kept making references to "slipping around on the Pareto welfare surface," and similar formulations about which I knew nothing. I knew I could not let my know-nothingness persist, so I pushed aside my memories of the previous class period and asked: "Mr. Buchanan, could you explain what you mean by slipping around on the Pareto welfare surface?" He responded nonchalantly: "Read 'On Welfare Theory and Pareto Regions,' by Ragnar Frisch (1959), published in *International Economic Papers*. Once you do that it will be clear to you."

Within a day or two, I started the morning sitting in the Alderman Library reading "On Welfare Theory and Pareto Regions." I was still sitting there at lunch time, and skipped lunch to continue reading because I did not yet understand what I was reading. Frisch's paper, dense with abstract formulations, was the most difficult thing I had read to that point in my life. It was mid-afternoon before I could say that I understood what I had been struggling to read. While this gave me a sense of accomplishment, it also inspired an epiphany about how Buchanan approached his teaching. Buchanan wasn't there to give an alternative presentation of what was already published. He was there to learn so as to create future publications, and we were there as participants in this adventure in learning. If something was already written, we could read it on our own. If we couldn't or if we weren't willing to make the effort, we should think about doing something else with our lives.

My day spent wrestling with Ragnar Frisch is nothing compared with wrestling with the devil for 40 days. All the same, however, it set my life on a different path from where it had been headed. I had always been a kind of bookworm along with having a normal adolescent interest in girls and sports, while also doing well in school with modest effort. It would have been around 1960 or 1961 when, while sitting in a doctor's waiting room, I read a magazine article written by the then President of the University of Minnesota, Meredith Wilson (not to be confused with the author of *The Music Man*) about the joys of a career in college teaching. What I took away from that article was that teaching wasn't highly paid but it offered much leisure to do as you wished. I was never highly materialistic; for instance, the only jewelry I have is a wedding ring, a watch, and two tie tacks. I went to Virginia with that attitude at the core of my consciousness, looking forward to three years of study, after which I would be a college professor with plenty of time for golfing, fishing, bowling, hiking, surfing, and the various other leisurely pursuits I was always ready to try.

After that day wrestling with Ragnar Frisch and reflecting on Jim Buchanan's approach to the classroom, I recognized that I got intense joy out of wrestling with ideas and trying to develop new articulations to replace long-standing articulations. While Jim Buchanan is known throughout the world for his scholarship, I hold him in particular esteem for showing me that the classroom could be a place of mutual learning where your position as instructor is one of *primus inter pares* and not one of an expert passing on knowledge to novices. Sure, Buchanan passed on knowledge, much of it, but he did so always in the context of searching for alternative ideas to articulate. If something had been written, a student can read it. Starting from that point of departure, the classroom is an arena for searching for new ideas to articulate. We typically think of ideas as macro entities, as illustrated by "rent seeking" for which Gordon Tullock (1967) should surely have been awarded a Nobel Prize. But if you take apart an idea, you will see that it is constituted through ordered strings of micro units of thought. Rent seeking, for instance, is constituted through combining ideas about competition, property rights, and contracting, among other ideas, and each of which can be conceptualized in a variety of ways. Ideas have a combinatorial quality, which means that the universe of potential thought is immense in relation to what is currently known. For instance, there are some 635 billion ways that a string of 13 cards can be drawn from a deck of 52 cards. If a publishable idea requires a string of 13 sub-ideas and 52 such sub-ideas are available, there are some 635 billion ideas awaiting articulation. Some of those might not turn out to be interesting or sensible, but a career as a university professor can provide an arena for lifetime learning. This I learned from Jim Buchanan during that fall of 1963, and the course of my life changed forever.

TEACHING BY DOING, WITH STUDENTS AS APPRENTICES

I don't know that Jim Buchanan ever articulated his vision of graduate education, but his conduct in the classroom certainly conveyed such a vision. My classroom experience with Jim came through two full semesters and nearly half of a third semester. That experience begin with his fall 1963 class in beginning public finance and continued with his spring 1964 class in advanced public finance. It further continued into the fall 1964 semester, when for six or seven weeks he replaced Warren Nutter in teaching advanced micro theory while Nutter was advising Barry Goldwater's presidential campaign.

If Buchanan were a carpenter, the classroom would be his shop. Students would be apprentices who were there to learn from Jim by watching him at work, by replicating what you saw him doing, and by creating your own constructions. You learned by doing, not by listening and watching. Sure, you did some listening and watching, but it was the doing that mattered. He would not take class time to show you how to drive a nail, level a plank, or miter an angle. You could practice doing these on your own. He assumed that you would acquire the basics of those techniques outside the classroom. The challenge inside the classroom was to deploy those skills and techniques in advancing construction projects.

Students were apprentices who were there to learn from Jim how to construct publishable work. Learning how to miter was something we acquired outside the classroom. In the classroom we observed and practiced the different ways that mitering might be incorporated into construction projects. Those projects, moreover, always had novel and creative aspects. After all, there is no market for simply duplicating what has already been written. While rehearsal in solving known problems can be useful in becoming familiar with your tools just as can practice mitering at different angles, these techniques are illustrated in books which students can study outside the classroom. The classroom was a forward-looking place for working on what was not yet a finished product. In this respect, Buchanan rarely recurred to things he had written in the past. He always looked forward, and Jim's forward-looking emphasis is something I have carried with me since those days in Charlottesville.

During a typical semester in the classroom, Buchanan would work on several projects, which we students would also work on by writing essays that touched upon the topics that Buchanan was working on. A good part of the fall 1963 semester was spent dealing with the material that became his well-cited paper on clubs (Buchanan 1965). One class session was devoted to Buchanan's musings about public goods, exclusion, and clubs, using a swimming pool as a concrete illustration. The classroom discussion revolved around a comparison between having your own pool and belonging to some group-owned pool. It was plain enough to see that the group pool would be cheaper but it could also entail crowding as well as having to share space with people you might prefer to avoid. The class session ended with Buchanan giving us an assignment for next week's class: set forth our ideas about how we would analyze the tradeoffs we had been discussing and debating.

For those written assignments, we typically spent more time trying to determine our approach to the problem than we did in actually writing the essay.

With our essays in hand, the first part of the following session was devoted to the presentation and discussion of our essays. Toward the end of the class, Buchanan passed out a rough draft of a paper that was destined to become Buchanan (1965). Our next assignment was to write a critical essay on the draft paper, as a kind of referee report we might be asked to write for a professional journal in our post-student days. Buchanan repeated this instructional scheme throughout the semester, though the paper on clubs was the only instance of repeated visitation and refinement over a few weeks. The other sessions were more on the order of one or two weeks exploring analytical possibilities, where Buchanan would lead a discussion on a topic, which we would follow by writing papers where we sought to articulate some theme that pertained to that topic, followed by presentation and discussion at the next session. Major tax reform was underway in 1963, and several class sessions were devoted to different facets of this topic, always with the emphasis placed on looking for new angles to pursue.

The spring 1964 semester proceeded in the same manner, only the course was more focused on Buchanan's interest in developing a book-length presentation of his catallactical orientation toward public finance, which he wanted to stand in contrast to Samuelson's (1954; 1955) claim that such an orientation could not be developed because of failures in preference revelation. The work that semester consisted mostly of reading draft chapters and preparing critical essays on those chapters, where our challenge was to find ways of carrying the argument forward. We were, in other words, enlisted as participants in the creation of an alternative orientation toward public finance, which is something to which Jim aspired from the start of his career, as Marianne Johnson (2014a) explains lucidly. The book of which I speak became *The Demand and Supply of Public Goods* (Buchanan 1968b).

This classroom experience was repeated the first part of the fall 1964 semester. Warren Nutter, who was traveling with Barry Goldwater's presidential campaign, was scheduled to teach the course on advanced micro theory. Buchanan replaced Nutter for the first six or seven weeks of the semester. Micro theory for Buchanan's half-semester was all about the relationship between cost and choice. I found the material fascinating, not least because Buchanan's presentation of the reciprocal character of cost and choice stood in sharp contrast to Nutter's Marshallian approach in the first micro course the preceding year. Once again, puzzles were posed, questions raised, and ideas put to paper. By the time Nutter returned to the classroom, Buchanan had assembled around 100 pages that eventually became *Cost and Choice* (Buchanan 1969a).

SUPERVISING DOCTORAL STUDENTS

While Buchanan is understandably known throughout the world for his scholarly writings which have influenced me greatly, I was also highly influenced through the example he established throughout his teaching activities, starting in the classroom and ending with the doctoral dissertation, which I wrote under his supervision. Over the course of my academic career, even extending back into the late years as an undergraduate, many people have told me stories of experiences with doctoral supervisors, both their experiences and experiences they have picked up second-hand. A good number of those stories and experiences were decidedly unpleasant when viewed from the student's perspective. One student might find it hard to get a meeting with the supervisor to discuss some points, bringing the process to a halt. Another student might submit a chapter, only to have the supervisor hold it for several weeks before returning it. In some cases, the comments offered on return were more cryptic than helpful, as illustrated by injunctions to elaborate a model without saying anything about what that elaboration might entail. In some cases there was a continuing parade of requests to do more or to do something different, with one draft leading the supervisor to ask the student to explore a different angle, and with this parade going on for several iterations. In such cases as these, dissertation supervision unfolded as a kind of adversarial process where the student had to overcome the supervisor's defensive activities to complete the dissertation.

In contrast, Jim's orientation toward supervising dissertations was that of a friendly but professionally serious advocate. This was clearly my experience, but that same experience was also relayed to me by several other people who wrote under Buchanan's supervision both in Charlottesville and in Blacksburg. Jim wanted students to succeed. He recognized that they differed in their talents and interests, and allowed them wide scope in developing those talents and interests. He was not a censor in that he did not insist that you do it his way in any detailed manner, though, of course, you had to write on a topic that interested him, but this is how it is with everyone. Through his supervisory efforts, you recognized that Jim wanted you to succeed, and that he was there more to help you avoid serious missteps than to pile on tasks that would convert you into a type of research assistant to explore questions he wanted addressed.

There is that line from Robert Browning: "Ah that a man's reach should exceed his grasp. Or, what's a heaven for." I would not have recognized the sense of that line when I carried my easy-going days from southern California into Charlottesville. By the time I finished my first year in Charlottesville, however, I was seized by the thrust of that line. My mentality had undergone transformation through my interaction with Jim Buchanan. Seized with sentiment Browning expressed, I began a dissertation project in the summer of 1965 that was far too big for the year I had in which to complete it. What I had proposed was a reconstruction of public finance that would unify the taxing and spending sides of the fiscal process. Early that summer, Jim told me he thought I was trying to do too much. I responded by saying that I wanted to do something big. I'm sure he appreciated the ambition I showed even if he didn't think I could realize what I wanted to do. On this judgment he was right, for I didn't even really approach the breadth of that proposed topic in a book-length treatment until my *Fiscal Sociology and the Theory of Public Finance* (Wagner 2007). While Jim was skeptical, he said I needed to reach that determination on my own, but also advised me to be thinking of how I could take a chunk of that project to create a smaller alternative that I could finish in the spring. By the end of the year, I realized that Jim was right. I reconfigured my dissertation to one on public housing and interest groups, and finished in May 1966.

Jim's treatment of dissertation supervision was a continuation of his classroom orientation toward students as apprentices. I began my first semester in Charlottesville already wanting to be like Jim, save that I had no idea that to do so I would have to make compromises with the laid-back mentality I had absorbed from my southern California days. After I recovered from a rough start the first few weeks of that fall semester, that initial desire did nothing but intensify. I finished my dissertation in May 1966 under Buchanan's supervision, and returned to my home territory in southern California by becoming an assistant professor at the University of California at Irvine, where I was filled with a driving ambition to be like Jim as best I could.

Jim kept contact with me, commented on ideas I advanced, sent me papers of his to review, and invited me into co-authoring adventures. One of those adventures was a little monograph on public debt, *Public Debt in a Democratic Society* (Buchanan and Wagner 1967), which a decade later had morphed into *Democracy in Deficit* (Buchanan and Wagner 1977). Co-authoring with students is a form of extra-classroom instruction that I think is especially good at transmitting some of the tacit knowledge that is essential for successful academic scholarship. Buchanan worked fast without a trace of procrastination, finishing projects in advance of deadlines. While you can always tell a student that it is important to submit work in timely fashion, that message is surely transmitted more strongly and memorably through example when your co-author or dissertation supervisor or instructor returns work quickly after you have submitted it. Here again, I found myself learning about the joint-supply characteristics of teaching and scholarship that Jim Buchanan exemplified.

During the fall quarter of 1967 (Irvine was on a quarter and not a semester system), Jim visited Irvine. While in Charlottesville, I had taken a course from Rutledge Vining on location theory. I came away from that course with a strong interest in central place theory. Just before Jim's arrival in Irvine, I had drafted a paper that tried to incorporate central place theory into the public finances of a federalist form of government. The main idea behind this effort was that any division of a map into distinct political entities will create differences in per capita incomes among those entities due merely to the uneven distribution of central places. In a conversation in my office, I showed Jim my paper and explained its logic. He pulled a paper out of his bag, written on yellow paper and typed on a manual typewriter, and explained to me what he was trying to do with respect to internal migration within a federal system. There was clearly much overlapping, and Jim invited me to join him in writing a paper for an NBER conference to which he was invited. That paper was published in a conference volume (Buchanan and Wagner 1970). Perhaps even more significantly, Jim's invitation gave me the opportunity to meet with such well-known scholars as Kenneth Arrow, Martin Bailey, Anthony Downs, Martin Feldstein, Julius Margolis, Mancur Olson, Jerome Rothenberg, Burton Weisbrod, Oliver Williamson, and William Vickrey, among others in attendance. And if that wasn't enough, Jim even let me present our paper, which I have to admit was intimidating at the time but good for me all the same. Once again, I learned lessons from Jim's example that I carried with me ever since about the importance of senior scholars helping junior scholars gain footholds within what in some cases can prove to be a treacherous scholarly landscape.

BUCHANAN AS COLLEAGUE

These post-doctoral glimpses of what it would be like to be a colleague of Jim Buchanan's became part of my reality when in 1973 I moved to Virginia Polytechnic Institute to join Buchanan, Tullock, and Charlie Goetz at the Center for Study of Public Choice that they started in 1969. I have earlier offered my recollections of and reflections on academic life at the Public Choice Center (Wagner 2004), and will not revisit that territory here. Without doubt, those six years in Blacksburg were the high point of my academic career with respect to enjoying the feeling of being amidst a set of highly energetic and creative people who were engaged in conquering new scholarly territory. The Public Choice Center was alive with activity seven days a week, though with a reduced schedule on weekends. The sounds echoing throughout the corridors were those of typewriters clacking, people talking, and pages turning—all directed at conquering scholarly territory from inside an energetic and interactive environment. Buchanan and Tullock were a truly dynamic combination in this respect, each seeking to wreak themselves upon the world and inviting interested parties to do the same.

Marianne Johnson (2014a) notes that Buchanan started his career by wanting to do public finance differently than it was then practiced, even in

Chicago where he did his graduate studies. This desire to be different commenced with Buchanan (1949), where he sought to locate public finance not as a tool of statecraft but as a component of a theory of political economy. This piece brought some ideas from continental public finance before an audience weaned on the Anglo-Saxon orientation (Backhaus and Wagner 2005a; 2005b). A distinctive Italianate style of public finance arose in the 1880s and pretty much disappeared during the 1930s (Fausto 2003). Buchanan's distinctive work in public finance throughout the 1950s and into the early 1960s culminated in the emergence of public choice as a distinct orientation toward political economy, even though that term was not officially established until 1968 when the Public Choice Society was officially formed and what had been *Papers on Non-Market Decision Making* was renamed *Public Choice*, still under Gordon Tullock's editorship.

With respect to the emergence of public choice and to Buchanan's expressed interest in doing public finance differently, I would offer a simple hypothesis. Start with someone well versed in the classical Italian scholarship of public finance as this was conveyed by such people as Antonio de Viti de Marco (1888; 1936), Maffeo Pantaleoni (1911), and Attilio Da Empoli (1941) and as conveyed through numerous papers published particularly in the *Giornale degli Economisti*. Imagine that this person falls into a deep sleep around 1940 in Rip Van Winkle fashion only to awaken around 1970. My hypothesis is that such a person would feel quite comfortable with the style of thought that was then being carried forward in Blacksburg under the rubric of public choice.

The animating thrust of Italian public finance was to treat public finance as a facet of social-economic theory and not as an instrument of statecraft. The analytical challenge was not to develop statements about good or optimal taxation and expenditure, but was rather to develop explanations of observed experience in terms of such universal categories as utility, cost, and profit. Public finance was not concerned with whether a state should provide electricity or how it should price such service if it did provide it. Rather it was concerned with bringing the universal economic categories to bear on explaining observed social formations. Hence, the same catallactical principles would be brought to bear on explaining the creation of a state enterprise and its pricing policies as would be brought to bear on explaining market relationships. To be sure, there are institutional differences between economic relationships organized through markets and those organized through governments. These differences don't deny the universal presence of catallactical relationships in society, but they do influence the particular pattern such relationships acquire.

While the Italian theorists were more oriented toward explanatory than hortatory questions, I should also note that they did not speak with some uniform voice. While Vilfredo Pareto thought in terms of and distinguished between economic equilibrium and political or social equilibrium, he did not do so in the same way as did his good friend, Maffeo Pantaleoni. For instance, Pantaleoni (1911) stresses similarity between the economic and the political by construing societies as operating with two systems of pricing, in which a system of political prices operates parasitically upon a system of market prices. In contrast, Pareto stressed the divergence between logical and non-logical action. Where logical action pertained to market interaction, non-logical action was the province of political processes. In this scheme of thought, Pareto was surely closer to Carl Schmitt (1932) and his emphasis on the autonomy of the political, in contrast to Pantaleoni who perhaps was closer to the classical liberal aspiration that politics could be reduced to some combination of ethics, law, and economics. Regardless of such differences in scholarly orientation, the Italian theorists sought mostly to explain the operation of political entities and processes from within a framework of economizing action. Buchanan's initial scholarship on public finance and political economy sought to carry forward this largely Italianate orientation, of which I was a very willing inheritor from Jim.

Jim Buchanan is, of course, the scholar who did the most to present Italianate public finance to English readers, especially with his 1960 essay on the Italians, but also in a line of thought that is represented well by his 1967 book, *Public Finance in Democratic Process*. To be sure, Buchanan's work showed decreasing Italianate connection as the years passed, but that is a different matter, one independent of the Italianate desire to treat state activity within the purview of social theorizing and not as a tool of statecraft. The Italianate challenge, carried forward by public choice, was to explain collective configurations according to the same underlying principles of cost and gain as used to explain market-generated configurations. Surely, an Italian Rip Van Winkle who awoke surrounded by public choice scholarship would feel quite at home in his new surroundings: while he would recognize that those surroundings differed a bit from what he remembered before falling asleep, they would seem comfortably familiar all the same.

TOO MUCH OF A GOOD THING?

While in my experience no place comes close to VPI under Buchanan's influence in terms of experiencing the joy of creative scholarly activity and while I recognized that quality while I was there, I left all the same in 1979. In one very personal respect, VPI offered too much of a good thing for me. By 1979, my daughters had become 10 and 12, and as my six years there passed I came increasingly to sense a difficult challenge in trying to balance my desire to be involved in my daughters' lives with my desire to participate robustly in Blacksburg's energetic and creative scholarly environment. Eventually, I realized I couldn't do both, and so left VPI even though I knew I would miss the academic intensity I had left behind. Had I been a bachelor, as was Tullock, or had my wife and I been childless, as was Buchanan and his wife, I could well have stayed in Blacksburg, though possibly not because leaving Blacksburg also gave me greater scholarly space to explore territory where my orientations diverged from Buchanan's. While Buchanan was open to different viewpoints, he, like everyone, had points of exception. I remember a seminar in late 1977 or early 1978 where I made some remark about the limited value of thinking in terms of veils of ignorance. This remark was not well received, which reinforced my growing sense that getting some geographical space might be instrumental in securing some analytical space. In this respect I never embraced Buchanan's concordant point of analytical departure for social theory, such as animated his *Limits of Liberty* (Buchanan 1975a). Instead, I embraced the discordant point of departure that Tullock (1975) set forth in *The Social Dilemma*. Indeed, in Wagner (2008), I contrasted Buchanan's and Tullock's orientations by asserting that Buchanan theorized from east of Eden while Tullock theorized from west of Babel.

In a perhaps ironic turn of circumstance, the differences between Buchanan and me, while small in the overall scheme of things, probably reflected my growing awareness of the classical Italian contributions that Buchanan (1960) did so much to bring to economists' attention. It was during my years in Blacksburg that I started to dig into the Italian literature that Buchanan emphasized when I was a graduate student. It was during this time that I my interest in Pareto at the suggestion of Jürgen Backhaus (1978) who was visiting at VPI. Aside from occasional references to Pareto efficiency and the like, Buchanan never dealt with Pareto during my student days, especially not his sociological work. Yet any theorist of social interaction will operate with some form of sociological theory, even if that theory might be implicit rather than explicit. Within sociological theory, there are two primary branches that seem relevant for economists. Randall Collins (1988) denotes these as the exchange and the conflict traditions. Buchanan's implicit sociology fits within the exchange tradition, as would the sociology of Herbert Spencer around Pareto's time. In contrast, Pareto's explicit sociology fits within the conflict tradition, as would the sociologies of Carl Schmitt or Isaiah Berlin, and also Gordon Tullock for that matter.

This difference in sociological orientations is not a matter of the presence or absence of conflict within societies, for conflict is always present. The difference resides in whether the analytical point of departure is grounded in concord or discord among the members of society. Is there some central point on which everyone can potentially agree, or does society operate without such a point? Buchanan's distinction between choice of rules and choice of strategies within rules is based on some point of potential agreement from which social life subsequently proceeds. In contrast, when Pareto was asked about the possibility of some state of maximal social welfare, he responded by asking: "how can you maximize happiness for a community when happiness for the wolf requires eating the lamb while happiness for the lamb requires the avoidance of being eaten?" Pareto recognized regions of gains from trade within society, of course, but such gains were always achieved within an environment rife with conflict. It is quite possible for societies to exist without those societies being reducible to some point of concord. Societies can exist with a reasonable modicum of civil peace and order even if they are also rife with antagonisms. At the time of the American constitutional founding, for instance, many people would have preferred to remain a British colony. Among the remainder, many opposed the new constitution and preferred to live under the Articles of Confederation. And at the Constitutional Convention, around one-third of the delegates opposed the new Constitution.

Pareto's scholarly path emerged out of his effort to understand why market-based relationships that were grounded in private ordering weren't more widely embraced within society. It was through his effort to understand this puzzle that Pareto ended up writing his 2,000 page *Treatise on General Sociology*. The lynchpin of this work was Pareto's distinction between logical and non-logical action, which is a distinction that has nothing to do with the distinction between rational and irrational action. Pareto didn't believe in irrationality. Rationality was the only option, for Pareto would surely have agreed with Thomas Szasz (1974) regarding *The Myth of Mental Illness*. While all action was rational, only a subset of action was logical in character.

By logical action, Pareto meant action that fit the pattern: "If I do A today, I can reasonably or plausibly expect B to obtain tomorrow." With logical action, there was a direct connection between an action and the object at which the actor aimed that action. Buchanan's (1969a) formulation in *Cost and Choice* reflected logical action in Pareto's scheme of thought: the cost of taking an action to attain an objective is whatever might have been attained had that action been aimed at a different objective. Economics for Pareto was the domain of logical action, and with prices being vehicles that aided the logical pursuit of objectives.

Logical action predominates in market interaction; non-logical action predominates in collective activity. It was this recognition that led Pareto to shift his focus from economics to sociology and also to distinguish conceptually between economic equilibrium and social equilibrium. Non-logical action pertains to actions where there is no logical basis for thinking that "if I do A today I can reasonably expect B to result tomorrow." People may well have grounds for thinking that the presence of B would be nice, but they have no logical basis for thinking that by doing A in place of some alternative action, B will result. Non-logical action is the domain of sentiment, as well as of derivations which are efforts to place the appearance of logic on what is non-logical.

In Pareto's view, one facet of human nature was a tendency to believe that actions carried out under impulse, habit, or sentiments are products of some underlying logic. Thus people create theories that demonstrate the logical nature of what they have done. In Pareto's framework, sentiment directs and reason yields. What does this Paretian excursion have to do with Buchanan's political economy, as well as with where political economy might go in the future? Plenty, I think. In his review of Italianate public finance, Buchanan (1960) noted that the Italian theorists diverged over whether the political and the social could be reduced to economics. Buchanan sided with the reductionists, as illustrated by Antonio de Viti de Marco and Luigi Einaudi, and did so by noting that they could generate deterministic answers through their formulations. Among the non-reductionists who gave scope for the autonomy of society and social processes were Pareto and Gino Borgatta, as well as such sociologists of ruling classes as Gaetano Mosca (1947) and Roberto Michels (1962). Buchanan often recurred to de Viti's treatment of the cooperative state, for that treatment fit well Buchanan's constitutional motif, as shown by Buchanan's discussion of de Viti in Mosca (2011, 109–14).

Buchanan's constitutional economics starts from the presumption that people want to live together in harmony, and need only to find the rules that will allow them to do so. Pareto's constitutional economics is skeptical about such harmony, and operates instead in terms of governance as a competition among elites using techniques of wit and power to seek domination over governed masses. Pareto's world was not Buchanan's world, and yet there are points of contact. For Pareto, governments try to extract as much as they can from taxpayers, with the only impediment to such extraction being the intensity of taxpayer resistance. This is a proposition Buchanan would doubtlessly accept. The difference between the two would surely reside in recognition that for Pareto this was the eternal way of the world while for Buchanan there was a constitutional remedy. I am skeptical that Buchanan really believed this, as distinct from holding to the proposition that without some such belief he would be describing a hopeless situation, and this was something Buchanan would never allow himself to do, so he clung to the conceptual unanimity on which he pinned his constitutional formulation.

Pareto's distinction between logical and non-logical action and the associated distinction between arguments that appeal directly to reason and arguments that appeal to sentiment in conjunction with allowing construction of a derivation that would cover the sentiment with the veneer of reason, points in a potentially productive direction with respect to a project of constitutional restoration. The Paretian orientation would be skeptical that reason alone could accomplish this. It would also hold, however, that sentiment supported by reasoned derivations might be sufficient for enabling liberal elites to gain ascendancy over collectivist elites. All the same, governance would be in the hands of elites within the Paretian scheme, which is not Buchanan's idealized scheme.

REMEMBERING JIM BUCHANAN

Some years after my first meeting with Jim Buchanan but long before now, I recall hearing a speaker remark with respect to getting older: "Remember the dreams of your past. You must fight to keep them alive." Jim Buchanan had a dream. He wanted to create a new orientation toward public finance. In this he surely succeeded, and fought to the end to keep that dream alive. I think from time to time he fell back too fully onto closed form models when advancing his dream might have been pursued more effectively by adopting more open ended modes of thought. We had many conversations about these points in the later years. While he would acknowledge my points and concerns, he also would remind me that the creation of scholarship is a social activity, and that it is necessary to speak the common language if you are to participate in that activity. The creative scholarly life entails working with a dialectical tension where you must use the language your colleagues use to change the language they use. Jim Buchanan embraced this challenge and vented himself upon the scholarly world with devotion and exuberance, and with an interest in helping his students and colleagues to do the same, and I consider myself a grateful inheritor of his scholarly example.

References

Atkinson, A.B. and Stiglitz, J.E. 1980. *Lectures on Public Economics*. New York: McGraw-Hill.

Auteri, M. and Wagner, R.E. 2007. "The Organizational Architecture of Nonprofit Governance: Economic Calculation within an Ecology of Enterprises." *Public Organization Review* 7: 57–68.

Backhaus, J.G. 1978. "Pareto and Public Choice." *Public Choice* 33: 5–17.

Backhaus, J.G. and Wagner, R.E. 2005a. "From Continental Public Finance to Public Choice: Mapping Continuity." *History of Political Economy*, Annual Supplement, 37: 314–32.

Backhaus, J.G. and Wagner, R.E. 2005b. "Continental Public Finance: Mapping and Recovering a Tradition." *Journal of Public Finance and Public Choice* 23: 43–67.

Baier, A. 1997. *The Commons of the Mind*. Chicago: Open Court.

Belloc, H. 1912. *The Servile State*. London: T.N. Foulis.

Berlin, I. 1953. *The Hedgehog and the Fox: An Essay on Tolstoy's View of History*. London: Weidenfeld and Nicolson.

Berlin, I. 1991. *The Crooked Timber of Humanity: Chapters in the History of Ideas*. New York: Knopf.

Bilo, S. and Wagner, R.E. 2015. "Neutral Money: Historical Fact or Analytical Artifact?" *Review of Austrian Economics* 28: 139–50.

Bish, R.L. 1971. *The Public Economy of Metropolitan Areas*. Chicago: Markham.

Bish, R.L. and Ostrom, V. 1973. *Understanding Urban Government: Metropolitan Reform Reconsidered*. Washington: American Enterprise Institute.

Bishop, E. 1967. *Foundations of Constructive Analysis*. New York: McGraw-Hill.

Black, D. 1958. *Theory of Committees and Elections*. Cambridge: Cambridge University Press.

Blankart, C.B. and Koester G.G. 2006. "Political Economics versus Public Choice." *Kyklos* 59: 171–200.

Blaug, M. 1996. *Economic Theory in Retrospect*, 5th ed. Cambridge: Cambridge University Press.

Boettke, P.J. 1998. "Economic Calculation: The Austrian Contribution to Political Economy." *Advances in Austrian Economics* 5: 131–58.

Boettke, P.J. 2001. *Calculation and Coordination*. London: Routledge.

Boettke, P.J. 2007. "Liberty vs. Power in Economic Policy in the 20th and 21st Centuries." *Journal of Private Enterprise* 22: 7–36.

Boettke, P.J. 2012. *Living Economics*. Oakland, CA: Independent Institute.

Boettke, P.J. and Marciano, A. 2015. "The Past, Present, and Future of Virginia Political Economy." *Public Choice* 163: 53–65.

Boudreaux, D.J. and R.G. Holcombe 1989. "Government by Contract." *Public Finance Quarterly* 17: 264–80.

Boulding, K.E. 1971. "After Samuelson, Who Needs Adam Smith?" *History of Political Economy* 3: 225–37.

Brennan, H.G. and Buchanan, J.M. 1980. *The Power to Tax: Analytical Foundations of a Fiscal Constitution*. Cambridge: Cambridge University Press.

Brennan, H.G. and Buchanan, J.M. 1985. *The Reason of Rules*. Cambridge: Cambridge University Press.

Brennan, G. and L. Lomasky. 1993. *Democracy and Decision: The Pure Theory of Electoral Preference*. Cambridge: Cambridge University Press.

Breton, A. 1965. "A Theory of Government Grants." *Canadian Journal of Economics and Political Science* 31: 175–87.

Buchanan, J.M. 1949. "The Pure Theory of Government Finance: A Suggested Approach." *Journal of Political Economy* 57: 496–505.

Buchanan, J.M. 1950. "Federalism and Fiscal Equity." *American Economic Review* 40: 583–99.

Buchanan, J.M. 1954a. "Social Choice, Democracy, and Free Markets." *Journal of Political Economy* 62: 114–23.

Buchanan, J.M. 1954b. "Individual Choice in Voting and the Market." *Journal of Political Economy* 62: 334–43.

Buchanan, J.M. 1958. *Public Principles of Public Debt*. Homewood, IL: Richard D. Irwin.

Buchanan, J.M. 1960. "The Italian Tradition in Fiscal Theory." In J.M. Buchanan, ed., *Fiscal Theory and Political Economy*. Chapel Hill: University of North Carolina Press, pp. 24–74.

Buchanan, J.M. 1961. "Predictability: The Criterion of Monetary Constitutions." In L.B. Yeager, ed., *In Search of a Monetary Constitution*. Cambridge, MA: Harvard University Press, pp. 155–83.

Buchanan, J.M. 1962. "Politics, Policy, and the Pigouvian Margin." *Economica* 29: 17–28,

Buchanan, J.M. 1963. "The Economics of Earmarked Taxes." *Journal of Political Economy* 71: 457–69.

Buchanan, J.M. 1964a. "What Should Economists Do?" *Southern Economic Journal* 30: 213–22.

Buchanan, J.M. 1964b. "Fiscal Institutions and Efficiency in Collective Outlay." *American Economic Review*, Proceedings 54: 227–35.

Buchanan, J.M. 1965. "An Economic Theory of Clubs." *Economica* 32: 1–14.

Buchanan, J.M. 1967. *Public Finance in Democratic Process*. Chapel Hill: University of North Carolina Press.

Buchanan, J.M. 1968a. "Knight, Frank H." In D.L. Sills, ed. *International Encyclopedia of the Social Sciences*, vol. 17. New York: Macmillan, pp. 424–28.

Buchanan, J.M. 1968b. *The Demand and Supply of Public Goods*. Chicago: Rand McNally.

Buchanan, J.M. 1969a. *Cost and Choice: An Inquiry in Economic Theory*. Chicago: Markham.

Buchanan, J.M. 1969b. "Is Economics a Science of Choice?" In E. Streissler, ed., *Roads to Freedom*. London: Routledge & Kegan Paul, pp. 47–64.

Buchanan, J.M. 1971. "Equality as Fact and Norm." *Ethics* 81: 228–40.

Buchanan, J.M. 1972 "Rawls on Justice as Fairness." *Public Choice* 13: 123–28.

Buchanan, J.M. 1975a. *The Limits of Liberty: Between Anarchy and Leviathan*. Chicago: University of Chicago Press.

Buchanan, J.M. 1975b. "The Political Economy of Franchise in the Welfare State." In R.T. Selden, ed., *Capitalism and Freedom: Problems and Prospects*. Charlottesville: University Press of Virginia, pp. 52–77.

Buchanan, J.M. 1976. "Methods and Moral in Economics: The Ayres-Knight Discussion." In W. Breit and W.P. Culbertson, eds., *Science and Ceremony: The Institutional Economics of C.E. Ayres*. Austin: University of Texas Press, pp. 163–74.

Buchanan, J.M. 1977. "The Samaritan's Dilemma." In E. Phelps, ed., *Altruism, Morality, and Economic Theory,* New York: Russell Sage, pp. 71–85.

Buchanan, J.M. 1978. "Markets, States, and the Extent of Morals." *American Economic Review*, Proceedings 68: 364–68.

Buchanan, J.M. 1982a. "The Domain of Subjective Economics: Between Predictive Science and Moral Philosophy." In I.M. Kirzner, ed., *Method, Process, and Austrian Economics*. Lexington, MA: D.C. Heath, pp. 7–20.

Buchanan, J.M. 1982b. "The Related but Distinct Sciences of Economics and Political Economy." *British Journal of Social Psychology* 21: 175–83.

Buchanan, J.M. 1982c. "Order Defined in the Process of Its Emergence." *Literature of Liberty* 5: 5.

Buchanan, J.M. 1983. "Monetary Research, Monetary Rules, and Monetary Regimes." *Cato Journal* 3: 143–46.

Buchanan, J.M. 1985a. "The Moral Dimension of Debt Financing." *Economic Inquiry* 23: 1–6.

Buchanan, J.M. 1985b. "Political Economy and Social Philosophy." In P. Koslowski, ed., *Economics and Philosophy*. Tübingen: J.C.B. Mohr, pp. 19–36.

Buchanan, J.M. 1986a. "Political Economy: 1957–1982." In J. M. Buchanan, ed., *Liberty, Market, and State*. Brighton, UK: Wheatsheaf, pp. 8–18.

Buchanan, J.M. 1986b. "Ideas, Institutions, and Political Economy." In K. Brunner and A. Meltzer, eds., *Real Business Cycles, Real Exchange Rates, and Actual Policies*. Amsterdam, North-Holland, pp. 245–58.

Buchanan, J.M. 1987a. "Keynesian Follies." In D. A. Reese, ed., *The Legacy of Keynes*. San Francisco: Harper & Row, pp. 130–45.

Buchanan, J.M. 1987b. "The Ethics of Debt Default." In J.M. Buchanan, C.K. Rowley, and R.D. Tollison, eds. *Deficits*. New York: Blackwell, pp. 361–73.

Buchanan, J.M. 1989. "On the Structure of an Economy: A Re-emphasis of Some Classical Foundations." *Business Economics* 24: 6–12.

Buchanan, J.M. 1990. "Born-Again Economist." In W. Breit and R.W. Spencer, eds., *Lives of the Laureates*. Cambridge, MA: MIT Press, pp. 163–80.

Buchanan, J.M. 1991. "Frank H. Knight: 1885–1972." In E. Shils, ed., *Remembering the University of Chicago: Teachers, Scientists, and Scholars*. Chicago: University of Chicago Press, pp. 244–52.

Buchanan, J.M. 1992. *Better than Plowing*. Chicago: University of Chicago Press.

Buchanan, J.M. 1995. "Federalism as an Ideal Political Order and an Objective for Constitutional Reform." *Publius: The Journal of Federalism* 25: 19–27.

Buchanan, J.M. 1997. "Economics as a Public Science." In S.G. Medema and W.J. Samuels, eds., *Foundations of Research in Economics: How Do Economists Do Economics?* Cheltenham, UK: Edward Elgar, pp. 30–36.

Buchanan, J.M. 1999–2002. *The Collected Works of James M. Buchanan*. Edited by G. Brennan, H. Kliemt, and R. D. Tollison, 20 vols. Indianapolis: Liberty Fund. [This collection contains the preponderance of his academic work through the late 1990s.]

Buchanan, J.M. 2005. "Afraid to be free." *Public Choice* 124: 19–31.

Buchanan, J.M. 2006. "The Virginia Renaissance in Political Economy: The 1960s Revisited." In R. Koppl, ed., *Money and Markets: Essays in Honor of Leland B. Yeager*. London: Routledge, pp. 34–44.

Buchanan, J.M. and Congleton, R.D. 1998. *Politics by Principle, Not Interest*. Cambridge: Cambridge University Press.

Buchanan, J.M. and Faith, R. 1987. "Secession and the Limits of Taxation: Towards a Theory of Internal Exit." *American Economic Review* 77: 1023–31.

Buchanan, J.M. and Forte, F. 1961. "The Evaluation of Public Services." *Journal of Political Economy* 69: 107–21.

Buchanan, J.M. and Goetz, C.J. 1972. "Efficiency Limits of Fiscal Mobility." *Journal of Public Economics* 1: 25–43.

Buchanan, J.M. and Lee, D.R. 1994. "On a Fiscal Constitution for the European Union." *Journal des Economistes et des Etudes Humaines* 5: 219–32.

Buchanan, J.M. and Musgrave, R.A. 1999. *Public Finance and Public Choice: Two Contrasting Visions of the State*. Cambridge, MA: MIT Press.

Buchanan, J.M. and Stubblebine, W.C. 1962. "Externality." *Economica* 29: 371–84.

Buchanan, J. M. and Thirlby, G.F., eds. 1973. *L.S.E. Essays on Cost*. London: Weidenfeld and Nicolson.

Buchanan, J.M. and Tullock G. 1962. *The Calculus of Consent: Logical Foundations of Constitutional Democracy*. Ann Arbor: University of Michigan Press.

Buchanan, J.M. and Wagner, R.E. 1967. *Public Debt in a Democratic Society*. Washington: American Enterprise Institute.

Buchanan, J.M. and Wagner, R.E. 1970. "An Efficiency Basis for Federal Fiscal Equalization." In J. Margolis, ed., *The Analysis of Public Output*. New York: National Bureau of Economic Research, 139–58.

Buchanan, J.M. and Wagner, R.E. 1977. *Democracy in Deficit*. New York: Academic Press.

Buchanan, J.M. and Yoon Y.J., eds. 1994. *The Return to Increasing Returns*. Ann Arbor: University of Michigan Press.

Buchanan, J.M. and Yoon, Y.J. 2015. *Individualism and Political Disorder*. Cheltenham, UK: Edward Elgar.

Buckley, F.H. 1999. *The Rise and Fall of Freedom of Contract*. Durham, NC: Duke University Press.

Budziszewski, J. 2003. *What We Can't Not Know*. Dallas, TX: Spence.

Burnham, J. 1943. *The Machiavellians*. New York: John Day.

Caplan, B. 2007. *The Myth of the Rational Voter*. Princeton, NJ: Princeton University Press.

Chaitin, G., N. da Costa, and Doria F.A. 2012. *Gödel's Way: Exploits into an Undecidable World*. London: Taylor & Francis.

Clinton, H.R. 1996. *It Takes a Village, and Other Lessons Children Teach Us*. New York: Simon & Schuster.

Coase, R.H. 1960. "The Problem of Social Cost." *Journal of Law and Economics* 3: 1–44.

Coase, R.H. 1974. "The Lighthouse in Economics." *Journal of Law and Economics* 17: 357–76.

Collins, R. 1998. *The Sociology of Philosophies: A Global Theory of Intellectual Change*. Cambridge, MA: Harvard University Press.

Da Empoli, A. 1926. *Teoria dell'incidenza delle Imposte*. Reggio Calabria: Vitalone.

Da Empoli, A. 1941. *Lineamenti teorici dell'economia corporativa finanziaria*. Milano: Giuffrè.

Dam, K.W. 1977. "The American Fiscal Constitution." *University of Chicago Law Review* 44: 271–320.

DeCanio, S. 2014. *Limits of Economic and Social Knowledge*. Houndmills, UK: Palgrave Macmillan.

De Jouvenel, B. 1961. "The Chairman's Problem." *American Political Science Review* 55: 368–72.

De Viti de Marco, A. 1888. *Il carattere teorico dell'economia* finanziaria. Rome: Pasqualucci.

De Viti de Marco, A. 1930. *Un trentennio di lotte politiche: 1894–1922*. Napoli: Giannini.

De Viti de Marco, A. 1934. *Principii di economia finanziaria*. Turin: Giulio Einaudi.

De Viti de Marco, A. 1936. *First Principles of Public Finance*. London: Jonathan Cape.

Edgeworth, F.Y. 1897. "The Pure Theory of Taxation." *Economic Journal* 7: 100–22.

Eisenstein, L. 1961 [2010]. *The Ideologies of Taxation*. New York: The Ronald Press.

Ellsberg, D. 1956. "Theory of the Reluctant Duelist." *American Economic Review* 46: 909–23.

Emmett, R.B. 2006. "Die gustibus est disputandum: Frank H. Knight's response to George Stigler and Gary Becker's 'die gustibus non est disputandum.'" *Journal of Economic Methodology* 13: 97–111.

Emmett, R.B. 2009. *Frank Knight and the Chicago School of Economics*. London: Routledge.

Epstein, R.A. 1985. *Takings: Private Property and the Power of Eminent Domain*. Cambridge, MA: Harvard University Press.

Epstein, R.A. 1995. *Simple Rules for a Complex World*. Cambridge, MA: Harvard University Press.

Epstein, R.A. 2014. *The Classical Liberal Constitution*. Cambridge, MA: Harvard University Press.

Eucken, W. 1952 [1990]. *Grundsätze der Wirtschaftspolitik*. 6th ed. Tübingen: J. C. B. Mohr.

Eusepi, G. and Wagner, R.E. 2010. "Polycentric polity: Genuine vs. spurious federalism." *Review of Law and Economics* 6: 329–45.

Eusepi, G. and Wagner R.E. 2011. "States as Ecologies of Political Enterprises." *Review of Political Economy* 23: 573–85.

Eusepi, G. and Wagner R.E. 2013. "Tax Prices in a Democratic Polity: The Continuing Relevance of Antonio De Viti de Marco." *History of Political Economy* 45: 99–121.

Eusepi, G. and Wagner, R.E. 2017. *Public Debt: An Illusion of Democratic Political Economy*. Cheltenham, UK: Edward Elgar.

Fasiani, M. 1949. "Contributi di Pareto all scienza delle finance." *Giornale degli Economisti* 8: 129–73.

Fausto, D. 2003. "An Outline of the Main Italian Contributions to the Theory of Public Finance." *Il pensiero economico Italiano* 11: 11–41.

Fawcett, H. 1871. *Pauperism: Its Causes and Remedies*. London: Macmillan.

Fried, C. 1982. *Contract as Promise: A Theory of Contractual Obligation*. Cambridge, MA: Harvard University Press.

Friedman, M. 1953. *Essays in Positive Economics*. Chicago: University of Chicago Press.

Frisch, R. 1959. "On Welfare Theory and Pareto Regions." *International Economic Papers* 9: 39–92.

Garvey, G. 1975. "Keynes and the Economic Activists of Pre-Hitler Germany." *Journal of Political Economy* 83: 391–405.

Gigerenzer, G. 2008. *Rationality for Mortals*. Oxford: Oxford University Press.

Gladwell, M. 2008. *Outliers: The Story of Success*. Boston: Little, Brown.

Greve, M.S. 2012. *The Upside-Down Constitution*. Cambridge, MA: Harvard University Press.

Grice-Hutchinson, M. 1978. *Early Economic Thought in Spain*. London: Allen & Unwin.

Grossman, S.J. and Stiglitz J.E. 1976. "Information and Competitive Price Systems." *American Economic Review* 66: 246–53.

Grossman, S.J. and Stiglitz J.E. 1980. "On the Impossibility of Informationally Efficient Markets." *American Economic Review* 70: 393–408.

Hansjürgens, B. 2000. "The Influence of Knut Wicksell on Richard Musgrave and James Buchanan." *Public Choice* 103: 95–116.

Harrod, R.F. 1951. *The Life of John Maynard Keynes*. London: Macmillan.

Hayek, F.A. 1937. "Economics and Knowledge." *Economica* 4: 33–54.

Hayek, F.A. 1945. "The Use of Knowledge in Society." *American Economic Review* 35: 519–30.

Hayek, F.A. 1960. *The Constitution of Liberty*. Chicago: University of Chicago Press.

Hayek, F.A. 1973–1979. *Law, Legislation and Liberty*, 3 vols. Chicago: University of Chicago Press.

Hebert, D. and R.E. Wagner 2013. "Taxation as a Quasi-Market Process: Explanation, Exhortation, and the Choice of Analytical Windows." *Journal of Public Finance and Public Choice* 31: 163–77.

Himmelfarb, G. 1983. *The Idea of Poverty*. New York: Alfred A. Knopf.

Himmelfarb, G. 1992. *Poverty and Compassion: The Moral Imagination of the Late Victorians*. New York: Vintage.

Hochman, H.M. and J.D. Rogers. 1969. 'Pareto Optimal Redistribution." *The American Economic Review* 59: 542–557.

Holcombe, R.G. 2002. *From Liberty to Democracy: TheTransformation of American Government*. Ann Arbor: University of Michigan Press.

Holcombe, R.G. and A.M. Castillo. 2013. *Liberalism and Cronyism: Two Rival Political and Economic Systems*. Arlington, VA: Mercatus Center.

Hughes, J.R.T. 1977. *The Governmental Habit: Economic Controls from Colonial Times to the Present*. New York: Basic Books.

Jacobs, J. 1992. *Systems of Survival*. New York: Random House.

Jacobs, J. 2004. *Dark Age Ahead*. New York: Random House.

Johnson, M. 2006. "The Wicksellian Unanimity Rule: The Competing Interpretations of Buchanan and Musgrave." *Journal of the History of Economic Thought* 28: 57–79.

Johnson, M. 2014a. "James M. Buchanan, Chicago, and Post War Public Finance." *Journal of the History of Economic Thought* 36: 479–97.

Johnson, M. 2014b. "Progressivism and Academic Public Finance, 1880 to 1930." *History of Political Economy* 46: 1–32.

Kenyon, D.A. and J. Kincaid, eds. 1991. *Competition among States and Local Governments*. Washington: Urban Institute.

Keynes, J.M. 1936. *The General Theory of Employment, Interest, and Money*. New York: Harcourt, Brace.

Klemperer, V. 2006. *The Language of the Third Reich*. New York: Continuum.

Knight, F. 1921. *Risk, Uncertainty, and Profit*. Boston: Houghton-Mifflin.

Knight, F.H. 1960. *Intelligence and Democratic Action*. Cambridge, MA: Harvard University Press.

Koppl, R. 2002. *Big Players and the Economic Theory of Expectations*. New York: Palgrave Macmillan.

Krause, M. 2015. "Buoys and Beacons in Economics." *Journal of Private Enterprise* 30: 45–59.

Kyle, R. 2012. *From Nashborough to the Nobel Prize: The Buchanans of Tennessee*. Murfreesboro, TN: Twin Oaks Press.

Lakatos, I. 1978. *The Methodology of Scientific Research Programs*. Cambridge: Cambridge University Press.

Landes, W.M. and Posner, R.A. 1987. *The Economic Structure of Tort Law*. Cambridge: Harvard University Press.

Latour, B. 2005. *Reassembling the Social: An Introduction to Actor-Network Theory*. Oxford: Oxford University Press.

Lave, C.A. 1985. "Speeding, Coordination, and the 55-MPH Limit." *American Economic Review* 75: 1159–64.

Leibowitz, A. and Tollison R.D. 1980. "A Theory of Legislative Organization." *Quarterly Journal of Economics* 94: 261–77.

Leipold, H. and Pies, I. (eds.) 2000. *Ordnungstheorie und Ordnungspolitik*. Stuttgart: Lucius & Lucius.

Levine, M.E. and Plott, C.R. 1977. "Agenda Influence and Its Implications." *Virginia Law Review* 63: 561–604.

Levy, D.M. and Peart S.J. 2013. "How the Virginia School Got Its Name." Richmond, VA: Jepson School of Leadership Studies.

Lindahl, E. 1958 [1919]. "Just Taxation—A Positive Solution." In R.A. Musgrave and A.T. Peacock, eds., *Classics in the Theory of Public Finance*. London: Macmillan, pp. 168–76.

Lovejoy, A.O. 1936. *The Great Chain of Being*. Cambridge, MA: Harvard University Press.

MacCallum, S. 1970. *The Art of Community*. Menlo Park, CA: Institute for Humane Studies.

Maine, H. 1864. *Ancient Law, 5th ed.* New York: Henry Holt.

Marlow, M.L. and Orzechowski, W.P. 1997. "The Separation of Spending from Taxation: Implications for Collective Choices." *Constitutional Political Economy* 8: 151–63.

Mazzola, U. 1890. *I dati scientifici della finanza pubblica*. Rome: Leoscher.

McCloskey, D.N. and Ziliak, S.T. 2008. *The Cult of Statistical Significance*. Ann Arbor: University of Michigan Press.

McCormick, R.E. and Tollison R.D. 1981. *Politicians, Legislation, and the Economy*. Boston: Kluwer Academic Publishers.

McIlwain, C.H. 1947. *Constitutionalism: Ancient and Modern*, rev. ed. Ithaca, NY: Cornell University Press.

McKean, R.N. 1965. "The Unseen Hand in Government." *American Economic Review* 55: 496–505.

McKean, R.N. 1968. *Public Spending*. New York: McGraw-Hill.

McLure, M. 2007. *The Paretian School and Italian Fiscal Sociology*. Houndmills, UK: Palgrave Macmillan.

Meckling, W.H. and Jensen, M.C. 1976. "Theory of the Firm: Managerial Behavior, Agency Costs, and Ownership Structure." *Journal of Financial Economics* 3: 305–60.

Medema, S.G. 2005. "'Marginalizing' Government: From La Scienza delle Finanze to Wicksell." *History of Political Economy* 37: 1–25.

Michels, R. 1962. *Political Parties: A Sociological Study of the Oligarchical Tendencies of Modern Democracy.* New York: Collier Books.

Mill, J.S. 1859. *On Liberty.* London: Walter Scott.

Mirrlees, J. 1994. "Optimal Taxation and Government Finance." In J.M. Quigley and E. Smolensky, eds., *Modern Public Finance.* Cambridge, MA: Harvard University Press, pp. 213–31.

Moberg, L. and Wagner, R.E. 2014. "Default without Capital Account: The Economics of Municipal Bankruptcy." *Public Finance and Management* 1: 30–47.

Moore, A. and Randazzo, A. 2016. "Causes and Cures of Public Pension Debt." Los Angeles, CA: Reason Foundation.

Mosca, G. 1939. *The Ruling Class.* New York: McGraw-Hill.

Mosca, G. 1947. *Elementi di scienza politica,* 4th ed. Bari: G. Laterza.

Mosca, M. 2011. *Antonio de Viti de Marco: Una storia degna di memoria.* Milano: Bruno Mondadori.

Mosca, M. 2016. *Antonio de Viti de Marco: A Story Worth Remembering.* New York: Palgrave Macmillan.

Montemartini, G. 1902. *Municipalizzazione dei publici servigi.* Milan: Società Editrice Libraria.

Munger, M.C. and Munger, K.M. 2015. *Choosing in Groups: Analytical Politics Revisited.* Cambridge: Cambridge University Press.

Murphy, L. and Nagel, T. 2002. *The Myth of Ownership.* Oxford: Oxford University Press.

Musgrave, R.A. 1939. "The Voluntary Exchange Theory of Public Economy." *Quarterly Journal of Economics* 53: 213–37.

Musgrave, R.A. 1959. *The Theory of Public Finance.* New York: McGraw-Hill.

Nutter, G.W. 1962. *The Growth of Industrial Production in the Soviet Union.* Princeton, NJ: Princeton University Press.

Nutter, G.W. 1983. *Political Economy and Freedom.* Indianapolis, IN: Liberty Press.

Oates, W.E. 1972. *Fiscal Federalism.* New York: Harcourt Brace.

Oates, W.E. 1999. "An Essay on Fiscal Federalism." *Journal of Economic Literature* 37: 1120–49.

Oi, W. 1971. "A Disneyland Dilemma: Two-Part Tariffs for a Mickey Mouse Monopoly." *Quarterly Journal of Economics* 85: 77–96.

Olasky, M. 1992. *The Tragedy of American Compassion.* Wheaton, IL: Crossway Books.

Ostrom, V. 1973. *The Intellectual Crisis in American Public Administration.* Tuscaloosa: University of Alabama Press.

Ostrom, V. 1984. "Why Governments Fail: An Inquiry into the Use of Instruments of Evil to Do Good." In J.M. Buchanan and R.D. Tollison, eds., *Theory of Public Choice II.* Ann Arbor: University of Michigan Press, pp. 422–35.

Ostrom, V. 1996. "Faustian Bargains." *Constitutional Political Economy* 7:303–8.

Ostrom, V. 1997. *The Meaning of Democracy and the Vulnerability of Societies: A Response to Tocqueville's Challenge.* Ann Arbor: University of Michigan Press.

Ostrom, V. 2008. *The Political Theory of a Compound Republic,* 3rd ed. Lanham, MD: Lexington.

Ostrom, V., Tiebout, C.M., and Warren, C. 1961. "The Organization of Government in Metropolitan Areas: A Theoretical Inquiry." *American Political Science Review* 55: 831–42.

Pantaleoni, M. 1911. "Considerazioni sulle roprieta di un sistema di prezzi politici." *Giornale degli Economisti* 42: 9–29, 114–33.

Patrick, M. and Wagner, R.E. 2015. "From mixed economy to entangled political economy: A Paretian social-theoretic orientation." *Public Choice* 164: 103–16.

Pareto, V. 1935 [1923]. *The Mind and Society,* New York: Harcourt Brace.

Peltzman, S. 1975. "The Effects of Automobile Safety Regulation." *Journal of Political Economy* 83: 677–726.

Pigou, A.C. 1920. *The Economics of Welfare.* London: Macmillan.

Pigou, A.C. 1928. *A Study in Public Finance.* London: Macmillan.

Plott, C.R. and Levine, M.E. 1978. "A Model of Agenda Influence on Committee Decisions." *American Economic Review* 68: 146–70.

Podemska-Mikluch, M. and Wagner, R.E. 2013. "Dyads, Triads, and the Theory of Exchange." *Review of Austrian Economics* 26: 171–82.

Polya, G. 1954. *Mathematics and Plausible Reasoning*, 2 vols. Princeton, NJ: Princeton University Press.

Potts, J. 2000. *The New Evolutionary Microeconomics*. Hants, UK: Edward Elgar.

Puviani, A. 1903. *Teoria della illusione finanziaria*, Palermo: Sandron. German translation: *Die Illusionen in der öffentlichen Finanzwirtschaft*, Berlin: Dunker & Humbolt, 1960.

Rajagopalan, S. and Wagner, R.E. 2013. "Constitutional Craftsmanship and the Rule of Law." *Constitutional Political Economy* 24: 295–309.

Ramsey, F.P. 1927. "A Contribution to the Theory of Taxation." *Economic Journal* 37: 47–61.

Rath, C. (1998), *Staat, Gesellschaft, und Wirtschaft bei Max Weber und bei Walter Eucken*. Egelsbach: Hänsel-Hohenhausen.

Reder, M.W. 1982. "Chicago Economics: Permanence and Change." *Journal of Economic Literature* 20: 1–38.

Reder, M.W. 1999. *Economics: The Culture of a Controversial Science*. Chicago: University of Chicago Press.

Resnick, M. 1994. *Turtles, Termites, and Traffic Jams: Explorations in Massively Parallel Microworlds*. Cambridge: MIT Press.

Riker, W. 1962. *The Theory of Political Coalitions*. New Haven, CT: Yale University Press.

Robbins, L. 1952. *The Theory of Economic Policy in English Classical Political Economy*. London: Macmillan.

Rodden, J.A. 2006. *Hamilton's Paradox: The Promise and Peril of Fiscal Federalism*. Cambridge: Cambridge University Press.

Romer, P.M. 1986. "Increasing Returns and Long-Run Growth." *Journal of Political Economy* 94: 1002–37.

Rosenberg, N. 1960. "Some Institutional Aspects of the *Wealth of Nations.*" *Journal of Political Economy* 68: 557–70.

Runst, P. and R.E. Wagner 2011. "Choice, Emergence, and Constitutional Process: A Framework for Positive Analysis." *Journal of Institutional Economics* 7: 131–45.

Salanié, B. 2003. *The Economics of Taxation*. Cambridge, MA: MIT Press.

Samuels, W.J. 1966. *The Classical Theory of Economic Policy.* Cleveland: World.

Samuelson, P.A. 1954. "The Pure Theory of Public Expenditure." *Review of Economics and Statistics* 36: 387–89.

Samuelson, P.A. 1955. "Diagrammatic Exposition of a Theory of Public Expenditure." *Review of Economics and Statistics* 37: 350–56.

Schelling, T.C. 1978. *Micromotives and Macrobehavior*. New York: Norton.

Schlicht, E. 1998. *On Custom and the Economy*. Oxford: Clarendon Press.

Schmitt, C. 1996 [1932]. *The Concept of the Political*. Chicago: University of Chicago Press.

Schmölders, G. 1959. "Fiscal Psychology: A New Branch of Public Finance." *National Tax Journal* 12: 340–45.

Schumpeter, J.A. 1954. *A History of Economic Analysis*. New York: Oxford University Press.

Shackle, G.L.S. 1961. *Decision, Order, and Time in Human Affairs*. Cambridge: Cambridge University Press.

Shackle, G.L.S. 1967. *The Years of High Theory*. Cambridge: Cambridge University Press.

Shackle, G.L.S. 1968. *Uncertainty in Economics and Other Reflections*, Cambridge: Cambridge University Press.

Shackle, G.L.S. 1972. *Epistemics and Economics*. Cambridge: Cambridge University Press.

Simmons, R. 2011. *Beyond Politics: The Roots of Government Failure*. Oakland, CA: Independent Institute.

Somin, I. 2013. *Democracy and Political Ignorance: Why Smaller Government Is Smarter*. Stanford, CA: Stanford University Press.

Stephen, J.F. 1873. *Liberty, Equality, Fraternity*. London: Smith, Elder.

Stigler, G.J. and Becker, G.S. 1977. "De Gustibus non est Disputandum." *American Economic Review* 67: 76–90.

Storing, J.J. 1981. *What the Anti-Federalists Were For*. Chicago: University of Chicago Press.

Streit, M.E. 1992. "Economic Order, Private Law, and Public Policy: The Freiburg School of Law and Economics in Perspective." *Journal of Institutional and Theoretical Economics* 148: 675–704.

Stringham, E.P., ed. 2005. *Anarchy, State, and Public Choice*. Cheltenham, UK: Edward Elgar.

Stringham, E.P. 2015. *Private Governance: Creating Order in Economic and Social Life*. Oxford: Oxford University Press.

Suits, B. 1967. "Is Life a Game We Are Playing?" *Ethics* 77: 209–13.

Szasz, T. 1961. *The Myth of Mental Illness*. New York: Harper & Row.

Tiebout, C.M. 1956. "A Pure Theory of Local Expenditures." *Journal of Political Economy* 64: 416–24.

Tullock, G. 1965. *The Politics of Bureaucracy*. Washington: Public Affairs Press.

Tullock, G. 1967. "The Welfare Costs of Tariffs, Monopolies, and Theft." *Economic Inquiry* 5: 224–32.

Tullock, G. 1975. *The Social Dilemma*. Blacksburg, VA: University Publications.

Tullock, G. 1989. *The Economics of Special Privilege and Rent Seeking*. Boston: Kluwer.

Tullock, G. 1997. "Origins of Public Choice." In A. Heertje, ed., *The Makers of Modern Economics*, vol. 3. Aldershot, UK: Edward Elgar, pp. 122–39.

Vanberg, V. 1988. "*Ordnungstheorie* as Constitutional Economics." *ORDO* 39: 17–31.

Vining, D.R. 1956. *Economics in the United States of America*. New York: UNESCO.

Vining, D.R. 1984. *On Appraising the Performance of an Economic System*. New York: Cambridge University Press.

Vriend, N.J. 2002. "Was Hayek an Ace?" *Southern Economic Journal* 68: 811–40.

Wagner, R.E. 1987. "Parchment, Guns, and the Maintenance of Constitutional Contract." In C. K. Rowley, ed., *Democracy and Public Choice: Essays in Honor of Gordon Tullock*. Oxford: Basil Blackwell, pp. 105–21.

Wagner, R.E. 1988. "*The Calculus of Consent*: A Wicksellian Retrospective." *Public Choice* 56: 153–66.

Wagner, R.E. 1992a. "Grazing the Budgetary Commons: The Rational Politics of Budgetary Irresponsibility." *Journal of Law and Politics* 9: 105–19.

Wagner, R.E. 1992b. "'Crafting Social Rules: Common Law vs. Statute Law, Once Again." *Constitutional Political Economy* 3: 381–97.

Wagner, R.E. 1993. *Parchment, Guns, and Constitutional Order*. Hants, UK: Edward Elgar.

Wagner, R.E. 2004. "Public Choice as an Academic Enterprise: Charlottesville, Blacksburg, and Fairfax Retrospectively Viewed." *American Journal of Economics and Sociology* 63: 55–74.

Wagner, R.E. 2006. "Retrogressive Regime Drift within a Theory of Emergent Order." *Review of Austrian Economics* 19: 113–23.

Wagner, R.E. 2007. *Fiscal Sociology and the Theory of Public Finance*. Cheltenham, UK: Edward Elgar.

Wagner, R.E. 2008. "Finding Social Dilemma: West of Babel, not East of Eden." *Public Choice* 135: 55–66.

Wagner, R.E. 2010. *Mind, Society, and Human Action: Time and Knowledge in a Theory of Social Economy*. London: Routledge.

Wagner, R.E. 2011. "Municipal Corporations, Economic Calculation, and Political Pricing: Exploring a Theoretical Antinomy." *Public Choice* 149: 151–65.

Wagner, R.E. 2013. "Choice versus Interaction in Public Choice: Discerning the Legacy of the *Calculus of Consent*." In D.R. Lee, ed., *Public Choice, Past and Present*. New York: Springer, pp. 65–79.

Wagner, R.E. 2014a. "James Buchanan's Public Debt Theory: A Rational Reconstruction." *Constitutional Political Economy* 25: 253–64.

Wagner, R.E. 2014b. "Richard Epstein's The Classical Liberal Constitution: A Public Choice Refraction." *New York University Journal and Law & Liberty* 8: 961–90.

Wagner, R.E. 2015a. "Virginia Political Economy: A Rational Reconstruction." *Public Choice* 163: 15–36.

Wagner, R.E. 2015b. "Welfare Economics and Second-Best Theory: Filling Imaginary Economic Boxes." *Cato Journal* 35: 133–46.

Wagner, R.E. 2016a. *Politics as a Peculiar Business: Insights from a Theory of Entangled Political Economy*. Cheltenham, UK: Edward Elgar.

Wagner, R.E. 2016b. "The Peculiar Business of Politics." *Cato Journal* 36: 535–56.

Wagner, R.E. and Yazigi, D. 2014. "Form vs. Substance in Selection through Competition: Elections, Markets, and Political Economy." *Public Choice* 159: 503–14.

Walker, G. 1990. *Moral Foundations of Constitutional Thought: Current Problems, Augustinian Prospects*. Princeton, NJ: Princeton University Press.

Walters, S.J.K. 2014. *Boom Towns: Restoring the Urban American Dream*. Stanford, CA: Stanford University Press.

Warren, C.O. 1932. *Congress as Santa Claus*. Charlottesville, VA: Michie.

Weaver, C.L. 1982. *The Crisis in Social Security: Economic and Political Origins*. Durham, NC: Duke University Press.

Weintraub, E.R. 1993. *General Equilibrium Analysis: Studies in Appraisal*. Ann Arbor: University of Michigan Press.

White, L.H. 1999. *The Theory of Monetary Institutions*. Oxford: Blackwell.

White, L.H. 2012. *The Clash of Economic Ideas*. Cambridge: Cambridge University Press.

Wicksell, K. 1896. *Finanztheoretische Untersuchungen*. Jena: Gustav Fischer.

Wicksell, K. 1958. "A New Principle of Just Taxation." In R.A. Musgrave and A.T. Peacock, eds., *Classics in the Theory of Public Finance*. London: Macmillan, pp. 72–118.

Wicksteed, P. 1910. *The Commonsense of Political Economy*, 2 vols. London: Macmillan.

Wildavsky, A. 1979. *Speaking Truth to Power: The Art and Craft of Policy Analysis*. Boston: Little, Brown.

Wilson, W. 1885. *Congressional Government*. Boston: Houghton, Mifflin.

Wittman, D. 1989. "Why Democracies Produce Efficient Results." *Journal of Political Economy* 97: 1395–1424.

Wittman, D. 1995. *The Myth of Democratic Failure*. Chicago: University of Chicago Press.

Yeager, L.B. 1958. "Immigration, Trade, and Factor Price Equalization." *Current Economic Comment* 20: 3–8.

Yeager, L.B., ed. 1962. *In Search of a Monetary Constitution*. Cambridge, MA: Harvard University Press.

Zodrow, G., ed. 1983. *Local Provision of Public Services: The Tiebout Model after Twenty-Five Years*. New York: Academic Press.

Index

action, logical vs. non-logical, 18, 65–66, 114–115. *See also* Pareto, V.
Adams, H.C., 26, 28
Atkinson, A., 29
Auteri, M., 67

Backhaus, J., 119, 185, 188
Baier, A., 7
Becker, G.S., 11, 19, 82, 157
Belloc, H., 134
Berlin, I., 3, 136, 188
Big Players, 42, 118
Bilas, R., 177
Bilo, S., 54
Bish, R., 89, 93
Bishop, E., 20
Black, D., 43
Blankart, C.B., 59
Blaug, M., 124
Blough, R., 26, 27, 28
Boettke, P.J., 12, 41, 61, 164, 171
Borgatta, G., 190
Boudreaux, D., 95
Boulding, K.E., viii, 8, 9
Brennan, G., 64, 66, 69, 121
Breton, A., 96, 98
Buchanan, J.M., 7, 11, 13, 14, 15, 16, 18, 25, 26, 28, 31, 32, 42, 43, 45, 46, 48–49, 50, 51, 52, 57, 58, 59–60, 61, 63, 64, 65, 67, 68–71, 72, 73, 77, 78, 80, 83, 85, 88, 90, 91, 95, 96, 97, 98,
99, 100, 101, 103, 104–105, 106–107, 109, 110, 111–113, 115, 119, 121, 122, 124–125, 129, 130, 131, 133–134, 136, 138–139, 140–141, 144, 149, 150–151, 154, 157–159, 160, 161, 162, 163–166, 172, 173, 174, 177–191; academic background of, 2; and assembly of Virginia political economy, 14–15; and economic theory between stasis and chaos, 19–22; and influence from Italian theorists, 39–41; and influence from Wicksell, 33–38; and origin of Virginia political economy, 7–10, 171; and the social philosophy toward which his work leads, 172–174; as hedgehog of a thinker, 3–4; as oak tree after 64 years, 3; as recipient of Nobel Prize, vii, 1. *See also* Berlin, I.
Buckley, F., 162
budgetary bridge between taxing and spending, 39, 41
Budziszewski, J., 174
Burnham, J., 31, 36

Calculus of Consent as Ur-text of Virginia political economy, 59–61
Caplan, B., 66
Castillo, A., 94
Center for Study of Public Choice, 3
centralized mindset, 40, 54, 67
Chaitin, G., 9

203

About the Author

Richard E. Wagner is the Holbert L. Harris Professor of Economics at George Mason University. He received his PhD in economics from the University of Virginia in 1966. He joined the faculty of George Mason University in 1988, after having held positions at The University of California at Irvine, Tulane University, Virginia Polytechnic Institute and State University, Auburn University, and Florida State University. While at George Mason University, he served for six years as chairman of the Department of Economics and twelve years as director of Graduate Studies.

Professor Wagner's fields of interest include public finance, public choice, political economy, and macroeconomics. He has authored more than 200 articles in professional journals and some 30 books and monographs, including *Inheritance and the State*; *Democracy in Deficit* (with James M. Buchanan); *Public Finance in a Democratic Society*; *To Promote the General Welfare*; *Parchment, Guns, and Constitutional Order*; *Fiscal Sociology and the Theory of Public Finance*; *Mind, Society, and Human Action*; *Deficits, Debt, and Democracy*; *The Peculiar Business of Politics*; and *Public Debt: An Illusion of Democratic Political Economy* (with Giuseppe Eusepi).